IEG WORLD BANK   IFC   MIGA
INDEPENDENT EVALUATION GROUP

MW01121534

Improving Effectiveness and Outcomes for the Poor in Health, Nutrition, and Population

An Evaluation of World Bank Group
Support Since 1997

http://www.worldbank.org/ieg
http://www.ifc.org/ieg
http://www.miga.org/ieg

2009
The World Bank
Washington, D.C.

Cover images:
Top left: As part of their efforts to reduce typhoid and save lives, the Junior Red Cross Club at Nasavusavu Public School in Savusavu, Fiji, has been running a handwashing campaign. Part of this campaign has involved making affordable soap dishes to hang at the school taps and painting a student-designed mural on the wall of their bath house. These projects were celebrated on October 15, 2008, the first ever Global Handwashing Day. Photo courtesy of Becky Huber Trytten, Peace Corps volunteer.

Top right: Doctor treating boy in Ghana. ©Mika/zefa/Corbis.

Bottom left: Indian woman with her children, who help her run her business. Photo by Curt Carnemark, courtesy of the World Bank Photo Library.

Bottom right: Mothers and infants at a World Bank-funded health facility on the island of Nias, off Sumatra, Indonesia. Photo courtesy of Nathalie M-H. Tavernier.

ISBN-13: 978-0-8213-7542-6
e-ISBN-13: 978-0-8213-7543-3
DOI: 10.1596/978-0-8213-7542-6

Library of Congress Cataloging-in-Publication Data have been applied for.

World Bank InfoShop
E-mail: pic@worldbank.org
Telephone: 202-458-5454
Facsimile: 202-522-1500

Independent Evaluation Group
Knowledge Programs and Evaluation Capacity
   Development (IEGKE)
E-mail: eline@worldbank.org
Telephone: 202-458-4497
Facsimile: 202-522-3125

 Printed on Recycled Paper

Contents

Figures

Tables

Abbreviations

AIDS	Acquired immune deficiency syndrome
CAS	Country Assistance Strategy
CASCR	CAS Completion Report
DOTS	Directly observed therapy, short course (for TB)
ESW	Economic and sector work
HAMSET	HIV/AIDS, malaria, sexually transmitted diseases, and TB
HIV	Human immunodeficiency virus
HNP	Health, nutrition, and population
IBRD	International Bank for Reconstruction and Development
ICR	Implementation Completion Report
IDA	International Development Association
IDI	Institutional development impact
IEG	Independent Evaluation Group
IFC	International Finance Corporation
M&E	Monitoring and evaluation
MDG	Millennium Development Goal
MIS	Management information system
PAD	Project Appraisal Document
PCR	Project Completion Report
PEPFAR	President's Emergency Plan for AIDS Relief (U.S.)
PER	Public expenditure review
PPAR	Project Performance Assessment Report
PPP	Public-private partnership
PRSC	Poverty reduction support credit
QAG	Quality Assurance Group
SIS	Integrated Health Insurance (Peru)
STD	Sexually transmitted disease
SWAp	Sectorwide approach
TB	Tuberculosis
TFR	Total fertility rate
UNAIDS	Joint United Nations Program on HIV/AIDS
UNDP	United Nations Development Program
USAID	United States Agency for International Development
WDR	World Development Report
WHO	World Health Organization
XPSR	Expanded Project Supervision Report (IFC)

A girl is weighed during a routine checkup at the Santa Rosa de Lima clinic in Nueva Esperanza, Honduras, which specializes in health care for children. Photo by Alfredo Srur, courtesy of the World Bank Photo Library.

Acknowledgments

This evaluation is a joint product of the World Bank and International Finance Corporation (IFC) departments of the Independent Evaluation Group (IEG). Martha Ainsworth (IEG-WB) was the task leader and coordinator of the joint evaluation, drafted the chapters of the report evaluating the World Bank, and was responsible for integrating the World Bank and IFC results. Hiroyuki Hatashima (IEG-IFC) led the evaluation of IFC. The evaluation was conducted under the overall direction of Vinod Thomas, Cheryl Gray, Marvin Taylor-Dormond, and Monika Huppi. The evaluation report is based on contributions from a team of IEG staff and consultants who conducted desk reviews, inventories, and interviews and data collection in the field.

The seven health, nutrition, and population (HNP) Project Performance Assessment Reports (PPARs) conducted for the evaluation of the World Bank were led and prepared by staff members Denise Vaillancourt (Egypt, Ghana) and Gayle Martin (Eritrea), and consultants Judyth Twigg (Kyrgyz Republic, Russia), Mollie Fair (Peru), and Patricia Ramirez (Peru). The PPARs on water supply and sanitation (Nepal) and roads (Romania) with health objectives were conducted by staff members Keith Pitman and Peter Freeman, respectively. The country case studies were prepared by R. Paul Shaw (Nepal), A. Edward Elmendorf and Flora Nankhuni (Malawi), and Alejandra Gonzalez (Egypt).

In-depth desk reviews of various aspects of the HNP portfolio over a decade were conducted by Mollie Fair, Judith Gaubatz, Manisha Modi, and Manuela Villar Uribe. Lisa Overbey contributed a desk review of the water supply and sanitation portfolio and Peter Freeman and Kavita Mathur provided a review of the transport portfolio. Additional specific reviews were provided by Mollie Fair (HNP strategy and timeline, population); Judith Gaubatz (Country Assistance Strategy review); Gayle Martin (communicable disease portfolio and inventory of HNP analytic work, with contributions from Manisha Modi and Marie-Jeanne Ndiaye); Manisha Modi (HNP portfolio analysis, staffing, and formal Bank analytic work, with inputs from Helena Tang and Saubhik Deb); Flora Nankhuni (health of the poor and staffing analysis); Shampa Sinha (Country Assistance Strategy review); Joan Nelson (health reform); Manuela Villar Uribe (monitoring and evaluation, impact evaluation and pilots, HNP in public expenditure reviews and poverty assessments); and Denise Vaillancourt (sectorwide approaches). IEG is particularly grateful to Christine Aquino and Samina Amin of the Human Resources department for facilitating access to and helping to interpret the data on staffing of the HNP sector.

The evaluation of IFC's operations in health was conducted under the guidance of Stoyan Tenev and Amitava Banerjee. The IFC evaluation team included Maria-Antonia Remenyi, Aygul Ozen, Chaoying Liu, Miguel Rebolledo Dellepiane, Nicholas Burke, and Vicky Viray-Mendoza.

The report team extends its gratitude to the hundreds of individuals in government, civil society, the donor community, the World Bank and IFC, and the private sector who were interviewed for the background papers, PPARs, country case studies, and IFC field visits. They are acknowledged individually in these respective reports. The team also extends its appreciation to World Bank HNP staff who served as peer reviewers for the portfolio work, and to those staff members who attended seminars on the findings of intermediate products and provided valuable feedback.

Ruth Levine and Susan Stout were the official peer reviewers; comments from the following individuals on the approach paper and various intermediate outputs were also greatly appreciated: Anabela Abreu, Olusoji Adeyi, Anders Agerskov, Julie Babinard, Cristian Baeza, Eni Bakallbashi, Arup Banerji, Alain Barbu, Nigel Bartlett, Chris Bennett, Alan Berg, Peter Berman, Anthony Bliss, Eduard Bos, Mukesh Chalwa, Laura Chioda, Safia Chowdhury, Mariam Claeson, Daniel Cotlear, Rooske De Joode, Jocelyne do Sacramento, Sheila Dutta, Maria Luisa Escobar, Shahrokh Fardoust, Armin Fidler, Deon Filmer, Ariel Fiszbein, Sundararajan Gopalan, Pablo Gottret, Davidson Gwatkin, Keith Hansen, April Harding, Eva Jarawan, Timothy Johnston, Marc Juhel, Christian Kammel, Arthur Karlin, Nicole Klingen, Pete Kolsky, Anjali Kumar, Christoph Kurowski, Kees Kostermans, Jerry LaForgia, Rama Lakshminarayanan, Jack Langenbruner, Bruno Laporte, Patrick Leahy, Maureen Lewis, Benjamin Loevinsohn, Akiko Maeda, Tonia Marek, John May, Julie McLaughlin, Tom Merrick, L. Richard Meyers, Michael Mills, Norbert Mugwagwa, Mary Mulusa, Homira Nassery, Son Nam Nguyen, Elaine Ooi, Ok Pannenborg, Ron Parker, Miyuki Parris, Christophe Prevost, Sandra Rosenhouse, Michal Rutkowski, Fadia Saadah, Pia Schneider, Julian Schweitzer, Meera Shekar, Agnes Soucat, Verdon Staines, Kate Tulenko, Vincent Turbat, John Underwood, Adam Wagstaff, Howard White, and Abdo Yazbeck.

The External Advisory Panel for this evaluation consisted of Augusto Galan (Former Minister of Health, Colombia), Anne Mills (London School of Hygiene and Tropical Medicine, UK), Germano Mwabu (University of Nairobi, Kenya), and Suwit Wibulpolprasert (Ministry of Health, Thailand). The evaluation team is enormously grateful for their sage advice and perspectives on the intermediate outputs and final report. The responsibility for interpreting the results and using this advice rests with the evaluation team, however.

William Hurlbut and Caroline McEuen edited the report and Marie-Jeanne Ndiaye provided logistical and production assistance throughout the preparation process. Heather Dittbrenner assisted with the photographs. Juicy Zareen Qureishi-Huq provided administrative and production support. Rose Gachina assisted in the processing of consultants. Nik Harvey set up the evaluation Web site (www.worldbank.org/ieg/hnp).

Finally, we wish to acknowledge the generous financial support of the Norwegian Agency for Development Cooperation (NORAD).

Director-General, Evaluation: *Vinod Thomas*
Director, Independent Evaluation Group-World Bank: *Cheryl Gray*
Director, Independent Evaluation Group-IFC: *Marvin Taylor-Dormond*
Manager, IEG Sector Evaluation: *Monika Huppi*
Task Manager: *Martha Ainsworth*

Foreword

The global aid architecture in health has changed over the past decade, with the adoption of the Millennium Development Goals (MDGs), expansion of the amount and sources of development finance, and new modes of international cooperation reflected in the 2005 Paris Declaration on Aid Effectiveness. Over this period, key health and nutrition outcomes have improved in every developing region, but many countries are off track for achieving the MDGs, and progress has been widely uneven among and within countries. Enormous challenges remain in reducing morbidity and mortality from infectious disease, high and rising noncommunicable disease, and pervasive malnutrition, as well as in lowering high fertility.

IEG's assessment of the efficacy of the World Bank Group's support for health, nutrition, and population (HNP) to developing countries since 1997 aims to help improve results in the context of the new aid architecture. The evaluation focuses on the Bank's policy dialogue, analytic work, and lending at the country level and the performance of IFC's health investments and Advisory Services. The evaluation also draws lessons from Bank Group experience in supporting several major approaches adopted by the international community—sectorwide approaches (SWAps), communicable disease control, health reform, and multisectoral action for health outcomes.

From 1997 to 2008 the World Bank provided $17 billion in country-level project financing, in addition to policy advice and analytic work for health, nutrition, and population. Bank support has helped build government capacity in the sector, and analytic work has contributed to better performance. About two-thirds of the Bank's HNP lending has had

satisfactory outcomes, often in difficult environments. The record also tells us that the Bank needs to intensify efforts to improve substantially the performance of the HNP portfolio. Factors that inhibit stronger performance include the increasing complexity of HNP operations, particularly in Africa, but also in health reform in middle-income countries; inadequate risk assessment and mitigation; and weak monitoring and evaluation. Over the same period, IFC has made important strategic shifts, committing $873 million in private health and pharmaceutical investments. IFC performance in health investments, mainly in hospitals, improved markedly from a weak start. The Corporation needs to invest more in activities that both make business sense and are likely to yield broader benefits for the poor. The accountability of Bank and IFC-financed HNP projects to ensure that results actually reach the poor has been weak. Non-health sectors, such as water supply and sanitation and transport, have weak incentives to obtain and demonstrate health benefits from their investments.

Though the Bank Group now funds a smaller share of the global financial support for HNP, it has stepped up its worldwide involvement, including its catalytic, lead, and support roles in many respects. The Group has a unique and substantial ability to help improve HNP results and outcomes for the poor. In delivering on this potential, the World Bank Group needs to strengthen its country support, renew the commitment to results for the poor, and give greater attention to reducing high fertility and malnutrition. Better results also hinge on supporting capacity and better governance for efficient health systems, enhancing the contribution of other sectors to HNP outcomes, and boosting monitoring and evaluation.

Vinod Thomas
Director-General, Evaluation

Through the hygiene education and good sanitation practices supported in the Bank's Rural Water Supply and Sanitation Project, this Nepalese woman believes her children are now healthier. Photo courtesy of George T. Keith Pitman.

Executive Summary

The global aid architecture in health has changed over the past decade, with the adoption of the Millennium Development Goals (MDGs) and a major expansion of the levels and sources of development assistance, particularly for low-income countries. While key health outcomes such as infant survival and nutritional stunting have improved over the decade in every developing region, nearly three-quarters of developing countries are either off track or seriously off track for achieving the MDG for reducing under-five mortality. Maternal mortality is declining at only 1 percent each year, a fifth of the rate needed to achieve the goal.

There are important differences in progress across countries, within regions, and within countries, with high levels of maternal mortality and malnutrition in Africa and South Asia. Enormous challenges remain in reducing morbidity and mortality from infectious disease, the high and rising share of noncommunicable disease, pervasive malnutrition, and high fertility, with its consequences for maternal mortality, maternal and child health, and poverty.

The World Bank Group's support for health, nutrition, and population (HNP) has been sustained since 1997—totaling $17 billion in country-level support by the World Bank and $873 million in private health and pharmaceutical investments by the International Finance Corporation (IFC). Beyond country-level support, the World Bank Group participates in nearly three dozen international partnerships in HNP, with indirect benefits to countries. This report evaluates the efficacy of the Bank Group's direct support for HNP to developing countries since 1997 and draws lessons to help improve the effectiveness of this support in the context of the new aid architecture.

Though the Bank Group now funds a smaller share of global HNP support than it did a decade ago, it still has substantial ability to add value if it can do a better job of helping countries deliver results, especially for the poor. World Bank support to countries in the form of lending, analytic work, and policy dialogue has helped build government capacity to manage the sector—critically important to improving aid effectiveness, given the increasing reliance of other donors on government systems.

About two-thirds of the World Bank's HNP lending has had satisfactory outcomes, often in difficult environments, but a third has not performed well. Contributing factors have been the increasing complexity of HNP operations, particularly in Africa but also in health-reform support to middle-income countries; inadequate risk assessment and mitigation; and weak monitoring and evaluation.

The performance of IFC's health investments has improved markedly from a weak start, but there remain important gaps in investing in activities that both make business sense and are likely to yield broader benefits for the poor. Accountability for results in these projects has been weak—the accountability of Bank and IFC-financed projects to ensure that results actually reach the poor, and the accountability of projects in the Bank's non-health sectors, such as water supply and sanitation and transport, for demonstrating their health benefits.

For the Bank Group to achieve its objectives of improving health sector performance and HNP outcomes among the poor, it needs to act in five areas: intensify efforts to improve the performance of the portfolio; renew the commitment to delivering results for the poor, including greater attention to reducing high fertility and malnutrition; build its own capacity to help countries to make health systems more efficient; enhance the contribution of other sectors to HNP outcomes; and boost evaluation to implement the results agenda and improve governance. By doing this, the Bank Group will contribute not only to meeting the MDGs but also to ensuring that the poor benefit, and that those benefits are sustained.

Since the late 1990s, when the World Bank Group was the largest source of HNP finance to developing countries, new aid donors and institutions have emerged, and development assistance for HNP has more than doubled, from an annual average of $6.7 billion in 1997/98 to about $16 billion in 2006. The international community has adopted global development targets, the most prominent of which are the MDGs, with a new emphasis on aid effectiveness, results orientation, donor harmonization, alignment, and country leadership, reflected in the 2005 *Paris Declaration on Aid Effectiveness* and the 2008 *Accra Agenda for Action*.

The World Bank Group, now one of many large players in international HNP support, accounts for only about 6 percent of the total—down from 18 percent in the 1990s—and is reassessing its comparative advantage in the context of the new aid architecture. At the same time, a call for greater engagement with the private health sector in developing countries presents new opportunities for IFC to extend its support.

The decline in its relative contribution aside, the World Bank Group commitment to HNP is still substantial. Since 1997, the World Bank (International Bank for Reconstruction and Development and the International Development Association) has committed nearly $17 billion to 605 HNP projects in more than 120 countries, sponsored analytic work, and offered policy advice. This support aimed to improve health and nutrition status and reduce high fertility; improve the access, quality, efficiency, and equity of the health system; reform health systems through changes in health finance, support for health insurance, decentralization, engaging the private sector, and other structural changes; and strengthen institutional capacity and sector management. In addition, the Bank has greatly expanded its participation in global partnerships for health; as of 2007, it was participating financially in 19 global partnerships and engaged in others ways in 15 more.

IFC has financed 68 private investment projects in the health and pharmaceutical sectors of developing countries—amounting to $873 million in total commitments—and offered advisory services on health to the private sector, including support for public-private partnerships.

The World Bank's 2007 strategy, *Healthy Development: The World Bank Strategy for Health, Nutrition, and Population Results,* aims, among other things, to improve HNP outcomes on average and among the poor; prevent poverty due to illness; improve health system performance; and enhance governance, accountability, and transparency in the sector. It points to several strategic directions or actions for the Bank to achieve the objectives, including:

- A renewed focus on HNP *results*
- Efforts to help countries *improve the performance of health systems* and to ensure *synergy with priority disease interventions*, particularly in low-income countries
- Strengthened Bank capacity to advise countries on *intersectoral approaches* to improving HNP results.

The 2002 IFC health strategy defines the sector's goals as improving health outcomes, protecting the population from the impoverishing effects of ill health, and enhancing the performance of health services. The strategy has both business and developmental objectives, among them promoting efficiency and innovation in the health sector. It also calls broadly for increasing the social impact of IFC investments.

The Scope of the Evaluation

This evaluation aims to inform the implementation of the most recent World Bank and IFC HNP strategies to enhance the effectiveness of future support. It covers the period since fiscal year 1997 and is based on desk reviews of the portfolio, background studies, and field visits. The evaluation of the HNP support of the World Bank focuses on the effectiveness of policy dialogue, analytic work, and lending *at the country level,* while that of IFC focuses on the performance of health investments and advisory services before and after its 2002 health strategy. The themes it covers are drawn from the two strategies and the approaches adopted by international donors in the past decade. IEG has previously evaluated several aspects of the Bank's HNP support. IFC's support for the health sector has never been fully evaluated.

Bank Support to the Public Sector for HNP

Over the past decade, the World Bank directly supported HNP outcomes in countries through lending and nonlending services. The largest source of lending was from projects managed within the Bank's HNP sector units ($11.5 billion, 255 projects). Almost all HNP-managed projects were investment lending. Beyond this, about $5 billion in lending for HNP outcomes was managed by other sectors. In nonlending services, since fiscal 2000 the Bank has spent $43 million of its own budget and trust funds on HNP-related economic and sector work (ESW). The number of professional HNP staff grew by a quarter, as did the share of health specialists among HNP staff.

The World Bank's Role

Although the World Bank finances a smaller share of country-level development assistance under the new international aid architecture, it still has significant potential to add value. But the value of that support is context-specific and depends on the Bank's ability to help countries deliver results. The World Bank brings important institutional assets to bear in helping countries make health systems work better and ensuring that health benefits reach the poor: long-term, sustained engagement in the sector; international experience; a history of support for building country capacity to implement programs; large-scale, sustained financing; strong links to finance ministries; and engagement with many sectors other than health with potential to contribute to HNP outcomes. The Bank's comparative advantage in a country is context-specific, depending on health conditions, government priorities and resources, and the activities of other development partners. To deliver on its comparative advantages, the Bank needs to improve the performance of its country-level support.

The Evolution and Performance of World Bank Support

While the overall level of HNP project approvals changed little, the composition of the lending portfolio saw some major shifts. The number of HNP-managed projects approved annually rose slowly, but new commitments declined. The share of communicable disease projects doubled over the decade, reaching about 40 percent of approvals in the second half of the period, as did the share of multisectoral projects, reaching half of all approvals. The share of Africa Region projects in the HNP lending portfolio also increased. These three trends were due primarily to an increase in multisectoral projects addressing acquired immune deficiency syndrome (AIDS). Projects supporting sectorwide approaches (SWAps) in health rose to a cumulative total of 28 operations in 22 countries, about 13 percent of the project portfolio. In contrast, the share of lending with objectives to reform the health system dropped by nearly half.

Attention to population and malnutrition was low, and support for population nearly disappeared. About 1 in 10 projects had an objective to reduce malnutrition, which disproportionately affects the poor, but the share of projects with nutrition objectives dropped by half over the decade. About two-thirds of nutrition projects were in countries with high levels of child stunting, but Bank nutrition support reached only about a quarter of all developing countries with high stunting. Lending to reduce high fertility or improve access to family planning accounted for only 4 percent of the lending portfolio, dropping by two-thirds between the first and second half of the decade, at a time when the need for such support remained high. Population support was directed to only about a quarter of the 35 countries the Bank identified as having the highest fertility (with rates of more than five children per woman). Analytic work and staffing to support population and family planning objectives nearly disappeared. Substantial analysis of population and nutrition issues rarely figured in poverty assessments, even though both issues are most acutely felt by the poor.

Two-thirds of HNP projects have had satisfactory outcomes, and the portfolio's performance has stalled. The evaluation highlights examples of good performance based on field assessments. Support for reducing malaria in Eritrea and schistosomiasis in the Arab Republic of Egypt, raising contraceptive use in pilot areas of Malawi, and reforming the health system in the Kyrgyz Republic, for example, showed good results. However, roughly a third of the HNP lending portfolio did not perform well, a share that has remained steady, while performance in other sectors has improved. The performance of HNP support in Africa was particularly weak, with only one in four projects achieving satisfactory outcomes. Complex projects—multisectoral projects and SWAps—in low-capacity environments were least likely to achieve their HNP objectives. However, health reform projects in middle-income countries also performed less well and are complex and politically volatile.

Poor-performing projects displayed common characteristics: inadequate risk analysis or technical design, inadequate supervision, insufficient political or institutional analysis, lack of baseline data on which to set realistic targets, overly complex designs in relation to local capacity, and negligible monitoring and evaluation. These problems are similar to those cited in IEG's 1999 evaluation of the HNP sector. The results of the recent De-tailed Implementation Review of HNP projects in India suggest that, even among projects that achieve their objectives, field supervision needs to be intensified to ensure that civil works and equipment are delivered as specified, in working order, and functioning.

Accountability of projects for delivering health results to the poor has been weak. Improving health outcomes among the poor is among the foremost objectives of the 2007 HNP strategy. Studies of the incidence of public expenditure have shown that in most countries, public health spending favors the non-poor; mere expansion of services cannot be assumed to improve access of the poor relative to the non-poor. While many projects targeted HNP support to geographic areas with a high incidence of poverty (including rural areas) or financed services or addressed problems thought to disproportionately affect the poor, only 6 percent of all HNP projects committed to deliver better health or nutrition among the poor in their statement of objectives, for which they were ultimately accountable. A third of projects with objectives to improve general health status (such as maternal and child health) had no targeting mechanism for reaching the poor. Among closed projects with objectives to improve HNP outcomes among the poor, most measured a change in average HNP status in project areas. Very few actually measured whether the poor (individuals or poor project areas) have benefited in relation to the non-poor or in relation to those in areas not reached by the project, and even fewer demonstrated that the poor *had* disproportionately benefited. In some cases, improvements in HNP status were only measured at the national level.

The Bank delivered several high-profile analytic products on HNP and poverty over the past decade—notably the *Reaching the Poor with Health, Nutrition, and Population Services* project and the *World Development Report 2004: Making Services Work for Poor People*. Nevertheless, the share of country poverty assessments with substantial discussion of health has declined, from 80 percent in fiscal years 2000–03 to only 58 percent in 2004–06. Only 7 percent of poverty assessments had substantial discussion of population, and major discussion of nutrition declined by more than half, from 28 to 12 percent. About a quarter to a third of Bank HNP analytic work—both ESW and research—was poverty-related, and this share has also declined in the decade since 1997.

Some aspects of monitoring have improved, but overall it remains weak, and evaluation is almost nonexistent, presenting a challenge for the HNP strategy's results orientation and commitment to better governance. Since 1997, an increasing number of projects have had monitoring indicators and baseline data when they were appraised. Yet, although nearly a third of projects supported *pilot* interventions or programs, or intended to evaluate the impact of a specific activity or program, few proposed evaluation designs in appraisal documents, and even fewer evaluations were actually conducted. Pilot projects or components without an evaluation design described in the appraisal document were never evaluated. Among the consequences of poor monitoring and evaluation and absence of baseline data were irrelevant objectives and inappropriate project designs, unrealistic targets—either too high or below the baseline value—inability to assess the effectiveness of activities, and lower efficacy and efficiency because of limited opportunities for learning. These findings are of great concern given the emphasis of the 2007 HNP strategy on results and good governance.

Approaches for Improving HNP Outcomes

The evaluation reviewed findings and lessons for three prominent approaches to raising HNP outcomes over the past decade—communicable disease control, health reform, and sectorwide approaches (SWAps). These approaches have been supported by the Bank as well as the international community and are not mutually exclusive. SWAps, for example, have included communicable disease control and health reform elements.

Support for communicable disease control can improve the pro-poor focus of health systems, but excessive earmarking of foreign aid for communicable diseases can distort allocations and reduce capacity in the rest of the health system. One of the strategic directions of the 2007 HNP strategy is to ensure synergy between priority disease interventions and strengthening the health system. The rationale for investing in infectious diseases is that they disproportionately affect the poor; their control has large, positive externalities; and control interventions have been shown to be cost-effective in many settings. Dedicated communicable disease projects have dramatically increased as a share of the overall portfolio over the past decade, and Bank support has directly built country capacity in national disease control programs. Support for communicable disease control, with the exception of AIDS projects, has shown better outcomes in relation to objectives than the rest of the HNP portfolio. Both equity and cost-effectiveness are particularly important to address in HIV/AIDS programs, given the huge commitments to that disease and that, unlike tuberculosis and malaria, HIV does not always disproportionately strike the poor. Care must be taken that, as the Bank enhances its support to systemwide reforms and SWAps, progress on communicable disease control remains a priority.

Since the initial increase in Bank-supported communicable disease control in the early 2000s, mainly for AIDS, the international community has also generously expanded funding through the Global Fund to Fight AIDS, TB, and Malaria and the (U.S.) President's Emergency Plan for AIDS Relief (PEPFAR), other bilateral contributions, and private foundations. In some low-income countries with high HIV prevalence, earmarked AIDS funds from international partners account for 30–40 percent or more of all public health funding. In an environment of scarce human resource capacity within the health system, care must be taken to balance the allocation of resources across health programs and budget lines, to ensure that large earmarked funds for specific diseases do not result in lower efficiencies or reduced care elsewhere in the health system. There is little evidence in recently approved Bank support for HIV/AIDS or the other high-priority diseases that this issue has been considered in funding decisions or in risk analysis.

Health reforms promise to improve efficiency and governance, but they are politically contentious, often complex, and relatively risky. Health system reform is central to the emphasis of the 2007 HNP strategy on strengthening health systems. About a third of HNP projects have supported reform or restructuring of the health system through changes in health finance, development of health insurance, decentralization of health systems, and regulation or engagement of the private health sector. These objectives affect efficiency and governance, which are valid objectives in their own right, even if they often do not directly affect health status in the short run. Reforms affecting health insurance help to prevent the impoverishing impacts of illness. Bank support for health system reforms has been mainly to middle-income countries, where health reform projects represent about half of the portfolio.

Many lessons have been learned over the past decade about the successes and pitfalls of support for health reform:

- First, the failure to assess fully the political economy of reform and to prepare a proactive plan to address it can considerably diminish prospects for success. Political risks, the interests of key stakeholders, and the risk of complexity—issues the evaluation case studies found to be critical—are often neglected in risk analysis in project appraisal documents for health reform projects.
- Second, reforms based on careful prior analytic work hold a greater chance of success, but analytic work does not ensure success.
- Third, the sequencing of reforms can improve political feasibility, reduce complexity, ensure that adequate capacity is in place, and facilitate learning. When implementation is flagging, the Bank can help preserve reform momentum with complementary programmatic lending through the Ministry of Finance, as it did in Peru and the Kyrgyz Republic.
- Finally, monitoring and evaluation are critical in health reform projects—to demonstrate the impact of pilot reforms to garner political support, but also because many reforms cannot work without a well-functioning management information system.

SWAps have contributed to greater government leadership, capacity, coordination, and harmonization within the health sector, but not necessarily to improved efficiency or better health results. Sectorwide approaches (SWAps) represent a reform in the way that government and international donors work together (the *approach*) to support the achievement of national health objectives (the *program*). They support the 2007 HNP strategy's objective to improve the organization, functioning, and sustainability of health systems. The *approach* promotes consensus around a common national strategy, country leadership, better harmonization and alignment of partners based on their comparative advantages, joint monitoring, the development and use of country systems, and, in many cases, the pooling of donor and government funds. The anticipated benefits include greater country sectoral leadership and capacity in managing health support, improved coordination and oversight of the inputs of all partners, reduced transaction costs, more efficient use of development assistance, more reliable support for the health sector, and greater sustainability of health programs.

The overwhelming focus of SWAps supported by the Bank has been on setting up and implementing the approach. Fieldwork found that country capacity has been strengthened in the areas of sector planning, budgeting, and fiduciary systems. However, weaknesses persist in the design and use of country monitoring and evaluation systems; evidence that the approach has improved efficiency or lowered transaction costs is thin, because neither has been monitored. Experience has shown that adopting the approach does not necessarily lead to better implementation or efficacy of the government's health programs: only a third of Bank projects that supported health SWAps have performed satisfactorily on meeting their health objectives. SWAps have often supported highly ambitious programs, involving many complex reforms and activities that exceed government implementation capacity. An important lesson is that programs need to be realistic and prioritized and that the process of setting up the SWAp should take care not to distract the players from ensuring the implementation and efficacy of the overall health program and a focus on results. SWAps have been most effective in pursuing health program objectives when the government is in a leadership position with a strongly owned and prioritized strategy (as in the Kyrgyz Republic). When this is not the case, there is a risk that the health program implemented will be less prioritized, reflecting the favored elements of the diverse partners, weakening effectiveness (as in Ghana).

The contribution of other sectors to HNP outcomes has been largely undocumented; the benefits of intersectoral coordination and multisectoral approaches need to be balanced with their costs in terms of increased complexity. Achieving the health MDGs will require complementary actions from sectors other than health, an explicit activity proposed within the 2007 HNP strategy. The contribution of other sectors to HNP outcomes has been captured through multisectoral HNP projects (projects that engage multiple sectors in a single operation with an objective to improve HNP outcomes) and parallel lending in projects managed by other sectors, in some cases with explicit health objectives. Multisectoral HNP operations have risen from a quarter of all HNP lending to half, greatly increasing the complexity of the portfolio. Most of the increase stems from multisectoral AIDS projects. The large number of sectors involved, the lack of specificity in design documents about the roles and responsibilities of each participating sector, the relatively new institutions put in charge, and other factors affecting lower performance in Africa all contribute to lower outcomes for multisectoral AIDS projects. Other multisectoral HNP projects with fewer implementing agencies have maintained stronger intersectoral collaboration and better outcomes.

Since 1997, the Bank has invested about $5 billion in smaller HNP components in 350 projects man-aged by other sectors, such as social protection, education, public sector management, water supply, and transport. Both the 2007 HNP strategy and its predecessor foresaw Country Assistance Strategies as the instrument for coordinating intersectoral action to improve HNP outcomes. However, this has not occured over the past decade. Lending activities in diverse sectors such as water supply and sanitation and education have been pursued—for the most part—independently of each other and of HNP operations, although this does not mean that they have not contributed to health outcomes.

Lending programs in other sectors may contribute directly or indirectly to HNP outcomes, in some cases by including health objectives or health components in projects. For example, half of all water supply and sanitation projects claim that health benefits will be generated, and 1 in 10 has an objective to improve health outcomes. But fewer water supply and sanitation projects include health objectives today than was the case 5–10 years ago; in fiscal 2002–06, only 1 in 20 water supply and sanitation projects had an objective to improve health for which they were accountable. Interviews with water supply and sanitation staff suggested that the sector has focused primarily on what is perceived to be "their" MDG, namely *increased access to safe water*. Yet research has shown that context matters; better access to safe water does not necessarily translate into better health. In contrast, the health content of transport projects has greatly increased, particularly in the field of road safety and HIV/AIDS prevention. While trends in accident statistics are relatively well documented for road safety components, there is very little in the way of documented outputs or results for HIV/AIDS components.

Water supply and sanitation and transport projects with health components or objectives rarely involved collaboration with Ministries of Health or the Bank's HNP sector (for example, the Rural Water Supply and Sanitation Project in Nepal). Delivery of health results in these and other sectors has been generally weak, except when an explicit health objective was identified at project appraisal.

There were virtually no results reported for health activities that were retrofitted into active projects.

IFC Support for Development of the Private Health Sector

About three-quarters of health expenditures in low-income countries and half in middle-income countries are private, and half of private health spending among the poor is for pharmaceuticals. IFC has made support to private investment in health one of its strategic priorities. Health is a relatively small and recent sector of IFC operations and involves the activities of two departments: Health and Education and General Manufacturing (for pharmaceuticals).

The performance of IFC's health investments, mostly hospitals, has substantially improved, following a learning process. Before 1999, four-fifths of all health investments performed poorly, and a majority of failed project businesses contributed to financial losses. The reasons for failure included the impact of financial crises in certain regions, delays in obtaining regulatory clearances from the authorities, and IFC's weaknesses in screening and structuring health sector deals owing to lack of sector-related experience. These experiences provided important lessons about hospital investments. More recent investments have realized good financial returns and performed better in achieving intended development outcomes. An evaluative framework for IFC's Advisory Services was only recently launched, so very few health projects have been evaluated, and their results should not be used to infer the performance of the whole portfolio. However, the few health Advisory Services projects that have been evaluated have performed lower than the IFC portfolio overall.

IFC has not been able to diversify its health portfolio as quickly as anticipated. In 2002, the sector set objectives to diversify the portfolio beyond hospitals and to improve the social impact of IFC health operations. IFC has continued to finance private hospitals; the share of pharmaceuticals and other life sciences investments has grown, though more slowly than envisioned in the strategy. IFC has also financed public-private

partnerships in health and expanded health Advisory Services with a focus on Africa. Investment numbers and volume increased from 2005 onward. However, to date IFC has not succeeded in financing any health insurance ventures and has financed only one project in medical education.

IFC's health interventions have had limited social impact, although efforts to broaden those impacts are increasing. IFC's investments in hospitals have targeted middle- and upper-income groups. Linkages to public insurance schemes will be necessary for IFC-supported hospitals to meet the health needs of a wider population. Expanded support to public-private partnerships, jointly with the World Bank, such as a recent output-based aid project to improve maternal care among some of Yemen's poorest people, and more strategic deployment of Advisory Services, such as recent efforts to assist social enterprises in Kenya and India, could lead to broadening of the social impact of investments in the health sector. These investments are too recent to evaluate.

Recent IFC health projects have had some positive results for efficiency, governance, and affordability. State-of-the-art facilities in some IFC-supported projects have attracted professionals with established, successful careers in developed countries. Many hospitals supported by IFC have posted fees and introduced control of doctors' side practices outside of the institutions. The majority of IFC-supported pharmaceutical projects have resulted in significant declines in the prices of generic drugs, thus enhancing affordability.

The need to collaborate closely with the World Bank's HNP sector is recognized as important in both the IFC and World Bank strategies to promote greater efficiency in the health sector through finance of private health care. The evaluation found some World Bank–IFC interaction, particularly in middle-income countries, but there is no real model of how that collaboration should occur in a situation where IFC health activities are few and very small in relation to the entire World Bank Group HNP sector in a given country.

Recommendations

The following recommendations for the World Bank and IFC are offered to help improve the implementation of their respective HNP strategies and further the mandate to reduce poverty and promote economic growth in the context of the new aid architecture.

1. Intensify efforts to improve the performance of the World Bank's support for health, nutrition, and population.

- Match project design to country capacity and reduce the complexity of support in low-capacity settings, particularly in Africa.
- Thoroughly and carefully assess the risks of proposed HNP support and strategies for mitigating those risks, particularly the political risks and incentives of stakeholders.
- Phase health system reforms to maximize the probability of success.
- Undertake thorough institutional analysis as an input into more realistic project design.
- Support intensified supervision in the field by the Bank and the borrower to ensure that civil works, equipment, and other outputs have been delivered as specified, are functioning, and are being maintained.

2. Renew the commitment to health, nutrition, and population outcomes among the poor.

The World Bank should:

- Boost *population, family planning* and other support to reduce high fertility.
- Incorporate the poverty dimension into project objectives.
- Increase support to reduce *malnutrition* among the poor, whether from the HNP sector or other sectors.
- Monitor health, nutrition, and population outcomes among the poor.
- Bring the health and nutrition of the poor and the links between high fertility, poor health, and poverty back into poverty assessments.

IFC should:

- Expand support for innovative approaches and viable business models that demonstrate private sector solutions to improve the health of the poor, including expansion of investments in low-cost generic drugs and technologies that address problems of the poor.
- Assess the external and internal constraints in achieving broad social impacts in the sector.

3. Strengthen the World Bank Group's ability to help countries to improve the efficiency of health systems.

The World Bank should:

- Better define the efficiency objectives of its support and how efficiency will be improved and monitored.
- Carefully assess decisions to finance additional freestanding communicable disease programs in countries where other donors are contributing large amounts of earmarked disease funding and additional earmarked funding may contribute to distortions in the health system.
- Support improved health information systems and more frequent and vigorous evaluation of reforms.

IFC should:

- Support public-private partnerships through Advisory Services to government and industry and through its investments, and expand investments in health insurance.
- Improve collaboration and joint sector work with the World Bank, leveraging Bank sector dialogue on health regulatory frameworks to engage new private actors, and more systematically coordinate with the Bank's policy interventions regarding private sector participation in health.

4. Enhance the contribution of support from other sectors to health, nutrition, and population outcomes.

The World Bank should:

- When the benefits are potentially great in relation to the marginal costs, incorporate health objectives into relevant non-health projects for which they are accountable.
- Improve the complementarity of investment operations in health and other sectors to achieve health, nutrition, and population outcomes, particularly between health and water supply and sanitation.
- Prioritize sectoral participation in multisectoral HNP projects to reduce complexity.
- Identify new incentives for Bank staff to work across sectors to improve health, nutrition, and population outcomes.
- Develop mechanisms to ensure that the implementation and results for small HNP components retrofitted into ongoing projects are properly documented and evaluated.

IFC should:

- Improve incentives and institutional mechanisms for an integrated approach to health issues across units in IFC dealing with health, including the way that health in IFC is organized.

5. Implement the results agenda and improve governance by boosting investment in and incentives for evaluation.

The World Bank should:

- Create new incentives for monitoring and evaluation for both the Bank and the borrower linked to the project approval process and the midterm review. This includes requirements for baseline data, evaluation designs for pilot activities in project appraisal documents, and periodic evaluation of main project activities as a management tool.

IFC should:

- Enhance its results orientation by developing clearly specified baseline indicators and an evaluation framework that adequately measures IFC's health sector objectives and results.

Management Response Summary

World Bank Group management welcomes IEG's evaluation of World Bank Group work in the health, nutrition, and population sector after 10 years of implementation of the 1997 health, nutrition, and population (HNP) strategy.

As a global development institution dedicated to supporting country and global efforts to achieve the better health outcomes that are central to reducing poverty and to achieve the 2015 Millennium Development Goals (MDGs), management appreciates the findings of this evaluation and other internal and external efforts to improve the World Bank Group's effectiveness in this key sector. (For the full-length Management Response and the detailed World Bank Management Action Plan, please see appendix J.)

This IEG report is consistent with the findings of the World Bank's own self-assessment, which prompted the Bank to adopt a new HNP strategy in mid-2007—*Healthy Development: The World Bank Strategy for Health, Nutrition, and Population Results.* In fact, IEG staff shared the preliminary results of their work with the strategy team that designed the subsequent 2007 strategy.

The new Strategy sharpened the Bank's focus on results on the ground; concentrated Bank contributions on health systems strengthening, health financing, and economics; supported government leadership and international community programs to achieve these results; and focused on enhanced engagement with global partners. Early implementation of the strategy has been promising. An example is the success of Rwanda's results-based approach to improving service delivery, with malaria incidence declining by 62 percent and child mortality decreasing by 30 percent.

Main Findings and Recommendations

The IEG evaluation covers a decade of Bank support, starting in 1997. The specific performance to date of the Bank's new strategy, adopted in mid-2007, is discussed in a separate Strategy Progress Report (World Bank 2009). Bank management has taken many of the findings and recommendations into account in the Progress Report and the Management Action Plan. While not detracting from the importance of the evaluation and its usefulness for the Bank's future work in health, nutrition, and population, management has observations on some of the findings.

Quality of the Bank HNP Portfolio—The principal finding of the IEG evaluation is that, while two-thirds of the Bank's HNP projects in the period 1997–2007 achieved their development objectives, one third, mostly in African countries, did not, clearly warranting close scrutiny. Current data on risky projects and programs in the HNP portfolio show that problems continue to be most acute in HIV/AIDS projects and in programs in the Africa Region. The HNP sector's performance in much of the rest of the world is now near the performance of other sectors, and the Africa Region has developed new strategic approaches to improving portfolio quality, including a focus on results and emphasis on health systems strengthening.

IEG notes the underperformance of HIV/AIDS projects during the height of the epidemic in southern Africa during the late 1990s, a period characterized by regional conflict and instability, and the internal displacement of millions of refugees across borders in the Great Lakes Region of the continent. Current projects, focusing on high-risk groups, also constitute a disproportionate number of projects at risk in the current portfolio. In order to redress this situation, a comprehensive approach has been adopted to improve the quality of the Bank's HIV/AIDS operations, including an umbrella restructuring of the Multi-Country HIV/AIDS Programs (MAPs).

Investing in Health Systems—The 2007 strategy underscores the need to focus on health system strengthening to ensure better health outcomes, particularly for the poorest and the most vulnerable. Over the past two years, projects with a primary focus on health systems have increased twofold. In line with the strategy, 67 percent of Bank programs approved since fiscal year 2007 that focused on priority disease areas also include strong components on health system strengthening. An Africa-focused initiative started in 2008 will improve the Bank's capacity to provide rapid advice and assistance on the ground, particularly in health finance, human resources, governance, supply chain management, and infrastructure planning.

Doing More in Population and Reproductive Health—Bank management agrees with IEG that it should do more in this key area. The Progress Report highlights plans for strengthening support for population and reproductive health, using a health systems approach that is critical to improving maternal and child survival rates.

Investing in Nutrition Support—We also agree with IEG's findings that the Bank needs to focus more on nutrition. The need for action is even more important today in the context of the ongoing crises in fuel, food, and fertilizers, as well as the escalating effects of the financial crisis. We are therefore investing significant resources in the next few years to ramp up the Bank's analytical and investment work and leverage resources from other donors. The agenda for scaling up nutrition is being catalyzed with additional budget and external resources, starting in 2009 and continuing for three years.

Improving Monitoring and Evaluation (M&E)—As noted in the Strategy Progress Report, this is an important part of strategy implementation, (including the work on retrofitting projects and improving the design of new projects). Routine health monitoring systems (including surveillance, facility reporting, vital registration, census data, resource tracking, and household surveys) may first need to be strengthened to provide the data and indicators that are needed. The Bank is working with partners, such as the World Health Organization, to develop better ways to monitor the health MDGs, including the estimation of trends in child and maternal mortality, for which updates have recently been issued.

The International Financial Corporation's HNP Footprint. IFC has considerably increased its footprint in HNP over the past decade and is prepared to intensify collaboration within the World Bank Group. There is a growing acknowledgement of the role of the private sector in health care in developing countries. The period under review has seen a marked increase in IFC's activity in health. During this time, many lessons have been learned, specialist knowledge has deepened, and performance has improved by any measure applied. As in other sectors, IFC continues to strive for greater development impact, and we therefore welcome all input that could help us to do better.

Management Action Record

Recommendations	Management response
1. Intensify efforts to improve the performance of the World Bank's health, nutrition, and population support.	
(a) Match project design to country context and capacity and reduce the complexity of projects in low-capacity settings through greater selectivity, prioritization, and sequencing of activities, particularly in Sub-Saharan Africa.	Management agrees that complexity can be at least partially addressed by adopting IEG recommendations, such as thorough technical preparation, including solid analytical underpinning, political mapping, high quality at entry, including prioritizing interventions relative to the institutional context, and establishing a good results framework, followed by in-depth supervision and parallel policy dialogue with client and partners.

However, HNP operations are rarely institutionally or technically simple, since the desired outcome depends on a complex and interacting set of social, cultural, and institutional factors. This is recognized by donors and policy makers, whether in low-income, middle-income, or high-income countries. The inherent complexity of the sector may be attributable to the political economy in a multi-stakeholder environment, the need for extensive coordination and partnership with national and international agencies and civil society organizations, and the often difficult technical and social nature of the subject. The recent international recognition of the need to invest in (complex) health systems in order to ensure the success of vertical disease control programs in low-income countriess is testimony to the fact that there are few easy ways to avoid systemic complexity. Investing in simple programs would not necessarily provide for lasting impact. |
(b) Thoroughly and carefully assess the risks of proposed HNP support and strategies to mitigate them, particularly the political risks and the interests of different stakeholders, and how they will be addressed.	Management agrees in principle to carry out political mapping exercises prior to investments in the sector where appropriate. As there are currently mandatory risk assessment and mitigation steps built into the project cycle and approval process, we anticipate improved risk mitigation strategies in newer HNP operations. These enable staff to identify major political and technical risks and devise with the client suitable risk-mitigation strategies. However, it is also evident that despite good assessments and risk-mitigation strategies, neither technical nor political risks can be completely offset.
(c) Phase reforms to maximize the probability of success.	Management agrees with this recommendation and would note that more projects are now taking this approach.
(d) Undertake thorough institutional analysis, including an assessment of alternatives, as an input into more realistic project design.	Management agrees with this recommendation.
(e) Support intensified supervision in the field by the Bank and the borrower to ensure that civil works, equipment, and other outputs have been delivered as specified, are functioning, and are being maintained.	Management agrees in principle with this recommendation. Supervision requirements, both in terms of staffing mix and budgeting, are being reassessed Bank-wide within the context of the ongoing review of investment lending. Given the inherent dispersed nature of many HNP investments, care must be taken during project design to ensure that the client assumes responsibility for ensuring that civil works, equipment, and other outputs have been delivered as specified, are functioning and being maintained, while the Bank audits/appraises/confirms that such monitoring is taking place so that detailed supervision of projects can be properly conducted within likely budget norms.

Management action: In response to the portfolio quality challenges, the HNP Sector Board has introduced a quarterly portfolio monitoring and benchmarking system, which is being used by the Sector Board and regional management to improve portfolio performance. |
| **2. Renew the commitment to health, nutrition, and population outcomes among the poor.** | |
| **WORLD BANK**

(a) Boost *population* and *family planning* support in the form of analytic work, policy dialogue, and financing to high-fertility countries and countries with pockets of high fertility. | Management agrees with this recommendation for high-fertility countries and regions—in particular as those areas have received less attention from other development partners as well over the past decade. Demand for stand-alone population (family planning) programs has declined over time. The Bank should increase support for reproductive health programs, which are usually better implemented when they are fully embedded into public health/clinical services. We would |

Management Action Record *(continued)*

Recommendations	Management response
	generally not support a return to stand-alone vertical family planning projects. Moreover, AIDS control projects (or components) and the work through UNAIDS have substantially contributed to reproductive health—and greatly expanded coverage of family planning for otherwise hard-to-reach population groups. In countries that are significantly advanced through the demographic transition, clients increasingly request advice and financing on financial protection, labor markets, and long-term care needs to address the ongoing demographic and epidemiological shifts resulting in an aging society. Finally, Development Grant Facility–financed programs such as the Special Program of Research, Development and Research Training in Human Reproduction (HRP), into which the Bank has substantial technical, financial, and managerial input, are contributing to the global reproductive health agenda.
(b) Incorporate the poverty dimension into project objectives to increase accountability for health, nutrition, and population outcomes among the poor.	Management generally agrees with the need to ensure that project design responds to the priorities and needs of the poor, and to measure the full impact of improved health services for the poor. Management will therefore seek to ensure that adequate attention is given to poverty dimensions in project design and supervision. However, direct assessments, where feasible, may be technically complex and expensive. The Bank publication *Attacking Inequality in the Health Sector—A Synthesis of Evidence and Tools* (Yazbeck 2009) lays out a policy menu (pro-poor policy reforms along six dimensions) and a list of the analytical tools for understanding the constraints to pro-poor targeting of public health investments in poor countries. As opposed to specific income groups, disease control programs must focus on the prevailing epidemiology (for example an AIDS program must focus on high-risk groups, irrespective of income). A malaria program focused solely on the poor would fail to eliminate malaria. Polio could only be eradicated from the Western Hemisphere by focusing on large, inclusive campaigns targeting all income groups. Such investments in public health and control of communicable diseases are global public goods, generating positive externalities for society, irrespective of income status. Investments in health systems should result in increased access and better quality of services—also benefiting the poor. Investment in social security and social safety net systems prevents the middle class from falling into poverty in case of a catastrophic health event. Management notes the substantive improvements over the past years in quantity and quality of HNP involvement in Poverty Reduction and Economic Management Network (PREM)–led analytical work, and agrees that HNP must be fully included in all Poverty Assessments and fully examined in the preparation of CASs.
(c) Increase support to reduce *malnutrition* among the poor, whether originating in the HNP sector or other sectors.	Management agrees with this recommendation. Particularly in the context of the global food crisis, the Bank needs to increase investments in nutrition, with a particular focus on maternal and infant nutrition. Management is therefore investing significant resources in the next few years to ramp up the Bank's analytical and investment work and leverage resources from other donors. The agenda for scaling-up nutrition is being catalyzed with additional budget resources, starting in 2009 and continuing for three years. The increased allocations are being utilized principally in Africa and South Asia, two Regions where the malnutrition burden is highest. These funds will be complemented by additional trust fund resources from Japan, and possibly from other donors that are currently engaged in discussions on this issue.
(d) Monitor health, nutrition, and population outcomes among the poor, however defined.	Management agrees in principle with this recommendation, and will seek to ensure adequate provision for data collection, where technically feasible, during quality-at-entry and supervision reviews, in particular as far as poverty targeting is concerned. In order to accomplish this in a sustainable manner, management believes that the first priority in many poor countries is to establish routine health monitoring systems (surveillance, facility reporting, vital registration, census data, resource tracking, household surveys, and the like). These data systems need to be strengthened in parallel to investing in project-specific management information systems, in order to provide data and indicators that are needed for program targeting and monitoring for (but not limited to) the poor.

Management Action Record *(continued)*

Recommendations	Management response
(e) Bring the health and nutrition of the poor and the links between high fertility, poor health, and poverty back into poverty assessments in countries where this has been neglected.	Management agrees. Substantial progress regarding this recommendation has been made in some regions over the past years, both in terms of the analytical underpinnings, the need for capacity building, and investment needs. Management will seek to improve cross-sectoral collaboration with the PREM Network at country level as a precondition to further improvements. Management action: Recent major analytical work for staff and policy makers prepared by the Human Development Network to improve effectiveness in reaching the poor includes: *Reaching the Poor with Health, Nutrition and Population Services—What Works, What Doesn't and Why* (Gwatkin, Wagstaff, and Yazbeck 2005) and *Attacking Inequality in the Health Sector—A Synthesis of Evidence and Tools* (Yazbeck 2009). It is expected that this work will help clients and staff achieve better results in reaching the poor with health services. Concerning nutrition, in addition to disseminating the new Nutrition Strategy (*Repositioning Nutrition as Central to Development—A Large Scale Action* [World Bank 2006c]) the Regional Reprioritization Fund will allocate US$4 million over fiscal years 2009–11 to strengthen Bank capacity to scale up nutrition support and leverage resources from other donors.

IFC

Recommendations	Management response
(a) Expand support for innovative approaches and viable business models that demonstrate private sector solutions to improve the health of the poor, including expansion of investments in low-cost generic drugs and technologies that address health problems of the poor.	Management agrees with working on innovative approaches and helping private providers to move down-market to serve lower-income groups and markets. IFC has several initiatives already under way to build on its work to date. Some examples include: • Health in Africa initiative. • Working with clients to invest expertise and capital from high-income to low- and lower-middle-income countries, e.g., Saudi-German Hospitals, based in Saudi Arabia, opened hospitals in Yemen, Egypt, and Ethiopia with IFC finance, creating a South-South investment. • Output-based aid projects in Yemen and Nigeria, in which poor people get subsidized care in IFC-financed private facilities that otherwise would not exist. • Creating finance facilities for health care small and medium-size enterprises in low-income countries by use of structured finance, combined with technical assistance, that IFC pioneered with banks in Africa and elsewhere to finance education facilities, and building on that knowledge to apply it in health. • Working with clients to move down-market within their country, e.g., working with Apollo Hospitals in India to create hospitals in secondary cities.
(b) Assess the external and internal constraints in achieving broad social impacts in the sector.	A number of continually changing factors are enabling greater activity in the sector. Among others, the private sector partners with whom IFC must work are continually evolving and developing more capacity and professionalism than was the case 10 years ago, due in part to IFC's involvement with them. Nevertheless, there is a lot still to be done and IFC needs more and larger partners with whom to work and is developing long-term partners and new approaches with a view to greater scale and impact. IFC's recent Health in Africa initiative also analyzed constraints and ways to address them across multiple countries in a particularly difficult region. This is indicative of the organization's evolving approach as both its knowledge and resources for addressing this recently entered sector expand.

3. Strengthen the World Bank Group's ability to help countries to improve the efficiency of their health systems.

WORLD BANK

Recommendations	Management response
(a) Better define the efficiency objectives of its support and how efficiency improvements will be improved and monitored.	Management generally agrees with this recommendation. The efficiency argument is a key rationale, in particular for working with health systems in middle-income countries. Since national health expenditures rise with national income, improving sector efficiency makes an important contribution to fiscal sustainability. However, in the health sector there are important efficiency-equity trade-offs. This points to the fact that efficiency gains should not be the sole objective of Bank-financed health programs.
(b) Carefully assess decisions to finance additional earmarked communicable disease activities in countries where other	Management agrees that it is necessary to carefully assess the need for additional finance where other donors are contributing substantial amounts. While fiscal space and potential

Management Action Record *(continued)*

Recommendations	Management response
donors are contributing large amounts of earmarked disease funding and additional funds could result in distortion in allocations and inefficiencies in the rest of the health system.	budget substitution by ministries of finance should be closely monitored, the empirical evidence of distortionary effects of large vertical disease programs is scanty. Proposals for Bank support for new disease-specific programs are closely coordinated with other donors and often fund complementary financing and institutional needs, for which financing was unavailable from other donors.
(c) Support improved health information systems and more frequent and vigorous evaluation of specific reforms or program innovations to provide timely information for improving efficiency and efficacy.	Management agrees partially with this recommendation: Technical support and financing for management information systems as well as routine surveillance and vital statistics systems should be ramped up. However, the outcomes of management information system investments may be hard to evaluate fully within the timeframe of a project, and multiple determinants influence health outcomes. Management also notes that the Paris and Accra Declarations and the new OP 13.60 emphasize the use of pooled funding and country-level M&E systems instead of ring-fenced funding and stand-alone M&E systems. Hence, the standard should be that sufficient evidence on outputs, intermediate outcomes, and outcomes should be collected to establish a credible story line to assess the link between Bank-financed investments and overall sector progress, including efficiency and efficacy gains.

Management action: The Human Development Network and the Regions have carried out major analytical work that will help policy makers and Bank staff to better understand challenges and trade-offs in health financing, risk pooling and insurance, the issue of fiscal space and external assistance (*Health Financing Revisited—A Practitioner's Guide* [Gottret and Schieber 2006]). Furthermore, the Bank is a lead sponsor of the International Health Partnership (IHP+). This is a country-led and country-driven partnership that calls for all signatories to accelerate action to scale up coverage and use of health services and deliver improved outcomes against the health-related MDGs, while honoring commitments to improve universal access to health. |
| **IFC**

(a) Support public-private partnerships through Advisory Services to government and industry and through its investments, and expand investments in health insurance. | IFC has supported pioneering health public-private partnerships (PPPs) in Romania and Lesotho and continues to work in this area. While health PPPs are a relatively recent development in emerging markets, there is increasing interest in health PPPs as a means to expand and improve services for the public. The work in Lesotho is at the leading edge for emerging-country health PPPs in several aspects. From the investment aspect, partners in health PPPs to date have often been construction companies rather than health providers and have not required capital from IFC. In some of the few cases where it is truly health services, rather than construction and facilities management, that have been provided by the private sector, IFC has financed providers of renal dialysis services and diagnostic services to public health systems.

Many of IFC's clients who provide health services have prepayment schemes for health care in operation and this makes the most business sense. In some instances, by creating more low-cost local capacity, IFC health-provider clients have made it possible for health insurers to offer new products with lower premiums. Experience to date has shown that the business case for direct investment in stand-alone private health insurance does not exist to the extent envisaged when the 2002 IFC health strategy was devised. The few health insurance operations found to date that actually needed capital have needed only very small amounts, too small to be viable transactions. This segment of the sector is intended to be addressed by the health-sector financing facilities now being developed and in early implementation. For the balance, typically the health insurer is one arm of a larger insurer that is well capitalized from its other operations such as life insurance or is a subsidiary or joint venture of a well-capitalized foreign parent company. |
| (b) Improve collaboration and joint sector work with the World Bank, leveraging Bank sector dialogue on regulatory frameworks for health to engage new private actors with value added to the sector, and more systematically coordinate with the Bank's policy interventions regarding private sector participation in health. | In some situations, such as the Health in Africa initiative and the Lesotho healthcare PPP, IFC and the World Bank are collaborating very closely. In practice, there are times when this is practical and possible and times when it is not. The imbalance in the size of human resources working on health in the two organizations, with the World Bank having many more people dedicated to health, requires IFC to be judicious in how it allocates its resources to work with the Bank. |

Management Action Record *(continued)*

Recommendations	Management response

4. Enhance the contribution of support from other sectors to health, nutrition, and population outcomes.

WORLD BANK

(a) When the benefits are potentially great in relation to the marginal costs, incorporate health objectives into non-health projects, for which they are accountable.

Management agrees in principle, but implementation can be challenging. For example, health is a secondary objective for many clients in water and sanitation operations and borrowers are reluctant to add potentially costly components. In addition, the current mandate, staffing, and budget of the water sector does not allow the sector to be "accountable for health benefits" as IEG suggests. Under IDA 15 guidelines, it is mandatory to track "safe and sustainable access to water and or sanitation services" as an outcome, with health benefits classified as impacts, rather than outcomes. Because it is difficult and expensive to track health impacts, the number of water projects with a health objective has declined, and this trend is likely to continue absent changes in policy and/or additional resources.

(b) Improve the complementarity of investment operations in health and other sectors to achieve health, nutrition, and population outcomes, particularly between health and water supply and sanitation.

Management generally agrees that we need to support client countries to seek improved complementarity of water and sanitation programs with health projects, in particular as clients are reluctant to burden all water and sanitation operations with potentially small (albeit cost effective) health impact objectives, and to demonstrate and document empirically such impact and outcomes in each case.

(c) Prioritize sectoral participation in multisectoral HNP projects according to the comparative advantages and institutional mandates, to reduce complexity.

Management agrees and notes that significant additional resources have been mobilized from fiscal year 2009 on to better respond to client and partner requests for embedding Bank support in multisector programs, or to provide just-in-time advice to countries and partners in development. Specifically, over US$3 million additional Bank budget will be allocated per year to ramp up Bank support for the 14 IHP+ countries, mostly in Africa, including the establishment and staffing of two regional technical support hubs in Africa. Additional resources are being provided by other donors.

(d) Identify new incentives for Bank staff to work cross-sectorally for improving HNP outcomes.

Management agrees, but notes that this is a concern across the institution that needs institutional analysis and solutions, including revisiting the incentives needed for improved cross-sectoral and cross-departmental collaboration.

(e) Develop mechanisms to ensure that the implementation and results for small health components retrofitted into projects are properly documented and evaluated.

Management agrees, subject to the limitations mentioned previously related to M&E and attribution.

Management action: the HNP sector continues to expand and deepen cross-sector engagement. Recent products include work on Social Safety Nets, Ageing and Demographic Change, Early Childhood Development and Poverty, Environment and Health. Ongoing initiatives include work with Water and Sanitation, Transport, Poverty Reduction and Economic Management, Agriculture and Rural Development, and Operations Policy and Country Services on global challenges ranging from global infectious threats, climate change (part of the 2010 *World Development Report*), road safety, and an Advanced Market Commitment to develop a pneumococcal vaccine suitable for use in Africa.

IFC

(a) Improve incentives and institutional mechanisms for an integrated approach to health issues across units in IFC dealing with health, including the way IFC is organized.

IFC is currently going through a period of reorganization aimed at achieving a number of goals. As part of this, industry clusters have been created and Health and Education are in the same cluster with Global Manufacturing and Services, which contains IFC's pharmaceutical activities. Communication and collaboration between teams working on health care and pharmaceuticals are frequent and ongoing. The market reality is that it is rare for one organization to invest in both health care provision and pharmaceutical manufacturing. The knowledge needed to work with these clients is also very different.

Information is also exchanged between the Infrastructure Advisory group, advising on health PPPs, and the Health and Education investment department. Care has to be exercised that such information is exchanged only at appropriate points in project life cycles to avoid conflicts of interest that could arise in being both advisor to a bidding process and financier of a winner of a bid. Integrating these two functions too closely would create a conflict for PPP work.

Management Action Record *(continued)*

Recommendations	Management response

5. Implement the results agenda and improve governance by boosting investment in and incentives for evaluation.

WORLD BANK

(a) Create new incentives for monitoring and evaluation for both the Bank and the borrower linked to the project approval process and the midterm review. This would include requirements for baseline data, explicit evaluation designs for pilot activities in project appraisal documents, and periodic evaluation of main project activities as a management tool.

Management agrees. We face the challenge that countries may be unwilling to borrow for M&E, particularly for expensive impact evaluations. These large-scale evaluations may require external (grant) financing in most cases, which can be particularly difficult to obtain in a middle-income country context. A second challenge is to ensure that data are readily available for public use. Some countries are not ready to fully share data and may be reluctant to include data in public documents, such as PADs, and the like. This can delay the establishment of appropriate baseline data and results frameworks prior to project approval.

Management action: The HNP Sector Board and the Human Development Network have made important progress to address M&E in the HNP portfolio: A number of Regions have carried out a complete portfolio review, including the retrofitting of all operations to assure an up-to-date results framework. Moreover, over US$2.8 million of Spanish Trust Fund (SIEF) resources are currently under implementation, benefiting impact evaluations of 15 HNP projects in all Regions, focusing on Pay for Performance in Health (5 projects, US$1.2m), Malaria Control (5 projects, US$600,000), HIV/AIDS Prevention (3 projects, US$750,000), and Innovations and "quick wins" (2 projects, US$300,000).

IFC

(a) Enhance its results orientation by developing clearly specified baseline indicators and an evaluation framework that adequately measures IFC's health sector objectives and results.

At the project level, IFC has implemented the Development Outcome Tracking System toward the end of the period under review. Over time, this is expected to improve such results orientation and specifying of baseline indicators.

IFC also agrees that where there is a sufficient critical mass of projects in the health sector in a specific country, it makes sense to try to asses IFC's development impact in the sector beyond aggregating project-level results. While recognizing that attributing sector development to IFC's intervention is an issue that needs to be carefully addressed, IFC is looking into ways of measuring results beyond the project level. Among others, the work IFC is undertaking with the IDA-IFC Secretariat in reviewing the CAS results matrix could lead to the establishment of a country-level sector development results framework that could be used in countries where IFC has a critical mass of projects in health. IFC is also exploring setting development impact and reach targets for investment departments, including health and education.

Chairperson's Summary: Committee on Development Effectiveness (CODE)

On January 28, 2009, the Committee considered the document *Improving Effectiveness and Outcomes for the Poor in Health, Nutrition, and Population: An Evaluation of World Bank Group Support since 1997* prepared by the Independent Evaluation Group (IEG) and the *Draft Management Response*.

Background

Following a self-assessment of its support in the health sector, the World Bank (the Bank) renewed its focus on the health sector in 2007 with an updated strategy, *Healthy Development: The World Bank Strategy for Health, Nutrition, and Population Results.* IFC outlined its health sector strategy in 2002.

IEG Evaluation

The report evaluated the efficacy, specifically the health, nutrition, and population (HNP) outcomes, of the World Bank Group (namely IBRD/IDA and IFC) country-level support since 1997 and drew lessons from that experience. It includes, for the first time, an evaluation of IFC's cumulative support for health. Based on the findings, the IEG made recommendations for the Bank and IFC grouped under five broad areas, which include: intensify efforts to improve the performance of the Bank's support for HNP; renew the commitment to HNP outcomes among the poor; strengthen the World Bank Group's ability to help countries to improve the efficiency of health systems; enhance the contribution of support from other sectors to HNP outcomes; and implement the results agenda and improve gover-nance by boosting investment in and incentives for evaluation.

The Draft Management Response

Management noted its agreement with many of the findings and recommendations that confirmed the Bank's own self-assessment, undertaken before its health sector strategy was updated. At the same time, it offered its views on several aspects of the evaluation, including coverage of the evaluation, targeting issues, the importance of not only focusing on health outcomes for the poor but also on preventing poverty due to financial costs from poor health, emerging issues such as the aging population in developing countries, challenges with respect to monitoring and evaluation, and actions being taken to address some of the issues identified by IEG.

Overall Conclusions

The Committee welcomed the discussion, noting the importance of the IEG evaluation findings. It also remarked on the centrality of the health sector to the Bank's mandate for poverty reduction and contribution to the Millennium Development Goals (MDGs), although the Bank's role has shifted to become a smaller financier in the sector. Concerns were expressed about the main IEG findings, including the under-performance of the HNP portfolio, particularly in the Africa Region; the weak accountability for ensuring that the results have reached the poor; and the continued weaknesses in monitoring and evaluation (M&E). Management was also asked to address the issue of excessive complexity of health programs while recognizing its multisectoral dimension.

Speakers raised questions and comments on a range of issues, including the need for more Bank support for nutrition and population, the importance of addressing maternal health, HIV/AIDS measures in health system strengthening, and the effectiveness of the sectorwide approaches (SWAps). They also remarked on the importance of establishing realistic targets, project supervision, local capacity building, reliable data, and appropriate staff skill mix and incentives to support the HNP strategy. Some speakers expressed interest in the development impact of IFC's health sector projects, particularly the inclusion of the poor. The Committee asked management to revise its response to address the various comments made at the meeting, including the request for an action plan to address the IEG recommendations. Several speakers also noted the need for a sound communication strategy before the disclosure of the IEG report.

Next Steps

The revised Management Response will be circulated for information to the Committee in advance of the Board's informal meeting to consider management's first report on the implementation of the new health sector strategy—*Health, Nutrition, and Population Strategy Implementation—An Interim Report.* The Committee will recommend to the Board that it consider the IEG evaluation report and the revised Management Response along with management's interim report, which is scheduled for an informal Board discussion on April 9, 2009. Management proposed to provide informal updates in response to speakers' interest in regular reports on the World Bank Group support for the health sector.

Main issues raised at the meeting were the following:

World Bank Group's Role. Members remarked on the changing environment of the health sector with an increase in institutions providing HNP support. In this regard, they emphasized quality over quantity of World Bank Group support. They also noted that the World Bank Group has an important role in donor coordination, ensuring efficient allocation and effective use of resources in the sector, and introducing innovations and generating knowledge to strengthen health systems and service delivery. Remarking on the inherent complexity and high risk of health sector support, a member emphasized the World Bank Group's continued role in this sector and also noted that the risks should be taken into account in assessing performance, to avoid providing staff with disincentives to invest in valuable but risky projects.

Bank's Portfolio Performance. The importance of addressing the Bank's comparatively lower portfolio performance in the health sector, including the poor results in Africa Region, was highlighted. Considering the Bank's comparative advantage as providing policy advice, strengthening health systems, and supporting institutional and human capacity building, several non-members queried about the growing share of programs addressing communicable diseases. A few members emphasized the importance of political analysis, which could be done during the preparation of country assistance strategies or through policy notes; project supervision; and learning, including for local implementation capacity building. Questions were raised about ensuring an appropriate staff skills mix to deliver HNP programs, especially in the Africa Region, taking into consideration the global competition for such skills. *Bank management elaborated on its review of all at-risk HNP projects, and work with the Quality Assurance Group to determine what actions are needed. It described the challenges and risks faced in the Africa Region and in the fragile states, and its efforts to improve performance in the Africa Region, including estab-*

lishing two technical hubs and staffing them with additional experts in epidemiology, health economics, and health management to support analytical work and project implementation. It said that it is scaling up technical assistance and capacity building at the country level.

A few speakers expressed interest in understanding the Bank's HNP portfolio performance across time, as compared to other sectors, and in the context of performance of other donor support to HNP. One of them also sought information on the Bank's HNP support against the principles of the 2005 Paris Declaration. *IEG responded that between fiscal years 1992 and 2001, the performance of both the HNP portfolio and other sectors had improved, but since fiscal 2002, the HNP portfolio performance has been flat, while that of other sectors has continued to improve. It referred to its evaluations of global program reviews in HNP, but noted that it did not have the same level of data on the effectiveness of HNP support by other donors.*

Reaching the Poor. Several speakers asked about the Bank's measures to strengthen the poverty focus of HNP sector support. While agreeing on the importance of reaching the poor, a member observed the greater challenges of assessing outcomes for the poor in the case of certain initiatives such as for communicable diseases, where focus is on groups at the highest risk or investment in vaccines. A few members expressed interest in IFC's efforts to improve the inclusion of the poor in its health projects, and in this regard also requested IEG to elaborate on its recommendation. *Bank management commented on its renewed focus on results, including for the poor, such as through the results-based financing mechanism. It also explained that investments in diseases of the poor, such as malaria, have a fully pro-poor targeted approach. IFC responded that it is supporting smaller health care institutions providing services to the poor through wholesaling or other arrangements with financial partners. It is also providing Advisory Services to promote public-private partnerships to provide services to the poor, as well as working with large-scale service providers to achieve cost efficiencies and to make services more affordable for the poor. IEG clarified that the impact of World Bank Group support on the poor is largely unknown, because outcomes among the poor have not been monitored. It suggested that IFC could improve the social impact of health initiatives by supporting investments that have greater benefits for the poor, such as supporting manufacturing and distribution of lower-cost, higher-quality generic drugs and research and development to treat diseases that disproportionately affect the poor.*

Project Design and Approach. A few members noted that the design of HNP projects could be simpler or phased, particularly in countries facing institutional and implementation capacity issues. At the same time, they also said the design should be based on country context and achievable objectives. Likewise, a member remarked that the level of multisectoral cooperation should be situation-specific, depending on capacity and availability of resources. *Bank management elaborated on how a health project with a seemingly simple objective and apparently easily measurable results (for example, providing mosquito nets to counter malaria) can require a complex solution, particularly in countries with limited infrastructure and capacity, and offer challenges in monitoring results. IEG emphasized the importance of setting achievable objectives and a clear results framework. It clarified that there was no evidence in the evaluation that simple health projects are less sustainable or those with more complex designs are more sustainable. It also said that the World Bank Group should not avoid investing in worthwhile but risky projects, but there is a substantial scope for minimizing risks through better ex ante risk analysis and mitigation measures.* A few speakers expressed interest in more analysis of the mixed results of the SWAps and IEG's recommendations for future use of this approach. *IEG responded that the context is important; SWAps work better in some contexts than in others. It also* *said that while SWAps have given much attention to the process, there could be more focus on HNP outcomes.*

Nutrition. A member welcomed the role of the Bank in emphasizing the importance of nutrition. Another member noted the importance of incorporating food security concerns in health sector projects.

Population and Reproductive Health. Several speakers encouraged the Bank to strengthen its focus on population and reproductive health. A few members remarked on the development challenge of high population growth from a global perspective and in Sub-Saharan Africa. Others urged the Bank to prioritize reproductive health and identify maternal health as a key target in its health programs. In addition, some speakers noted the importance of a gender-based approach to, and integrating HIV/AIDS measures in, health system support, particularly in the area of reproductive health. The need for adequate staffing and analytical work to support initiatives addressing population and reproductive health was emphasized. *Bank management said that it is currently considering how to strengthen the focus on population issues in its health system support and it intended to elaborate on this in the forthcoming HNP interim report to the Board in April.*

Monitoring and Evaluation. Members and non-members underlined the importance of improving M&E to enable a better understanding of the Bank's performance in the sector. They commented on the need for a clear results framework and M&E plan in all initiatives, for establishing and strengthening country-based M&E systems, and for appropriate incentives within the World Bank Group as well as for promoting country ownership. The lack of reliable health data, challenges of data collection, and reluctance of countries to share data were discussed. A member supported a prag-

matic and realistic approach to M&E, taking into consideration the local capacity and financial resource constraints. *Bank management elaborated on the serious attention it is giving to M&E, noting that the Human Development Network has the biggest impact evaluation program in the Bank. It described its work with other partners to jointly strengthen data at the country level and to strengthen the country's M&E systems. IFC said it is setting project-level baselines and monitoring relevant development impact indicators through the Development Outcome Tracking System.*

Response to the IEG Evaluation Report

Members and non-members requested that management revise its response to the IEG evaluation report to address members' comments, including the requests for an action plan addressing IEG's recommendations that may be monitored. *IEG noted that the evaluation report would be disclosed with the revised Management Response.* Several speakers stressed the importance of communicating, particularly to IDA donors, that management's response will urgently and effectively address the evaluation findings and recommendations. In this context, the chairperson referred to another speaker's observation about the issue of timing of the IEG evaluation with respect to the Bank's 2007 HNP strategy. It was widely felt that the IEG recommendations may be incorporated in the interim report on health, nutrition, and population strategy implementation, scheduled to be discussed at the Board on April 9, 2009. In this respect, members and non-members requested that the Board consider the IEG evaluation report together with the revised Management Response, alongside the management's paper on *Health, Nutrition, and Population Strategy Implementation—An Interim Report*. The general preference was to discuss the reports in one meeting.

Giovanni Majnoni, Chairman

Advisory Panel Statement

The external advisory group welcomes this report on World Bank Group support for health, nutrition, and population outcomes since 1997. In an era when health has been very high on the international agenda, it is vital that development agencies such as the World Bank Group rigorously scrutinize the effectiveness of what they do and learn from such scrutiny to improve practices.

From its involvement during the process of the evaluation, the advisory group was satisfied that the processes were transparent, independent, constructive, and evidence-based. The evaluation's approach and methods made the most of what evidence was available, and the overall analyses, conclusions, and recommendations are sound. Below we highlight and comment on key findings.

The decade has seen a remarkable increase in international assistance for health, and a marked decline in the Bank's share of total assistance, from 18 percent in the 1990s to 6 percent. While we echo the view of the evaluation that the Bank still has a very important role to play, we were taken aback by the extent to which the Bank followed the trend of increased support to communicable disease control. At a time when disease-specific programs were getting greatly increased support from elsewhere, we were surprised that the Bank did not provide a countervailing trend. Indeed, there was a fall of nearly half in the share of projects with objectives to reform the health system. We endorse the view in the report of the Bank's comparative advantage—that it can provide long-term, sustained engagement, a focus on building country capacity in the sector, strong links to Ministries of Finance, and engagement across many sectors—and fully agree that its focus should be on making health systems work better and ensuring that benefits reach the poor.

In this context, it is a source of considerable concern that the performance of the HNP portfolio overall has been below average, and that within this the health sector reform type of projects have tended to perform less well. The report provides much food for thought in exploring why this might have been the case. We strongly endorse the recommendations that project design should be matched to country context and capacity, that complex projects should be avoided in low capacity settings, and that thorough institutional analysis and exploration of political economy issues should be part of project design and implementation. The strong preparatory analytical work that the report calls for should help ensure that projects are relevant to country needs. Although the advisory group agrees that it is important to seek to explore the determinants of project outcome ratings, the regression results summarized in the text and presented in an appendix table should be interpreted with care.

The evaluation did not undertake any extensive analysis of the past analytical work done in HNP. However, it is notable that 41 percent of the analytical work was on health system performance, and yet many projects in this area encountered difficulties. Further exploration of the analytical work would be valuable, to assess the extent to which it was relevant to country programs and to see whether lessons can be learned in terms of ensuring that analytical work supports high-quality project design and implementation.

Another area that would have benefited from greater attention is that of sustainability and building country capacity. Although sustainability was an objective in both the 1997 and 2007 HNP strategies, this aspect has not been sufficiently explored in the report. There are a number of aspects of capacity that need building at the country level—human resources are absolutely key and yet whether or not they were adequately addressed by projects was not explored. There are similar considerations with respect to health information systems and national monitoring and evaluation capacity. No evidence is presented on the extent to which local capacity was used or built to ensure projects are sustained into the future, or on whether projects were managed in the most efficient way. If there are inadequate attempts to use or build internal capacity, it is highly likely that the projects will not be effectively sustained.

The report comments that while half of all Water Supply and Sanitation projects cited potential for health benefits, only 10 percent had an objective to improve health. This is presented as a weakness, but it need not be: the projects can improve other things that have large effects on health, so failure of a project to state that it is improving health or its failure to do things that directly improve health may not be bad for health. For example, SWAPs encourage projects to do things that indirectly improve health.

The report highlights a clear problem of accountability for results. Despite the Bank's mandate for poverty reduction, a very small share of projects had explicit objectives relating to improving HNP outcomes among the poor, and of closed projects with these objectives, very few were able to demonstrate improvements. Similarly, many projects were termed *pilots*, implying they were intended at least in part for learning, but few projects actually evaluated results. A widespread weakness in monitoring and evaluation and in evaluation was identified.

It is notable that these weaknesses have been identified in previous evaluations, and recommendations made to improve monitoring and evaluation. Improvements are noted—for example, in terms of availability of baseline data—but weaknesses remain. Failure to respond sufficiently to previous recommendations suggests that there are pervasive incentives in the Bank that work against investing sufficiently in monitoring and evaluation and evaluation. This is a vital area for management action to consider how to create stronger incentives. The issue of whether staff are drawing in the necessary expertise in evaluation research methods also needs consideration—issues of appropriate research design and data analysis methods are complex.

The World Bank Group has many strong assets, including its analytical and synthesis capacity, its strong relationship to country financial policy makers, its extensive networks at the country level in all regions, its massive financial and social capital, and its skill in managing development funds. These assets are extremely important in helping the group successfully formulate, implement, evaluate, and reformulate its HNP projects. If applied properly and efficiently, these assets will allow the World Bank Group to build up sustainable capacity within developing countries and support health systems development that is more pro-poor, more efficient, and more sustainable. However, given the now highly complex aid environment in health, it is vital that the World Bank position itself clearly with respect to what others are doing. To address the problem of fragmentation within countries, it should also seek to support interagency coordination.

Finally, there is a need to strengthen the IEG evaluation team and resources. Insufficient human resources, financial support, and time inevitably limited the work that could be done for the evaluation report. The IEG staff have done their best, given limited resources, to come up with an excellent assessment with much rich detail. But more could be done with better support.

Augusto Galán-Sarmiento, former Minister of Health, Colombia
Anne Mills, London School of Hygiene and Tropical Medicine, United Kingdon
Germano Mwabu, University of Nairobi, Kenya
Suwit Wibulpolprasert, Ministry of Public Health, Thailand

Chapter 1

Evaluation Highlights

- Because of fundamental changes in the global aid architecture, the World Bank is no longer the largest external source of health finance.
- Health outcomes have improved in every region, but averages conceal differences across and within countries.
- The Bank has committed about $28.7 billion and IFC about $951 million to HNP since 1970.
- The 2007 HNP strategy, *Healthy Development,* aims to strengthen health systems, prevent impoverishment due to poor health, and improve the health of the poor.
- This evaluation considers the effectiveness of both World Bank and IFC activities in HNP over the past decade and points to lessons of that experience.

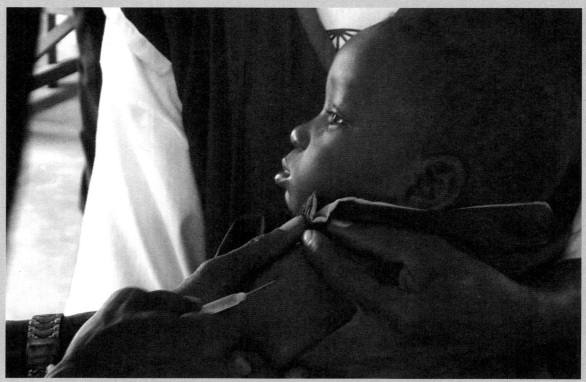

Child being immunized in Liberia. Support for communicable disease control rose dramatically during the evaluation period. Photo courtesy of Melanie Zipperer.

Introduction

The past decade has seen fundamental changes in the global aid architecture in health, with potential implications for the World Bank Group's work and its comparative advantages relative to other sources of health, nutrition, and population (HNP) support.

In the late 1990s, the World Bank was the largest single external source of finance for HNP in developing countries, accounting for about 18 percent of global HNP aid.[1] Since then, new aid donors and institutions have emerged, both public and private (see Timeline in appendix A). Development assistance for HNP has risen from an annual average of $6.7 billion in 1997–99 to about $16 billion in 2006, most of it for low-income countries (Michaud 2003; World Bank 2008a). The international community has adopted global development targets; the most prominent are the Millennium Development Goals (MDGs), set for 2015.

There is also a new international emphasis on aid effectiveness, results orientation, donor harmonization, alignment, and country leadership, reflected in the 2005 *Paris Declaration on Aid Effectiveness*. Hence, the World Bank is now one of many large players in international HNP support, accounting for about 6 percent of the total in 2006.[2] The Bank is in the process of reassessing its comparative advantage in the context of the new aid architecture, while a call for greater engagement with the private health sector in developing countries presents new opportunities for the International Finance Corporation (IFC) to extend its support.

There have been improvements in some health outcomes over the past decade, but progress is uneven and in many cases too slow to meet the MDGs by the target date

of 2015. Key health outcomes, such as the infant mortality rate, have improved in every developing region since 1990 (figure 1.1). The prevalence of stunting among children under five has declined dramatically in Asia and Latin America since 1980, though only modestly in Africa (Shekar, Heaver, and Lee 2006, p. 5). These improvements have been attributed to rising average levels of income and education, coupled with improvements in health technology and expanded public health interventions (see, for example, Jamison 2006;

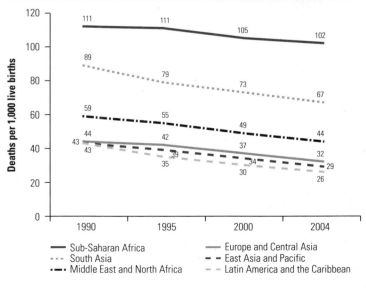

Figure 1.1: Infant Mortality Rates Have Declined in Every Region, but Disparities across Regions are Large

Source: UNICEF 2006.

Levine and others 2004). Despite this progress, nearly three-quarters of developing countries are either off track or seriously off track for achieving the MDG of reducing under-five mortality by two-thirds. Maternal mortality is declining by only about 1 percent annually, a fifth of the rate needed to achieve the goal of reducing it by three-quarters by 2015 (World Bank 2008a).

Further, average outcomes conceal important differences in progress across countries, within regions, and within countries. Under-five mortality rates in 30 countries have stagnated or increased since 1990;[3] in some countries, high fertility rates have remained unchanged or even increased slightly since the 1990s (Wagstaff and Claeson 2004, p. 36). Despite some progress in Bangladesh and India, undernutrition remains very high in South Asia, while in 26 countries, primarily in Africa, malnutrition is increasing (Shekar, Heaver, and Lee 2006, p. 3). Maternal mortality remains extremely high in Africa, where the average woman faces a nearly 1 percent risk of dying from pregnancy and childbirth, and very high fertility repeatedly exposes women to these high risks.[4]

Despite improvement in some key health outcomes since 1990, there are important differences across and within countries.

Communicable diseases account for about a third (36 percent) of the disease burden in developing countries (Jamison and others 2006b); within countries, the burden of morbidity and mortality is greatest among the poor (Gwatkin and Guillot 2000). In some countries, HNP outcomes have improved disproportionately among the poor, while in others they have improved primarily among the non-poor. The gaps between the poor and non-poor, even when closing, often remain substantial, in part reflecting lower access of the poor to public services (Gwatkin, Wagstaff, and Yazbeck 2005; Filmer 2003). The burden of disease is distributed differently within developing Regions, with communicable disease and maternal, perinatal, and nutritional conditions as a group predominating in Africa, while in the remaining five developing Regions, the burden of non-communicable disease is equal or greater (figure 1.2).

The Bank committed about $28.7 billion and IFC about $951 million to HNP from 1970 to mid-2008.

Rationale for World Bank Group Investments in Health, Nutrition, and Population

The mandate of the World Bank Group is to reduce poverty and promote economic growth. Poor health and malnutrition contribute to low productivity of the poor, so improving HNP outcomes is seen as a major way of reducing poverty. But poverty is also a prime cause of poor health, malnutrition, and high fertility. The poor have low access to preventive and curative care (both physically and financially) and are more likely to be malnourished, have unsafe water and sanitation, lack education, have large families and closely spaced births, and engage in activities that may put them at heightened health risk.

Within the World Bank Group, the World Bank (International Bank for Reconstruction and Development [IBRD] and the International Development Association [IDA]) have committed about $28.7 billion to help governments improve HNP outcomes in 132 countries since 1970 (figure 1.3).[5] In addition, **IFC has invested $951 million in the private health and pharmaceutical sectors of developing countries.**[6] The World Bank supports *government* HNP policies and programs. The *World Development Report 1993: Investing in Health* (World Bank 1993c) highlighted the major rationales for a government role in the health sector; many of these also apply to nutrition and population:

- To provide public goods and invest in HNP services with large positive externalities, which the private sector would have no incentive to provide in adequate quantity
- To enhance equity by ensuring provision of cost-effective HNP services to the poor, who are otherwise unlikely to gain adequate access to essential clinical services or insurance[7]
- To address uncertainty and multiple market failures in health, including problems of adverse selection, moral hazard, and asymmetry in information between providers and patients.[8]

IFC supports investments and Advisory Services to the *private sector* in health and pharmaceuti-

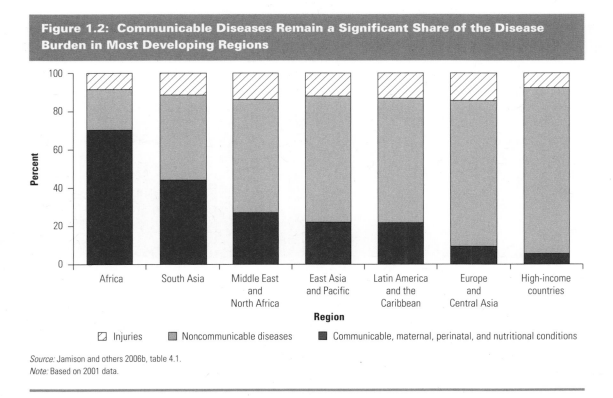

Figure 1.2: Communicable Diseases Remain a Significant Share of the Disease Burden in Most Developing Regions

Source: Jamison and others 2006b, table 4.1.
Note: Based on 2001 data.

cals to build institutional and systemic capacity and promote efficiency and innovation in the health sectors of developing countries.

World Bank Group Strategies in Health, Nutrition, and Population

This evaluation aims to inform the implementation of the most recent HNP strategies of the World Bank and IFC and to help enhance the impact of future support. The *World Bank's* policies, strategies, and lending for HNP have evolved in phases (box 1.1). Its current strategy, *Healthy Development: The World Bank Strategy for Health, Nutrition, and Population Results*, was launched in 2007, with objectives to improve HNP outcomes on average and among the poor and prevent the impoverishing impact of illness by improving health system performance, including governance, and intersectoral approaches (table 1.1). The strategy includes an increased emphasis on demonstrating outcomes by incorporating a detailed results framework for the entire sector. The goals of IFC's current health strategy, *Investing in Private Health*

Care: Strategic Directions for IFC, adopted in 2002, are: improve health outcomes, protect the population from the impoverishing effects of ill health, and enhance the performance of health services (table 1.2) (IFC 2002, p. 3). These strategies provide a vision of the sector as a whole. The extent to which their objectives are specifically addressed in a given country depends on the borrower's interest and the country context.

Since 1997, IEG has issued three evaluations of the development effectiveness of the Bank's support for HNP; it has never evaluated IFC's cumulative support for the health sector.[9] *Investing in Health: Development Effectiveness in the Health, Nutrition, and Population Sector* (IEG 1999) found that the Bank had been more successful in expanding health service delivery systems (physical objectives) than in improving service quality and efficiency or achieving policy and institutional change. The lending portfolio had grown rapidly, and the most complex

Since 1997, IEG has evaluated aspects of the World Bank's HNP sector three times; IFC's cumulative support for health has never been evaluated.

Figure 1.3: Trends in World Bank Group Commitments and Project Approvals

A. World Bank

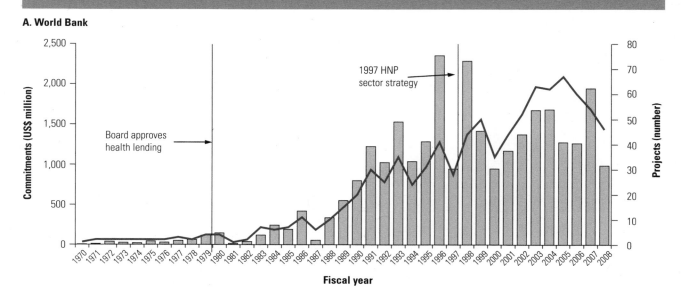

B. IFC

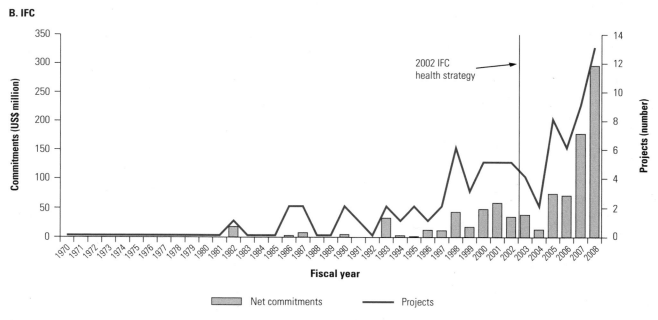

Net commitments   ——— Projects

Source: World Bank Group data.
Note: The commitment for the entire project is attributed to the fiscal year of approval. IFC data excludes investments made under the Africa Enterprise Fund/Small Enterprise Fund.

projects were approved in countries with the weakest institutional capacity. The evaluation recommended that the Bank be more selective in its engagement and focus on improving the quality of HNP operations, particularly through stronger monitoring and evaluation (M&E) and institutional analysis. In addition, the evaluation recommended strengthening health promotion and

Box 1.1: Six Phases of World Bank Engagement in HNP

Population lending, 1970–79

The Bank focused on improving access to family planning services because of concern about the adverse effects of rapid population growth on economic growth and poverty reduction. A handful of nutrition projects was also approved following a 1973 nutrition policy paper, and throughout the decade health components were included in agriculture, population, and education projects as important links between health, poverty, and economic progress were established.

Primary health care, 1980–86

The 1980 *Health Sector Policy Paper* (World Bank 1980a) formally committed the Bank to direct lending in the health sector with the objective of improving the health of the poor by improving access to low-cost primary health care. The rationale for this policy change was contained in the *World Development Report 1980: Poverty and Human Development* (World Bank 1980b), which emphasized that investment in human development complements other poverty reduction programs and is economically justifiable. However, over this period systemic constraints were encountered in providing access to efficient and equitable health services.

Health reform, 1987–96

Following the release of *Financing Health Services in Developing Countries: An Agenda for Reform* in 1987 (Akin, Birdsall, and De Ferranti 1987), the Bank addressed two new objectives: to make health finance more equitable and efficient and to reform health systems to overcome systemic constraints. The message was further refined by the *World Development Report 1993: Investing in Health* (World Bank 1993c), which highlighted the im-

portance of household decisions in improving health, advocated directing government health spending to a cost-effective package of preventive and basic curative services, and encouraged greater diversity in health finance and service delivery.

Health outcomes and health systems, 1997–2000

The 1997 *Health, Nutrition, and Population Sector Strategy Paper* (World Bank 1997b) focused on health outcomes of the poor and on protecting people from the impoverishing effects of illness, malnutrition, and high fertility. However, it continued to emphasize support for improved health system performance (in terms of equity, affordability, efficiency, quality, and responsiveness to clients) and securing sustainable health financing.

Global targets and partnerships, 2001–06

The Bank's objectives, rationale, and strategy remained unchanged, but major external events, the surging AIDS epidemic, and the Bank's commitments to specific targets and to working in partnerships led to an increase in finance for single-disease or single-intervention programs, often within weak health systems.

System strengthening for results, 2007–present

In the context of changes in the global health architecture, *Healthy Development: The World Bank Strategy for Health, Nutrition, and Population Results* (World Bank 2007a) emphasizes the need for the Bank to reposition itself, with a greater focus on its comparative advantages, to more effectively support countries to improve health outcomes. It adheres closely to the 1997 strategy's objectives and means for achieving them, with increased emphasis on governance and demonstrating results.

Source: Fair 2008.

intersectoral interventions, greater emphasis on economic and sector analysis, a better understanding of stakeholder interests, and strategic alliances with regional and global development partners.

IEG's 2004 evaluation of the Bank's approach to global programs (IEG 2004a; Lele and others 2004), including health programs, recommended that the Bank engage more selectively in global programs, favoring those that exploit the Bank's comparative advantages and provide global public

goods, and that the links between global programs and the Bank's Regional and country operations be strengthened.

IEG's 2005 evaluation of the Bank's support for the fight against HIV/AIDS (IEG 2005a) found that the Bank had contributed to raising political commitment and improving access to services. However, evidence of results for health behaviors and outcomes is thin because of a failure to monitor and evaluate. IEG recommended that the Bank be more strategic and selective, focusing on

Table 1.1: Objectives and Strategic Directions of *Healthy Development,* the 2007 World Bank HNP Strategy

Objectives	Strategic directions
• Improve the level and distribution of key HNP outcomes (for example, MDGs), outputs, and system performance at the country and global levels in order to improve living conditions, particularly for the poor and vulnerable. • Prevent poverty due to illness (by improving financial protection). • Improve financial sustainability in the HNP sector and its contribution to sound macroeconomic and fiscal policy and to country competitiveness. • Improve governance, accountability, and transparency in the health sector.	• Renew Bank focus on HNP results. • Increase Bank contribution to client country efforts to strengthen and realize well-organized and sustainable health systems for HNP results. • Ensure synergy between health-system strengthening and priority disease interventions, particularly in low-income countries. • Strengthen Bank capacity to advise client countries on an intersectoral approach to HNP results. • Increase selectivity, improve strategic engagement, and reach agreement with global partners on collaborative division of labor for the benefit of client countries.

Source: World Bank 2007a, p. 7.

efforts likely to have the largest impact for their cost; strengthen locally adapted institutions to manage the long-term response; and invest heavily in M&E capacity and incentives as the basis for evidence-based decision making.

Objectives and Scope of this Evaluation

This report evaluates the efficacy, specifically the HNP outcomes, of World Bank Group country-level support for HNP over the past decade and draws lessons from that experience. The objectives of the evaluation of the World Bank are to assess the effectiveness of the Bank's support in improving HNP outcomes at the country level since 1997, particularly among the poor, and to identify lessons from that experience that can be employed to improve the efficacy of the Bank's support in the next decade. Support to countries includes policy dialogue, analytic work, and lending. The evaluation focuses on assessing the effectiveness of support under the supervision of the HNP sector, as well as support with likely health benefits supervised by the water supply and sanitation and the transport sectors.[10]

The evaluation of the Bank addresses four main questions:

• **What have been the objectives, effectiveness, and main outcomes of the World Bank's country-level HNP support over**

the past decade and what accounts for this performance? How effective has the Bank's support been in helping countries improve HNP outcomes, on average and among the poor? To what extent has the Bank improved its M&E performance and used evaluation to improve the evidence base for decision making in HNP? These findings are intended to contribute to more effective implementation of the 2007 HNP strategy's objective of improving HNP outcomes among the poor and of its results focus.

• **What lessons have been learned about the efficacy, advantages, and disadvantages of three approaches to improving HNP outcomes in different settings:** control of communicable diseases that disproportionately affect the poor; programs to "strengthen" or "reform" the health system; and sectorwide approaches designed to improve ownership, reduce transaction costs, and improve the allocation of resources? These three approaches, which are not mutually exclusive, are closely related to the HNP strategy's objectives of health system strengthening and are relevant to the balance between investments in communicable diseases and health systems.

• **What has been the contribution of activities in other, complementary sectors to improving HNP outcomes?** In particular, to what extent have Country Assistance Strategies been used as a vehicle to coordinate the

Table 1.2: Business and Developmental Objectives of IFC's 2002 Health Strategy

Business objectives	Developmental objectives
• Provide value-added financing. • Mobilize private resource flows. • Invest in financially viable projects. • Improve managerial and financial capacity.	• Contribute to institutional and systematic building of capacity in the health sector by expanding the capacity of the sponsoring institution to serve patients, either through the creation of new facilities or the expansion or improvement of existing operations. Capacity building is also served when IFC clients transfer technical expertise from private providers to the public facilities. • Promote efficiency and innovation within the institution and the health sector. • Support country and World Bank health sector objectives. • Financial protection through: — Expanding access and quality of health services to those who would otherwise receive inadequate or no care — Investing in health insurance schemes. • Reduce the brain drain by improving the quality and quantity of local facilities, contributing to the supply of attractive local employment opportunities. • Reduce pressure on the overburdened public sector.

Source: IFC 2002, pp. 32–37.

activities of other sectors to maximize the impact on HNP outcomes? Have projects in non-HNP sectors with plausible health benefits delivered on them? How effective has multisectoral lending managed by the HNP sector been at capitalizing on synergies between sectors in producing health outcomes? This question is intended to inform efforts of the recent strategy to implement an effective multisectoral approach and will also provide evidence on the extent to which the Bank has a comparative advantage in multisectoral action.

• **What have been the observed value added, comparative advantages, or contributions of World Bank support for HNP in developing countries over the past decade, and how is that changing?**

Over the past decade, the World Bank increasingly has become involved in global partnerships. An appendix to the 2007 HNP strategy lists 19 global health initiatives and partnerships to which the Bank contributes financially and another 15 in which the Bank participates with no financial contribution.[11] While it is beyond the scope of this evaluation to assess the Bank's participation and contribution to these activities in the aggregate,

IEG has recently reviewed 2 of the 19 partnerships financed by the Bank—the Medicines for Malaria Venture and the Population and Reproductive Health Capacity Building Program, summarized in appendix I.

This report evaluates the efficacy of World Bank Group country support for HNP over the past decade.

The evaluation of IFC's health activities has three objectives: assess the relevance, effectiveness, and efficiency of IFC's health operations since 1997; assess the design and implementation of IFC's 2002 health sector strategy; and identify lessons from that experience to improve the efficacy of future IFC support to the health sector. *Health operations* in IFC include both lending and Advisory Services for health and investments, both in health services, managed by the Health and Education Department, and pharmaceuticals, managed by the Global Manufacturing Department.

Evaluation Design and Methodology

The evidence for the evaluation was distilled from desk reviews, background papers, country case studies and field visits, IEG project assessments, and in-depth interviews, in addition to published and unpublished research and evaluation literature (box 1.2). Some of the evidence is compre-

---

Box 1.2: Evaluation Building Blocks

World Bank

- Review of strategy documents and construction of a timeline of World Bank HNP support and policies and international events.
- Desk review of Country Assistance Strategies (CASs) with respect to their prioritization of health, attention to health outcomes among the poor, and planning of multisectoral operations.
- Desk review of the objectives, strategies, and *development effectiveness*[a] of all 220 HNP projects approved during fiscal years 1997–2006 under the responsibility of the HNP sector, as well as analysis of projects with HNP objectives or components under the responsibility of the transport and water supply and sanitation sectors.
- Field evaluations (Project Performance Assessment Reports, PPARs) of completed HNP projects in Bangladesh, the Arab Republic of Egypt, Eritrea, Ghana, Kyrgyz Republic, Peru, the Russian Federation, and Vietnam; a road safety project in Romania; and a rural water supply and sanitation project in Nepal that had objectives to improve HNP outcomes. Field-based country case studies to evaluate the entirety of World

Bank lending and nonlending support in Egypt, Malawi, and Nepal.
- Background papers reviewing the evidence from the portfolio review and field studies on key evaluation themes, such as communicable diseases, sectorwide approaches, and M&E.

IFC

- Review of IFC health sector strategies.
- Review of the objectives, characteristics, design features, and implementation status of the portfolio of all 54 committed health investment projects approved between fiscal 1997 and 2007 and an assessment of the performance of mature health projects against established benchmarks and their stated objectives.
- Desk review of all completed and ongoing Advisory Service projects in health and follow-up interviews with World Bank and IFC staff, as appropriate.
- Field visits to Argentina, China, Egypt, Philippines, and Turkey to interview IFC clients and other stakeholders, and to review the performance of 12 investment projects, IFC support for public-private partnerships, and IFC-World Bank collaboration.

a. Development effectiveness is the extent to which a program has attained its major relevant objectives efficiently.

---

hensive—representing 100 percent of the lending portfolio—while other evidence is culled from in-depth investigation of purposive samples. The samples of projects reviewed are described in appendix B, and the World Bank HNP sector projects and IFC health projects included in the portfolio review are listed in appendixes C and D.

The evaluation also draws on findings and lessons from other IEG evaluations that are relevant to the World Bank Group's HNP support, in particular, evaluations of social funds (IEG 2002b), middle-income countries (IEG 2007b), public-sector reform (IEG 2008f), economic and sector work (IEG 2008h), and an impact evaluation of maternal and child health and nutrition in Bangladesh (IEG 2005b).

Organization of the Report
The evaluation results are presented in six chapters. Chapters 2–4 evaluate the World Bank's support since 1997 with respect to the key evaluation themes.

- Chapter 2 examines the evolution and outcomes of the portfolio of HNP lending and analytic work. Key issues include: trends in the objectives, composition, and performance of the HNP portfolio; the poverty focus and outcomes for the poor of the Bank's investments; and whether M&E of HNP activities have improved the evidence base for decision making.
- Chapter 3 distills the performance and lessons from a decade of experience supporting three approaches that are closely related to the strategic actions to be taken in the 2007 HNP strategy: communicable disease control, health system reform, and sectorwide approaches (SWAps) in health, which aim to improve the efficiency and effectiveness of donor assistance in support of developing country health objectives.
- The 2007 HNP strategy maintains that multisectoral action to improve HNP outcomes is a comparative advantage of the World Bank.[12] Chapter 4 highlights the contribution of other sectors to HNP results: the extent to which

Country Assistance Strategies (CASs) have been used as a vehicle for generating synergies across sectors to improve health outcomes; the results from HNP lending operations that tried to coordinate and bring to bear the actions of multiple sectors on improving outcomes; and the health impact of investments in the water supply and sanitation and transport sectors.

Chapter 5 assesses IFC's health investments and Advisory Services since 1997, the implementation of the 2002 health strategy, and the lessons learned from IFC's health investments and Advisory Services. Health is a relatively new area of investment for IFC, so the portfolio is small and relatively young.

Chapter 6 reflects on the value added of World Bank and IFC support for HNP outcomes, as revealed by the experience of the past decade, and offers recommendations for improving the effectiveness of both agencies of the World Bank Group.

Chapter 2

Evaluation Highlights

- The Bank has committed nearly $17 billion to HNP since 1997; $11.5 billion was managed by the HNP sector.
- Lending has shifted in favor of HIV/AIDS, multisectoral, and Africa Region projects.
- Support and staffing for population and nutrition have eroded.
- About two-thirds of HNP projects overall—but only a quarter of HNP projects in Africa—have had satisfactory outcomes.
- Performance of HNP projects has stalled, while it has improved in other sectors; complexity and low quality at entry have contributed.
- M&E remain weak, despite an increase in monitoring indicators and baseline data.
- The portfolio has a generally pro-poor focus, but few projects could show improved outcomes for the poor.

Family health clinics such as these in the Kyrgyz Republic, which cater to men, women, and children, increasingly replaced inefficient specialized care as part of the *Manas* health reform program supported by the World Bank and other donors. Photo courtesy of Judyth Twigg.

Evolution and Performance of the World Bank's Country Support for Health, Nutrition, and Population

Since 1997, the World Bank has committed nearly $17 billion for HNP in 605 projects, about 6.5 percent of all Bank commitments over that period. This includes projects managed by the HNP sector—about three-quarters of all HNP commitments—and HNP components embedded in projects managed by other sectors.

Beyond this, the Bank has spent some $43 million of its own budget and trust funds on economic and sector work (ESW) tasks in HNP that generated reports, policy notes, conferences, workshops, consultations, and country dialogue.[1] This chapter and the next focus on the commitments managed by the HNP sector, while chapter 4 assesses multisectoral approaches and the HNP support managed by other sectors.

Two-thirds of HNP projects have had satisfactory outcomes, but the findings in this chapter point to several challenges for the implementation of the 2007 HNP strategy: the low performance of HNP support overall and in Sub-Saharan Africa, in part due to the complexity of multisectoral operations and sectorwide approaches; weak M&E that could undermine the strategy's results orientation and commitment to improve governance; and a lack of evidence that the Bank's HNP support is really delivering results to the poor.

The Health, Nutrition, and Population Portfolio and Its Performance

From 1997 through 2008, the portion of World Bank HNP commitments managed by the HNP sector has amounted to about $11.5 billion in 255 projects. The number of HNP projects approved annually has risen slowly, while new annual commitments have declined (figure 2.1). The projects managed by the HNP sector are almost exclusively investment projects.[2] IEG conducted an in-depth review of the lending portfolio managed by the HNP sector and approved during the 10-year period from fiscal 1997 through 2006, based on review of project appraisal documents (PADs), implementation completion reports (ICRs) for those that had closed, and tabulation of key characteristics. During that period, 220 HNP-managed projects were approved, of which 110 had closed as of June 30, 2008 (appendix C). This portfolio review forms much of the evidence base for the discussion here, as well as in chapters 3 and 4.

Improving health status was the most frequently cited objective of HNP projects, followed by improving the access, quality, efficiency, or equity of the health care system, collectively cited by more than half of the projects approved from fiscal 1997 through 2006 (table 2.1). A third of projects

Figure 2.1: The Number of HNP-Managed Projects Has Risen Slowly, While Commitments Have Declined

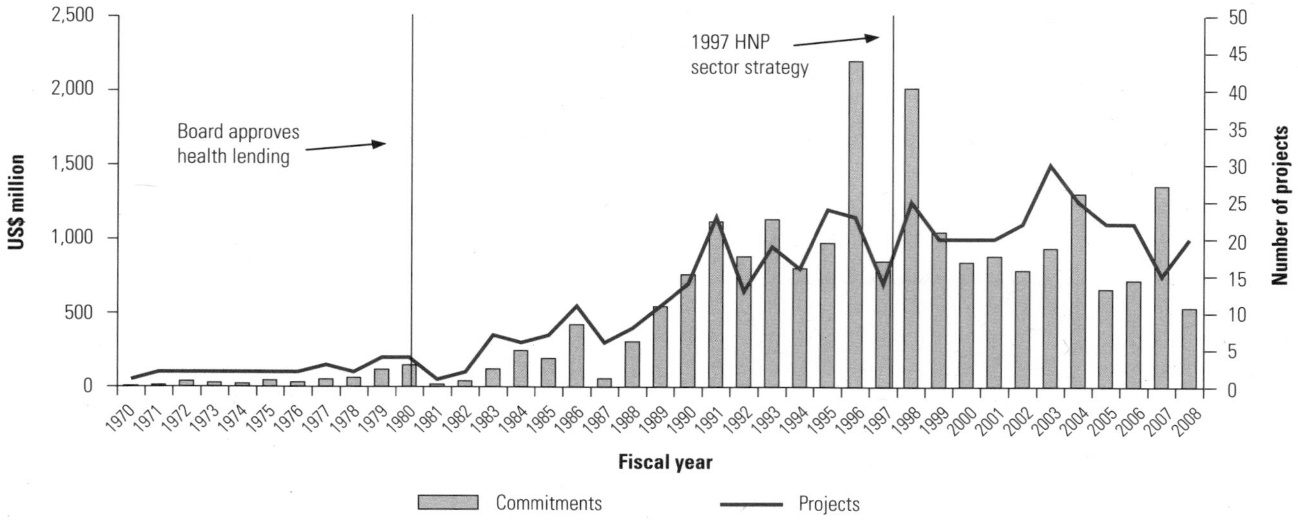

Source: World Bank data.

Note: The peaks in commitments in fiscal years 1996 and 1998 are due to a few projects in large countries—in 1996, one project each in Argentina, Brazil, India, Mexico, and Russia, and in 1998, five projects in Bangladesh, Egypt, India, and Mexico. In both years the projects in these large countries accounted for 70 percent of commitments.

Table 2.1: Objectives of HNP Projects Approved in Fiscal 1997–2006

Objective	Number[a]	Percent
Improve health status	**135**	**61**
Reduce the burden of communicable disease[b]	78	35
Promote child growth/reduce malnutrition	21	10
Reduce high fertility/promote family planning	8	4
Improve access, quality, efficiency, or equity of the health system	**126**	**57**
Improve access	70	32
Improve quality	76	35
Improve efficiency	61	28
Improve equity	16	7
Health system reform and financing	**73**	**33**
"Health reform"	41	19
Health financing	32	15
Health insurance	16	7
Decentralization	15	7
Private sector	8	4
Build/strengthen institutional capacity	**68**	**31**
Improve management	**39**	**18**
Improve participation[c]	**26**	**12**
Learning	**21**	**10**

Source: IEG portfolio review.

a. Total projects = 220.

b. Includes AIDS (29 percent); malaria (5 percent); TB (5 percent); and other communicable diseases such as leprosy, polio, and avian influenza (6 percent).

c. Community participation and/or empowerment, multisectoral or intersectoral action.

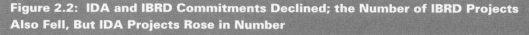

Figure 2.2: IDA and IBRD Commitments Declined; the Number of IBRD Projects Also Fell, But IDA Projects Rose in Number

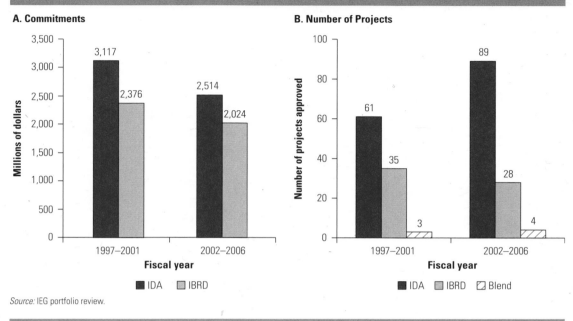

Source: IEG portfolio review.

aimed to reduce communicable disease, while only 1 in 10 had nutrition objectives and only 4 percent had an objective to reduce high fertility. Health reform–related objectives collectively were addressed by a third of the projects.

Trends in the Level and Composition of Health, Nutrition, and Population Support, Fiscal 1997–2006

Although IDA and IBRD commitments fell, the number of IDA projects rose, resulting in a larger number of small projects in the portfolio by the end of the decade. IDA's share of commitments remained about the same, accounting for 55 percent of total commitments in the second period (figure 2.2A). The total number of HNP projects approved increased from 99 to 121 between fiscal 1997–2001 and 2002–06. All of this increase was created by IDA project approvals; the number of IBRD projects declined (figure 2.2B).[3]

There were other major developments in the composition of the HNP portfolio over the decade. Africa's share of HNP project approvals increased from more than a quarter in fiscal years 1997–2001 to more than a third in fiscal 2002–06. The number of new HNP projects in Africa rose by more than 60 percent (from 28 to 45), and in Latin America and the Caribbean by 30 percent (from 20 to 26). The share of communicable disease and multisectoral HNP projects also increased dramatically. **The increase in Africa Region, communicable disease, and multisectoral projects reflected a rise in HIV/AIDS project approvals; in the second half of the period, the HIV/AIDS projects reached nearly 40 percent of the HNP portfolio.** In line with international efforts to improve donor harmonization and alignment, the share of HNP projects financing SWAps in health also climbed.[4]

Although more HNP projects were approved during the second half of the decade, both the share and the absolute number of projects financing health reform–type objectives declined (table 2.2, lower panel).[5] This includes projects with objectives of reform, financing, insurance, decentralization, and government actions with respect to the private health

While commitments declined over the period, the number of projects increased, as did the share in Africa.

Communicable disease projects rose to 44 percent of approvals, while health reform objectives declined.

Table 2.2: Key Developments in the HNP Portfolio

lio	Percent of the portfo-	
Development	1997–2001[c]	2002–06[c]
Share increased		
IDA projects[a]	62	74
Projects in Africa	28	37
Multisectoral HNP projects	25	49
Free-standing communicable disease projects	25	44
HIV/AIDS projects[b]	*17*	*39*
Projects supporting SWAps	9	15
Share decreased		
Projects with health reform/financing/insurance objectives	44	24
Projects with objective to improve health care quality	49	22
Projects with objective to improve efficiency and cost-effectiveness of health care	37	20
Projects with nutrition objectives	12	7
Projects with population objectives	6	2
Number of projects approved	99	121

Source: IEG portfolio review.

a. The share of IDA commitments was unchanged.

b. Projects with an objective to prevent the spread of HIV/AIDS or mitigate its impact.

c. Fiscal year of approval.

Figure 2.3: The Number of Sector Specialists Rose over the Decade

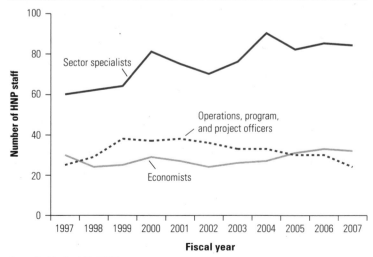

Source: Nankhuni and Modi 2008.

sector. The share of projects with explicit objectives to improve the quality and efficiency of health care also dropped.

Lending to reduce fertility, population growth, or unwanted births remained low and became scarcer, dropping from only 6 percent of the portfolio to 2 percent (table 2.2, lower panel). Over the decade, only 14 projects were approved with objectives to lower fertility or increase use of contraception, or with family planning components. The Bank's population support was directed to only about a quarter of the 35 countries identified by the strategy (World Bank 2007g) as having a total fertility rate of 5 or higher (appendix E).

Lending with objectives to improve nutritional status dropped by half, from 12 to 7 percent of the portfolio (table 2.2, lower panel). Bank support to reduce malnutrition was directed to only about a quarter of countries with child stunting of 30 percent or more; malnutrition is a significant problem among the poor in many more countries, though its causes are diverse (appendix F).

Total staffing in the sector rose, particularly the number of health specialists. Total professional staff[6] affiliated with the HNP sector grew by a quarter, from 136 in fiscal 1997 to a peak of 185 in fiscal 2004, and then had declined slightly, to 169, by fiscal 2007 (appendix H). Virtually all of this increase was among sector specialists, who increased by about 40 percent; the number of economists remained about the same and the number of operations officers declined (figure 2.3).

While the overall number of sector specialists rose, the count of specialists in nutrition and population declined. The number of population specialists plummeted, from 24 in 1997 to 7 in 2003, while the number of nutrition specialists dwindled from 8 to 5 over the decade (appendix H).[7]

The increase in staff affiliated with the Regions was not in proportion to the increase

in HNP projects. The number of HNP projects in Africa increased by 60 percent from the first to the second half of the decade, while the number of HNP staff affiliated with the Region rose by only about 12 percent (appendix H). The number of HNP projects in the Latin America and Caribbean Region rose by 30 percent, and HNP staff rose by half. The number of HNP staff affiliated with Europe and Central Asia more than doubled, yet the number of HNP projects in the two periods remained about the same.

Performance of Health, Nutrition, and Population Support

Over the past decade, about two-thirds of completed HNP-managed projects had satisfactory outcomes. The performance of HNP projects has stagnated, while the outcomes of projects in other sectors have continued to improve (figure 2.4).[8] The growing gap between the performance of HNP and other sectors is *not* due to underlying shifts in the composition of the portfolio. The share of development policy loans relative to investment projects over time within the HNP sector and other sectors was stable.[9] According to the 2008 *Annual Review of Development Effectiveness* (IEG 2008a), project outcomes in Africa trail those in other Regions across the board, not just in the HNP sector.[10] The share of Africa Region projects among closing projects also does not explain the divergence in outcomes between HNP and other sectors: the share of Africa Region projects in other sectors declined from 28 to 24 percent, but *by an even larger percentage among exiting projects in the HNP sector,* from 35 to 26 percent.[11] If one compares the outcomes of HNP lending to lending in all other sectors—excluding projects in Africa from both—the performance of the HNP portfolio declines from 78 to 74 percent satisfactory between the first and second half of the period, while the performance of other sectors collectively rises from 78 to 81 percent satisfactory.[12]

The quality of project preparation by the Bank and the borrower's overall performance in preparing and executing the project strongly predict better outcomes. The Bank's performance, and to a lesser extent the borrower's performance, also

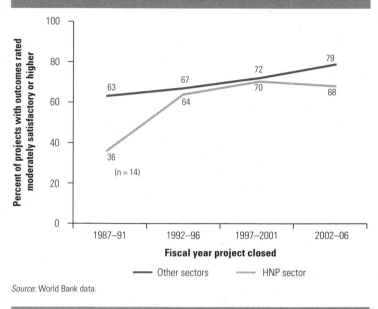

Figure 2.4: Performance of HNP Projects Has Stagnated, while Outcomes in Other Sectors Continue to Improve

Source: World Bank data.

shows a widening gap between HNP and other sectors (appendix H).[13] Multivariate analysis of the outcomes of HNP projects approved during fiscal 1997–2006[14] found that the performance of the borrower (which includes government and the implementing agency), as well as the Bank's role in quality at entry, are strongly correlated with better outcomes (appendix H). Eighty-three percent of projects with satisfactory borrower performance ultimately achieve satisfactory outcomes, compared with only 7 percent of projects with unsatisfactory borrower performance. Seventy-six percent of projects with satisfactory quality at entry achieve satisfactory outcomes, compared with only 19 percent of those with unsatisfactory quality at entry.

Given the importance of quality at entry in determining outcomes, it is worrisome to note that both the costs and duration of project preparation dropped precipitously over fiscal 1997–2001 and

Support to reduce malnutrition was low; support to address high fertility nearly disappeared.

Staffing in the sector rose, particularly health specialists.

While performance in other sectors has improved, HNP outcomes have stagnated.

The borrower's performance and the quality of project preparation strongly predict outcomes.

have only partially recovered to previous levels (appendix H). In contrast, average annual supervision costs for HNP investment projects have been rising since 2001, as have supervision costs for investment projects in other sectors, with HNP supervision costs exceeding those in other sectors in fiscal 2004–06 (appendix H).[15]

Projects with unsatisfactory outcomes are more likely to cite certain Bank performance factors than are projects with satisfactory outcomes: inadequate risk analysis (relative risk for unsatisfactory projects = 10:1);[16] inadequate technical design (8:1); inadequate supervision (5:1); inadequate political or institutional analysis (3:1); lack of baseline data that can be used to set realistic targets (3:1); overly complex design (2:1); and an inadequate M&E framework or poor data quality (2:1, appendix H). In addition, 12 percent of unsatisfactory projects cited inadequate prior analytic work, while none of the satisfactory projects cited this factor. IEG's recent evaluation of Bank-wide analytic and advisory activities found that prior analytic work led to higher project quality at entry (IEG 2008h). Fieldwork for this evaluation confirmed the value added and influence of analytic work in the case study countries (box 2.1).

Inadequacies in risk assessment, political analysis, technical design, and supervision are among the factors lowering outcomes.

HNP projects in Africa do not have lower performance simply because of the concentration of low-income countries in the Region. Only a quarter of the closed HNP projects in the Africa Region had satisfactory outcomes, compared with three-quarters of the closed projects in other Regions. All closed projects in Africa were in low-income countries and were financed by IDA grants or credits. However, HNP projects financed by IDA in other Regions managed to perform substantially better, often as well as or better than IBRD-financed HNP projects in middle-income countries (figure 2.5). The performance of AIDS projects in Africa has been particularly weak—only 18 percent have had satisfactory outcomes. But even if AIDS projects are excluded, only 27 percent of HNP projects in the Africa Region have had satisfactory outcomes.[17]

The complexity of HNP operations in Africa and among IDA recipients is contributing to low outcomes. Multisectoral investment lending, in which multiple sectors are involved in managing and/or implementing activities, is associated with lower outcomes in IDA countries, but not in countries receiving IBRD support. SWAps[18] are also associated with lower outcomes, and most of them have occurred in Africa. Thus, the problem of highly complex operations in low-capacity countries found in IEG's 1999 HNP evaluation continues. The review of Bank performance, cited above, showed that while project complexity raises the risk of low outcomes, some complex projects *do* have satisfactory results. Among the factors found not to affect HNP out-

---

Box 2.1: Analytic Work Supported Better Outcomes in Four Countries

Analytic work sponsored by the Bank—one of the major forms of country support in addition to policy dialogue and lending—was highly influential in four of the countries where IEG conducted in-depth fieldwork.

In Nepal, a burden-of-disease analysis showing that 70 percent of life years lost were taken by preventable communicable diseases that disproportionately affect the poor helped the government to improve the pro-poor allocation of public health expenditures.

In Malawi, the 2005 health public expenditure review led to a more realistic assessment of the resource needs for the first SWAp in health.

In Peru, *Improving Health Care for the Poor* (Cotlear 2000) provided the analytic framework and major recommendations that guided health reforms in that country and was valued highly by government.

Five major pieces of influential analytic work were supported in preparation for the second health reform project in the Kyrgyz Republic.

Sources: Shaw forthcoming: Elmendorf and Nankhuni forthcoming; IEG 2009b, forthcoming.

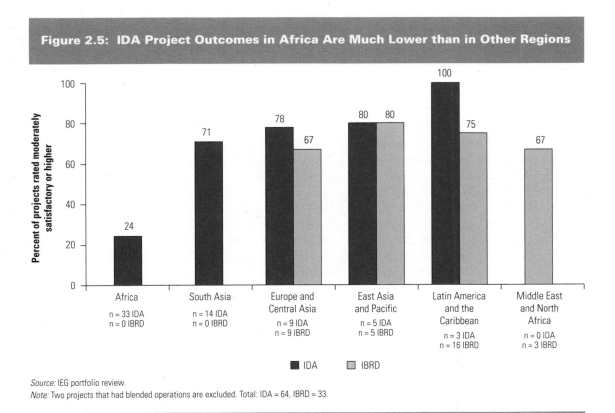

Figure 2.5: IDA Project Outcomes in Africa Are Much Lower than in Other Regions

Source: IEG portfolio review.

Note: Two projects that had blended operations are excluded. Total: IDA = 64, IBRD = 33.

comes were the source of finance (IDA versus IBRD, when Region is controlled for), the size of the support, the borrower's population size, and the year of approval (there was no time trend when other factors were controlled for).

Although they comprised a small part of the overall portfolio, projects with population and nutrition objectives also had lower-than-average outcomes compared with the rest of the portfolio. None of the projects with explicit fertility or population objectives achieved them: modern contraceptive use and fertility were barely affected in Guinea, India, Kenya, and Mali. In Bangladesh, Gambia, and Senegal, fertility declined somewhat, but it is doubtful that the results stem from population programs or Bank support.[19] Three projects with population and family planning components (but no population objective) partially achieved their objectives, showing that it is possible to raise contraceptive use in difficult environments when both demand and supply-side factors are addressed (box 2.2). Among the 15 nutrition projects that had closed,

only 2—the Indonesia Iodine Deficiency Control and the Senegal Nutrition Enhancement Projects—were able to substantially meet their objectives and show a change in nutritional outcomes. The performance of the population and nutrition portfolios is discussed in greater depth in appendixes E and F, respectively.

Population and nutrition projects often did not achieve their objectives.

Complex designs, the lack of up-front risk and institutional analysis, and the absorption of these services into a basic package along with other health care were all implicated in the low results. Project complexity was particularly acute in the nutrition projects, cited as contributing to shortcomings in more than half of the weak-performing projects. Nutrition projects tend to involve several sectors in implementation and are often managed outside the Ministry of Health, in some cases by new or inexperienced institutions (as in Mauritania). In Uganda, the added complexity arose from expanded geographical coverage of what was supposed to be a pilot activity.

Project complexity in IDA countries has contributed to low outcomes.

Box 2.2: Family Planning Can Be Successful in Difficult Environments

Support to Egypt and Malawi demonstrates that intensive efforts to raise contraceptive use and lower fertility in high-fertility rural areas can show results.

The Egypt Population Project (1996–2005) financed activities to increase the demand for smaller families and the supply of contraception in rural Upper Egypt.[a] Community development associations designed and managed subprojects in 148 of the poorest villages. The subprojects financed home visits, community conferences on healthy behaviors, and microcredit and literacy classes for women and promoted local maternal and child health/family planning services, in order to improve women's family planning and reproductive health knowledge, stimulate demand for smaller families, and raise modern contraceptive use. The project also improved the quality and supply of family planning services offered in the health system in the project villages. The modern contraceptive prevalence rate (CPR) rose from 40 to 45 percent between 2000 and 2005, compared with an increase from 56 to 59 percent nationwide, while the total fertility rate (TFR) declined by 0.8 children, from 4.7 to 3.9, compared with a national decline from 3.5 to 3.1. Attribution of these results to the project is difficult because M&E was limited and other donors (mainly the United States and the European Union) were supporting similar

interventions in the same part of Egypt. It was found that the project contributed to the collective impact of these efforts and that its design influenced other donors in adopting demand-side interventions.

The Malawi Population and Family Planning Project (1999–2004) aimed to demonstrate that a community-based distribution approach to family planning could raise contraceptive use in three high-fertility pilot areas in rural Malawi. Public sector community-based distribution agents (CBDA) provided family planning counseling and contraceptives and referred clients for long-term or permanent methods. Information, education, and communication activities aimed to generate demand. The percent of contraceptive users with CBDAs as their source rose from 1 to 24 percent and contraceptive use rose by twice as much in the pilot districts as in the three matched control districts (see figure, below). While the evaluation demonstrated that this community-based approach, emphasizing both demand and supply-side activities, could raise contraceptive use in high-fertility rural areas, the model was not replicated more widely. Certain lessons were incorporated into the government program, but by 2004, the government and donors were fully engaged in launching a health SWAp.

The Modern CPR Increased in Pilot Districts in Rural Malawi, Relative to Control Districts, 1999–2003

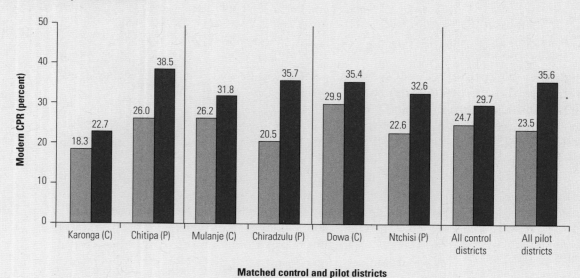

Sources: IEG 2008b; Elmendorf and Nankhuni forthcoming.

a. The changes in the CPR and the TFR in rural Upper Egypt are both statistically significant.

Complexity was also cited as a factor in poor-performing population projects, in addition to lack of up-front risk analysis and mitigation and institutional analysis. Absorption of family planning programs into basic packages of services supported by SWAps and health reform projects also may have contributed; field visits in Egypt confirmed the finding of a previous study that emphasis on a basic package of services had often reduced the availability and quality of family planning (appendix E).

Results from a Detailed Implementation Review of five health projects in India suggest that even projects that meet their objectives may be performing at substantially lower levels than their outcomes would suggest.[20] The review found that the Bank often relies on the borrower's reporting systems to confirm the delivery of such key outputs as civil works and equipment, without independent verification by the Bank of the quality of project goods and services and their delivery. For example, more than half of the pieces of equipment procured for the Food and Drug Capacity Building Project were not delivered or not installed,[21] and "severe construction deficiencies" were found in the Orissa Health Systems Development Project in buildings that the construction supervisors had reported to be complete and performing according to specification.[22] The review found that "supervision generally did not involve comprehensive site visits or physical inspections."[23] It is not known how representative these India projects are of the overall HNP portfolio, but there is an important lesson here about the need to conduct supervisory field visits to verify the implementation data provided by the borrower. Better supervision has the potential to enhance the impact of Bank support on outcomes, if addressed.

To summarize, while the overall levels of lending in HNP have not changed much over the past decade, the composition of the portfolio has shifted rather dramatically toward communicable disease projects, particularly AIDS; projects in the Africa Region; and, to a lesser extent, support for SWAps. Support for health reform (as measured by the projects' stated objectives) has de-

clined but is still significant, particularly in middle-income countries, while support for population and nutrition, already low, has declined further. Performance of the lending portfolio has stalled, with only about two-thirds of projects showing satisfactory outcomes. While some of the activities are inherently risky, several factors that can be addressed were implicated—excessive complexity, particularly in low-capacity environments; lack of institutional analysis and relevant analytic work linked to lending; inadequate baseline data and M&E; and inadequate assessment of the risks and mitigation strategies.

Bank supervision is missing some key implementation deficiencies.

Monitoring, Evaluation, and the Results Agenda

The 2007 HNP strategy highlights delivering results and improving governance, both of which depend critically on strong M&E for success. Two previous IEG evaluations of HNP and HIV/AIDS support concluded that weak M&E had contributed to lower efficacy and less learning. The 2007 HNP strategy acknowledges these shortcomings and maintains that inadequate M&E precludes a thorough analysis of the efficacy of Bank support over the past decade.

An increasing share of projects since 1997 has had monitoring indicators and baseline data at the time they are appraised, in part because of changes in the requirements for PADs. Around the time that the 1997 HNP strategy was approved, a required "logical framework" was added to the PAD. In fiscal 1997–98, all active projects were retrofitted with performance indicators. Thus, it should not be a surprise that HNP projects approved in 2007 had more indicators and were more likely to have baseline data than projects approved in 1997 (table 2.3).[24]

An increasing share of projects since 1997 have monitoring indicators and baseline data.

Despite these improvements, too few projects have baseline data at appraisal. In fiscal 2007, the share of HNP projects that planned to collect baseline data *after* the project was approved was about the same as a decade earlier (40

Table 2.3: More Project Appraisal Documents Have Baseline Data, but There Is Still Some Distance to Go, Fiscal Years 1997 and 2007

Characteristic	Percent of projects approved/fiscal year	
	1997	2007
Baseline values for all outcome indicators	14	47
Baseline values for none of the outcome indicators	71	27
Targets set for indicators	43	80
Baseline data already collected at the time of the PAD	14	27
Planned to collect baseline data after approval	43	40
Number of projects	14	15

Source: IEG portfolio review.

Yet more than half of indicators have no baseline value and 40 percent of projects plan to collect baseline data after they are approved.

versus 43 percent). A quarter of projects approved in fiscal 2007 still had no baseline values in the PAD, and only about half had baseline values for all outcome indicators. A recent analysis of 12 projects in South Asia found that baseline data were collected for only 39 percent of indicators and that there was little evidence of improvement in M&E between projects approved before and since 2001 (Loevinsohn and Pande 2006).

M&E of recently closed HNP projects—almost all of them approved since fiscal 1997—has been weak. Since mid-2006, IEG has been systematically rating the performance of closed projects on M&E, with a "quality of M&E" rating, based on M&E design, implementation, and use of the data. It is rated on a four-point scale: negligible, modest, substantial, or high. The M&E of 45 projects managed by the HNP sector has been reviewed since mid-2006; M&E was substantial or high for only 27 percent of the projects, slightly lower than the rate Bank-wide (35 percent), which is also quite low (figure 2.6).[25] Nearly half of the ICRs for these HNP projects had no baseline data when the projects were approved, and baseline data were never collected at all for five projects.

A significant number of the Bank's ongoing impact evaluation initiatives are addressing HNP themes.

Lack of M&E has had consequences for the design and efficacy of projects and for improved governance, an objective of the 2007

HNP strategy. According to a review of ICRs of closed projects with low M&E ratings, the lack of baseline data has reduced the relevance and feasibility of projects' objectives and design. Unrealistic targets were set—either too high, or below levels later found to prevail at the start of the project. Weak M&E not only makes it difficult to assess the effectiveness of activities, but also contributes directly to lower efficacy and efficiency because it limits opportunities for learning and fine-tuning implementation for better results.

The Bank has launched major initiatives in impact evaluation, and a significant number of these address HNP themes. These include the Development Impact Evaluation Initiative from the Bank's Development Economics Department; the Spanish Trust Fund for Impact Evaluation, which is dedicated to the evaluation of innovative programs to improve human development; and the Africa Impact Evaluation Initiative. In the databases for these initiatives, IEG identified 101 ongoing or complete HNP impact evaluations—most with an experimental design.[26] It is too early to assess the results and long-run impact of the initiatives in institutionalizing or providing greater incentives for evaluation. Moreover, many of the activities and reforms supported by the Bank are not amenable to the randomized design or even quasi-experimental designs used by impact evaluations. The recently launched Africa Results Monitoring System will provide public access to information from both country and Bank systems on data from countries

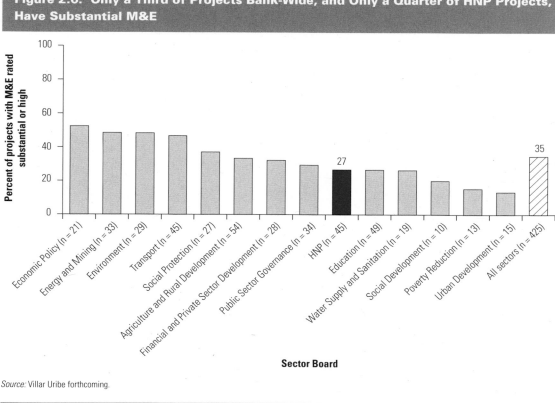

Figure 2.6: Only a Third of Projects Bank-Wide, and Only a Quarter of HNP Projects, Have Substantial M&E

Source: Villar Uribe forthcoming.

and World Bank operations from national accounts, administrative sources, and surveys.

Notwithstanding these initiatives, a large share of the Bank's HNP support finances pilot interventions or programs, or intends to evaluate the impact of a specific activity or program, but few do. Sixty-five projects—about 30 percent of the total HNP portfolio—were labeled as pilot projects, had pilot interventions or pilot regions, had an objective to test an approach or intervention, declared an intent to evaluate the impact of an intervention or program, or had an intent to conduct an impact evaluation, according to the PAD.[27] The objective was generally to test the effectiveness or acceptability of an activity, and on this basis improve or expand it. However, only 17 projects mentioned a control group, 12 described an evaluation design in the PAD, 8 had baseline data in the PAD, and 7 identified an explicit control group or planned an economic analysis (figure 2.7).[28]

All of the pilot and impact evaluations that were eventually conducted had an evaluation design in the PAD. About half of the 65 approved projects with planned pilot or impact evaluations had closed. Only 7 of them had a detailed design in the PAD, and only 4 actually conducted the proposed evaluation of a pilot (figure 2.7), including an impact evaluation of early childhood interventions in the Philippines (box 2.3).[29] Among the 25 pilot and impact evaluation projects that did not have an evaluation design described in the PAD, *none* conducted the planned evaluation.

There is great scope for improving the efficacy of the Bank's HNP support by incorporating rigorous evaluation into projects that already have some pilot feature. Projects can also do more to ensure that public policy is making a difference by incorporating periodic

Much of the Bank's HNP support finances pilot interventions or intends to evaluate impact, but few projects actually do so.

The evaluations that did occur had a design in the PAD.

Figure 2.7: The Discrepancy Between Plans, Evaluation Design, and Implementation of Pilots and Impact Evaluations in HNP Projects Approved in Fiscal Years 1997–2006

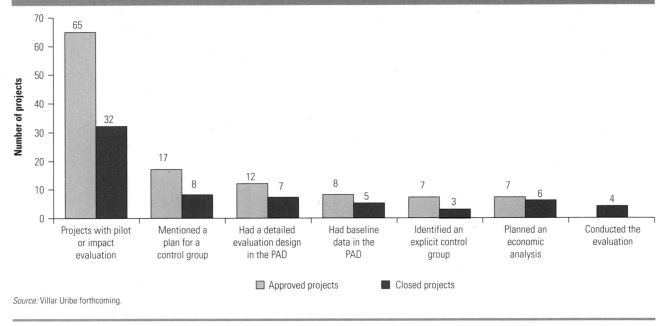

Source: Villar Uribe forthcoming.

Box 2.3: Early Childhood Interventions Improved Cognitive Development and Nutritional Status in the Philippines

The objective of the Philippines Early Childhood Development (ECD) Project (fiscal 1998–2006) was to ensure the survival and promote the physical and mental development of Filipino children, particularly the most vulnerable and disadvantaged. The project implemented expanded immunization, integrated management of childhood illness (IMCI), prevention and control of micronutrient malnutrition, a service to inform parents on growth monitoring and ECD, and a first grade early childhood education/development program in three regions. The project did not introduce new services but sought to integrate and deliver existing ones through center- and home-based interventions.

The impact evaluation conducted longitudinal surveys annually from 2001 to 2003 on 6,693 children aged 0–4 in randomly selected households of two project experimental regions, and one control region without the interventions. The design included baseline and endline surveys: a general population-based sample survey of ECD status and services; nutrition surveys integrated into the National Nutrition Surveys; surveys of ECD-related knowledge, attitudes, and practice; and provincial-level surveys of ethnic groups. The end-project survey in 2003 repeated the 1998 baseline survey in full.

The evaluation found a significant improvement in the cognitive, social, motor, and language development and the short-term nutritional status of children residing in ECD program areas compared with those in nonprogram areas, particularly for children under four. The share of children under four with worms and diarrhea was significantly lower in program areas than in nonprogram areas, but higher for older children. These results, as well as other studies sponsored by the project, helped guide improvement in ECD interventions, build capacity for evidence-based policymaking, and assured the continuation of the ECD program.

Source: Armecin and others 2006.

evaluation of specific elements into the project design and making continued finance of those elements contingent on their evaluation. For example, the efficacy of training programs in changing provider behavior can be measured. It is also important to collect, in parallel with the results framework, information on other key determinants of outcomes that are outside of the project.

One of the main reasons for lack of M&E throughout operations is said to be a lack of incentives. The project appraisal and approval process is one such incentive that does seem to be operating—projects that do not have evaluation designs for pilot projects in the PAD, or those that do not have baseline data collected at the PAD stage, often do not implement them. Making project approval contingent on evaluation designs for specific elements of a program, and making baseline data a requirement, should result in more frequent evaluation.

To summarize, logframes and results frameworks, such as the one in the 2007 HNP strategy, have created greater incentives for monitoring inputs, outputs, outcomes, and impacts and offer guidance to select the right indicators. However, the incentives are still not sufficient to ensure adequate incentives for baseline data and *evaluation*, which is key to understanding effectiveness and impact. Strengthening M&E is one of the key elements of achieving the strategy's objective of better governance in the sector.

Is Health, Nutrition, and Population Support Reaching the Poor?

In keeping with the Bank's mandate for poverty reduction, improving health outcomes among the poor is one of the major objectives in the 2007 HNP strategy, as it was in the 1997 strategy. Numerous studies have shown that it would be dangerous to assume that simply expanding health services would extend benefits primarily to the poor; instead, most have found a strong bias in government health expenditure in favor of the non-poor (box 2.4). Over the past decade, most CASs and about half

of the health portfolio had a generally pro-poor focus, but evidence that the poor actually benefited is weak. The number of country strategies and projects that set explicit objectives regarding the poor is small, and the evidence that the poor have benefited absolutely or relative to the non-poor is thin.

Nearly three-quarters of CASs specifically discussed health issues among the poor (Sinha and Gaubatz 2009). Attention to the poor increased slightly from the first to second half of the period—from 70 to 79 percent of CASs. However, only half articulated a definition of the poor, and fewer than a quarter cited a method to reach them. Even among the subset of CASs that emphasized health issues for the poor, only 15 percent set explicit targets for them. While this share is low, it has increased over time, from 11 to 21 percent.

While two-thirds of HNP project support is for the poorest countries, only about half of the lending portfolio could be said to have a poverty focus *within* countries. This would include projects that explicitly target the poor in their objectives, those that have an objective to improve access to health services more generally, those that seek to prevent and control communicable diseases known to disproportionately affect the poor,[30] and projects with objectives to improve health outcomes of the population but with a design that favors poor geographic areas or services for the poor. Using this definition, about half of the portfolio (107 projects) could be said to have a pro-poor focus. This definition of *poverty focus* could be overly generous, as one could argue and it has been shown that increasing access to services often disproportionately benefits the non-poor (World Bank 2003b; Gwatkin, Wagstaff, and Yazbeck 2005). At the same time, the PADs for almost all HNP lending operations discuss the welfare of the poor or are linked to poverty reduction, even if the project is not ex-

Making project approval contingent on evaluation designs and baseline data should result in more frequent evaluation.

Nearly three-quarters of CASs discussed health issues among the poor.

Only about half of the lending portfolio could be said to have a poverty focus within countries.

Box 2.4: Is Public Health Spending Pro-Poor?

Assuring that the poor have access to health services is often an objective of government spending, but studies of the incidence of government health expenditure in developing countries have consistently found that the *wealthiest* quintiles generally benefit the most from public health subsidies.[a]

In Ecuador, for example, the poorest quintile received 8 percent of health subsidies compared with a 38 percent share for the richest quintile.[b] In Uzbekistan the poor received 13 percent of health spending, while the rich got 39 percent.[b]

A comparison of 11 Asian countries found a pro-rich bias in 9 countries and that the bias was particularly acute in the lowest-income countries.[c] In most cases there was a strong pro-rich bias

in the distribution of hospital care; there was less pro-rich bias in basic health services and in *higher*-income countries, where there are private alternatives and the rich can self-select out of the public sector.

Aggregation of findings in countries across Regions suggest that the bias of public spending against the poor is most acute in some of the *lowest*-income Regions—Sub-Saharan Africa and South Asia—while the bias is also strong in Europe and Central Asia (see figure below). Even in Latin America, where government health spending is pro-poor on average, there are countries where this is not the case.

Government Health Expenditure in Most Regions Is Biased toward the Non-Poor

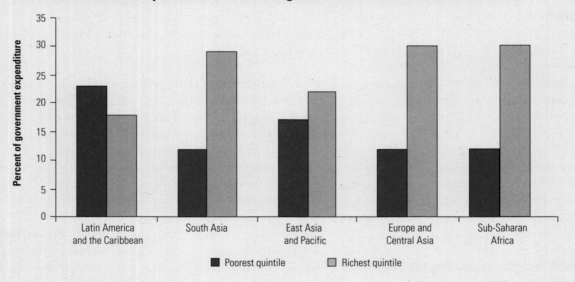

Source: World Bank 2008a, based on calculations from Filmer 2003.

a. For example, Van de Walle 1995; Castro-Leal and others 1999; Mahal and others 2000; Sahn and Younger 2000.

b. Filmer 2003, table 1, p. 1.

c. O'Donnell and others 2007, table 2, p. 100.

pected to yield direct benefits for the poor in the short run.

A remarkably small share of projects had objectives to improve health outcomes among the poor. Only one in eight projects (13 percent) had an objective to target health status, access, use,

quality, or demand, or to provide health insurance *specifically among the poor* (table 2.4).[31] Beyond this, an additional 7 percent of projects had an objective to improve equity, most often expressed in terms of equity in the distribution of resources in the health system, in access to health services, or in health status.[32]

Two-thirds of projects with objectives to affect outcomes for the poor used geographic targeting in design—that is, they aimed to improve outcomes among the poor by implementing activities in poor regions. About 1 in 10 planned to reach the poor by providing services that the poor would use disproportionately (basic health package, nutrition, primary health care, communicable disease control), and 14 percent planned to target individual households using administrative data. The remainder planned to reach the poor by targeting specific population groups presumed to be poor or making health care more affordable. Surprisingly, 7 percent of the projects with objectives targeting the poor advocated addressing the needs of the whole population—that is, there were no plans to ensure that the poor would be reached.

Very few of the closed projects with pro-poor or equity objectives were able to demonstrate an improvement in HNP outcomes among the poor. Among the 108 closed projects that have ICRs, 12 (11 percent) had objectives targeting the poor.[33] Of these, only 2 projects collected outcome data in both the (poor) project and control areas, and in both cases improvements in health were shown across the board. In half of the cases, data were collected only in project areas, with no information on comparison areas (or, in two cases, the comparison was national data). In two cases, no outcome data were collected at all. In a project in Bangladesh, where the targeting mechanism was expansion of an essential services package that would most benefit the poor, all of the outcome targets improved at the national level, but no data were collected to represent access of the poor. Whenever health outcomes were measured, the results showed an improvement. However, the attribution to project outputs in these cases was weak. Without information on what happened elsewhere, it is difficult to attribute these improvements to the programs supported by the Bank.

Fieldwork for the evaluation revealed both success and challenges in reaching the poor. In Egypt, the Schistosomiasis Control Project successfully reached the poor because the disease

Table 2.4: Few HNP Projects Have Objectives That Explicitly Mention the Poor	
Objective	**Percent**
Any specific HNP objective mentioning the poor	13
Improved health status among the poor	6
Increased access to health care among the poor	5
Improved quality of health care for the poor	4
Increase in demand or utilization of services by the poor	3
Providing health insurance for the poor	2

Source: IEG portfolio review.
Note: Projects approved from fiscal 1997 to 2006.

disproportionately affects the rural poor in areas with limited water management infrastructure. The Population Project noted earlier targeted low-income rural communities in Upper Egypt, where fertility rates were higher than the national average. The Eritrea HIV/AIDS, Malaria, Sexually Transmitted Diseases, and TB (HAMSET) Control Project asserted that community-managed subprojects would benefit the poor, but there was no specific effort to monitor the incidence of benefits among the poor, and the TB control activities, thought to disproportionately benefit the poor, had the weakest performance. The Basic Health and Nutrition and Health Reform Projects in Peru had explicit objectives to improve the health of poor women and children over a decade. Health insurance was extended to the poor nationwide. Yet only average health outcomes could be tracked, and these were not even for the specific areas targeted by the projects. The links between health reform projects more generally and benefits for the poor were complex and uncertain (box 2.5).

Of projects with objectives to improve outcomes for the poor, two-thirds used geographic targeting to reach the poor.

Few projects with pro-poor or equity objectives were able to demonstrate improvements among the poor.

About two-thirds of poverty assessments delivered over fiscal years 2000–07 featured a chapter or subchapter on health. An important value added of Bank support for HNP analytic work is in drawing the link between health and poverty and policies to address both. However, about a third of poverty assessments have no substantial discussion of health, as evidenced by a health chapter or subchapter, and the share

---

Box 2.5: Links Between Health Reform Projects and the Health of the Poor Were Complex and Uncertain

The first and second Health Reform Projects in the Kyrgyz Republic (1996–2006) improved the efficiency of the health system, but were less successful in redistributing funds in favor of the poor or addressing their health needs. Primary care was strengthened, broadened, and made more available, with clear improvements in access to care for the poorer populations. Copayments were made more predictable, and the outpatient drug package made prescription drugs more affordable. However, the guaranteed benefits were not universally implemented because of a shortage of funds. The centralization of fragmented pooling arrangements should have enhanced opportunities for efficiency and cross-subsidization, but it is not clear that this actually benefited the poor. During the second project, anticipated redistribution of resources from relatively rich and over-serviced Bishkek to the poorer oblasts did not occur. Neither project tracked health outcomes among the poor.

The Egypt Health Reform Program (1998–present) intended to improve the health of the poor, yet chose to concentrate initially on relatively affluent governorates to increase the chances of success. The poor within these areas would benefit by rationalizing health infrastructure investment with an emphasis on underserved neighborhoods. But fewer than 40 percent of facilities followed the pro-poor rationalization guidelines; positive gains were undermined by enrollment and service fees without proper mechanisms to exempt the poor. Public-sector health providers interviewed by IEG had a vision of a competitive market where potential users preferred other options (nongovernmental organizations or the private sector) on quality grounds; they saw it as their role to compete with these providers, as opposed to enrolling and serving the poor. Concern for the failure to enroll the poor was not voiced until 2004; tracking of the enrollment of the poor was not added as an indicator for the project until late 2007.

Sources: IEG 2008d, Gonzalez-Rosetti forthcoming.

About two-thirds of poverty assessments over fiscal 2000–07 had significant sections on health; few addressed nutrition or population, which greatly affect the poor.

of poverty assessments with a health focus declined from 80 percent over the period fiscal 2000–03 to 58 percent over 2004–07 (figure 2.8).

Very few poverty assessments address nutrition or population. Only 19 percent of poverty assessments had a nutrition chapter or subchapter, and this percentage declined by more than half over time, from 28 percent in fiscal 2000–03 to 12 percent in fiscal 2004–07. The treatment of population was even lower: only 8 percent of poverty assessments had a chapter or subchapter on population, fertility, or family planning. Of the 20 poverty assessments conducted for countries with a total fertility rate of five or more, only one had a subchapter on population (Mozambique, total fertility rate of 5.2).

The poverty orientation of HNP analytic work has declined over the past decade.

The inventory of analytic work assembled by IEG also shows a decline in the poverty-orientation of HNP analytic work over the past

decade. Overall, poverty-related analytic work accounted for a third of all analytic work during fiscal 1997–2006 if multicountry studies are treated as separate studies, and about a quarter if multicountry studies are treated as a single study (table 2.5).[34] Irrespective of the inclusion of multicountry studies, the share of poverty-related analytic work declined.

To summarize, the Bank has supported HNP outcomes in developing countries over the past decade in an environment of shifting international priorities and approaches. Composition of the lending portfolio has shifted in favor of HIV/AIDS and multisectoral projects, and a greater share of projects in Africa.

The shift of the Bank's lending for communicable diseases has added to a huge international influx of resources for HIV/AIDS, TB, and malaria. The share of projects with health system reform objectives has shrunk both relatively and absolutely, though global resources for these objectives do not seem to have increased nearly as much. Attention to nutrition has remained relatively low; attention to population dropped from low to negligible, but appears to be reversing.

About half of the lending portfolio is focused explicitly or implicitly on improving health for the poorest people within countries, yet accountability for actually delivering health results is lacking. We know very little about the success of Bank support in delivering on its institutional mandate of poverty reduction within the HNP sector. Attention to HNP in poverty assessments appears to be slipping.

Only two of every three HNP projects have satisfactory outcomes, and there has been no improvement, in part because of the increased complexity of projects in countries with low implementation capacity, as well as shortcomings in institutional and risk analysis. M&E remain weak and evaluation is scarce, even in projects with evaluation objectives or pilot activities that were planned for evaluation.

The Bank's HNP support in many countries has had significant positive impacts, and additional examples will be highlighted in the chapters that follow. Yet these findings for the portfolio at large

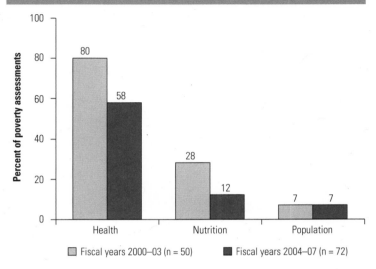

Figure 2.8: The Share of Poverty Assessments with a Focus on HNP Declined

Source: IEG review of analytic work.

pose major challenges to the sector in turning around performance and in pursuing the 2007 HNP strategy, with its aim of delivering results on health outcomes among the poor, health system performance, and better governance.

Table 2.5: The Poverty Focus of HNP Analytic Work Declined

	Fiscal years		
	1997–2001	**2002–06**	**1997–2006**
Multicountry treated separately			
Number of publications	559	899	1,458
Share poverty-related (%)	52	20	32
Multicountry treated as one			
Number of publications	380	899	1,279
Share poverty-related (%)	29	20	23

Source: IEG inventory of analytic work.
Note: Analytic work includes official economic and sector work, research, and Working Papers and publications by Bank staff.

Chapter 3

Evaluation Highlights

- Results of support for TB, malaria, schistosomiasis, and leprosy control have often been substantial; those for HIV/AIDS control have been more modest, limited by project complexity, especially in Africa.
- Excessive earmarking of donor support for diseases can distort sector resource allocations.
- Health system reform projects—about a third of the portfolio—are concentrated in middle-income countries and tend to perform less well than other HNP projects.
- Failure to assess and address the political economy of reform has reduced the performance of health reform support.
- Support for SWAps has strengthened sector capacity, but M&E remains weak, and the impact on transaction costs is unclear.
- There is no necessary relationship between adopting the SWAp approach and better HNP outcomes.

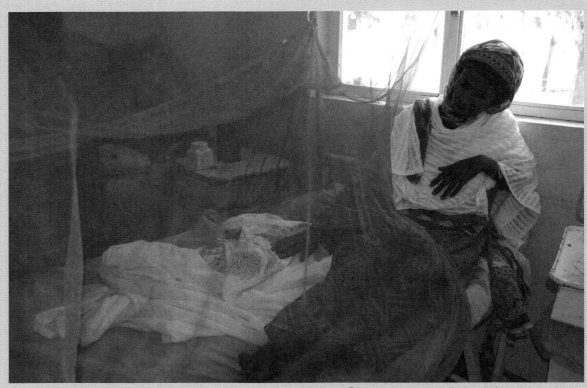

Eritrean mother tends to her child, shielded by an insecticide-treated mosquito net. Eritrea made enormous gains in malaria control over the evaluation period. Photo courtesy of the Eritrea National Malaria Control Program.

Lessons from Three Approaches to Improve Outcomes

Since 1997, the Bank has supported a number of approaches to improve health status and health system performance that figure prominently in the action plan of the 2007 HNP strategy. The rapid increase in support for *communicable disease control* was not only a strategy for improving health outcomes among the poor, but also has led to efforts in the action plan to ensure synergy between infectious disease programs and health systems. Experience with *health reforms* and *sectorwide approaches* (SWAps) are at the heart of improving the performance of health systems, a second major theme of the 2007 strategy.

This chapter presents findings and lessons from Bank support for communicable disease control, the reform of health systems, and health SWAps. While discussed separately, it is important to note that these efforts are not mutually exclusive, and Bank support for one or more may be found in the same country at the same time.

Communicable Disease Control

Eighty percent of the 15 million people who die every year from communicable diseases live in developing countries. The World Health Organization (WHO) estimates that there were 247 million cases of malaria worldwide in 2006 and 881,000 deaths, most of them among African children (WHO 2008). Tuberculosis (TB) kills 1.6 million people annually. As of the end of 2007, 33 million people worldwide were living with HIV/AIDS, more than 90 percent of them in developing countries (UNAIDS 2008). Three-quarters of the 2 million people who died of AIDS in 2007 were living in Sub-Saharan Africa.

Communicable diseases account for about a third (36 percent) of the disease burden in the developing world (Jamison and others 2006b), but the burden of morbidity and mortality is greatest among the poor (Gwatkin and Guillot 2000). The 1993 *World Development Report: Investing in Health* (World Bank 1993c) highlighted this burden and advocated investing in a package of cost-effective, basic public health measures that included communicable disease control. The World Bank has long supported communicable disease control components as part of health projects; freestanding disease projects date back to 1988.[1]

World Bank commitments for communicable disease control accounted for $3.5 billion, or about a third of all HNP-managed commitments approved during fiscal 1997–2006.[2] The World Bank approved a total of 93 communicable disease projects, including 63 free-

Commitments for communicable disease control were $3.5 billion—about a third of all HNP-managed commitments over fiscal 1997–2006.

Figure 3.1: AIDS Accounted for More than Half of Communicable Disease Projects Approved in Fiscal Years 1997–2006

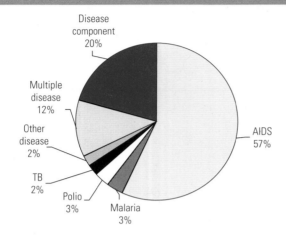

n = 93 communicable disease projects approved

Source: IEG portfolio review.

Note: Includes projects with objectives to control communicable disease or with a communicable disease component. *Other disease* includes leprosy and avian influenza (one project each).

standing single-disease projects, 11 projects addressing multiple diseases, and 19 projects with communicable disease components. Communicable disease control was thus funded in at least 42 percent of the HNP projects approved over the period. Freestanding AIDS projects accounted for nearly 60 percent of all communicable disease projects approved over the decade (figure 3.1) and a quarter of all approved HNP projects.

Support for communicable disease control has produced demonstrable results for TB, malaria, schistosomiasis, and leprosy.

Between the first and second half of that decade, the share of communicable disease projects (including freestanding single- and multiple-disease projects and components) among all approvals rose from a third to half of all projects and from 30 to 43 percent of all HNP commitments.

The most common rationales offered for supporting public communicable disease control involved the positive externalities and public-good nature of disease control, the understanding that most communicable diseases disproportionately affect the poor, and the cost-effectiveness of com-

municable disease interventions.[3] AIDS projects in Africa were largely launched in an emergency mode in light of exploding HIV transmission rates, the high mortality rate from AIDS, and the adverse economic and social impact of the disease in a very poor Region.[4]

The surge in Bank support for communicable disease control was in step with major new international initiatives for communicable disease control. In 2000, the G8 Summit in Japan committed to implement an ambitious plan to prevent infectious disease, including AIDS, malaria, and TB, and the Bank agreed to triple IDA financing for those diseases.[5] Communicable disease control was considered an international public good, and the international community rallied behind it. The UN Millennium Development Goals were adopted with a goal for AIDS and malaria. Initiatives were launched to eradicate polio and guinea worm. An outbreak of Severe Acute Respiratory Syndrome (SARS) and avian influenza reminded the world of its vulnerability to new infectious agents.[6] The Global Fund to Fight AIDS, TB, and Malaria was created in 2002; it has committed $15.0 billion and disbursed $6.9 billion to date.[7] The U.S. President's Emergency Plan for AIDS Relief (PEPFAR) committed $12.8 billion for AIDS from fiscal 2004 to 2007. Support from bilateral aid agencies expanded, and major private foundations have become involved. Bank strategies on HIV/AIDS and on malaria have been developed, and the Bank continues to be involved in global international partnerships such as Stop TB, Roll Back Malaria (RBM), and the Global Alliance for Vaccines and Immunization (GAVI),[8] in addition to its role as a cosponsor of the Joint United Nations Program on HIV/AIDS (UNAIDS). Communicable diseases feature prominently in the Bank's global public good strategic theme, one of six identified in 2007 by Bank President Zoellick.

Efficacy of Support for Communicable Disease Control

Evidence on the efficacy of Bank support for communicable disease control can be gleaned from an in-depth portfolio review of the 93 approved projects (Martin 2009), IEG Project Performance Assessments of freestanding communicable disease projects or projects with communicable disease components,[9] and country case studies. In 2005, IEG evaluated the development effectiveness of the entire HIV/AIDS portfolio.

Support for communicable disease control, both in freestanding projects and components, has produced demonstrable results for TB, malaria, schistosomiasis, and leprosy. In Bangladesh, the Fourth Population and Family Health Project supported the National Leprosy Elimination Program (IEG 2006b). The prevalence of leprosy declined from 13.6 to less than 1 per 10,000 population. Bank support through two projects contributed to dramatic results in reducing malaria in Eritrea (box 3.1). Support for TB Control in India (1997–2006) expanded coverage of directly observed treatment short-course (DOTS) by training half a million government staff and enlisting the help of 10,000 private practitioners, more than 1,600 nongovernmental organizations, 100 private enterprises, and a wide network of community volunteers. Information, education, and communication investments spread the word that TB is curable and sought to reduce stigma. More than twice as many people were treated as planned, the cure rate rose from 35 to 86 percent, and death rates in areas with DOTS were reduced sevenfold relative to non-DOTS areas (World Bank 2006a). In Egypt, support for schistosomiasis control helped to reduce the prevalence of *S. mansoni* (the cause of intestinal schistosomiasis in Lower Egypt) from 14.8 to 1.2 percent, and of *S. haematorbium* (the cause of urinary schistosomiasis in Middle and Upper Egypt) from 6.6 to 1.2 percent over the period 1993–2006 (IEG 2008c).

In contrast, the performance of the HIV/AIDS portion of the communicable disease portfolio, which was responsible for the enormous growth in communicable disease projects over the decade, has been modest. Only 29 percent of the freestanding HIV/AIDS projects approved and completed during fiscal years 1997–2006 had satisfactory outcomes, compared with 89 percent for the

Box 3.1: Successful Malaria Control in Eritrea

Following a severe malaria outbreak in Eritrea in 1998, two successive Bank projects[a] supported a three-pronged strategy to reduce malaria: distribution of insecticide-impregnated bednets; targeted indoor residual spraying; and reduction in vector breeding sites. Malaria morbidity decreased by 74 percent, mortality by 85 percent, and the case fatality rate by 78 percent. The number of cases per 100,000 population nationally dropped from 7,546 to 568 between 1998 and 2006. While the early part of the response also corresponded to a period of declining rainfall, which would have contributed to these trends, malaria cases continued to fall even when the rains resumed in 2003.

Source: IEG 2009a.
a. Eritrea Health Project, Eritrea HAMSET Control Project. The Bank was the largest single source of funding to the National Malaria Control Program. Other important sources of funding were the U.S. Agency for International Development (USAID); the Italian Cooperation; and, since 2003, the Global Fund.

Figure 3.2: HIV/AIDS Projects Have Performed Less Well than Other Communicable Disease Projects

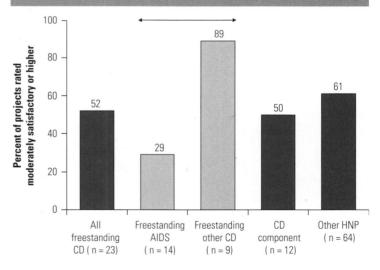

Source: IEG portfolio review.

freestanding projects for other diseases[10] (figure 3.2). Thus, while the performance of the HIV/AIDS portfolio has been much lower than that of other HNP projects, performance of freestanding proj-

The performance of the HIV/AIDS portion of the portfolio has been modest.

ects for other communicable diseases has been substantially higher.[11] AIDS projects in Africa—where the crisis is most acute—have had particularly modest performance: Only 18 percent of the projects in the Africa Multicountry AIDS Program (MAP) have had satisfactory outcomes.[12]

The advantage of support for one or more communicable diseases is that the project can be less complex. Communicable disease support can have better defined boundaries; the objective is easier to understand; the results chain leading from outputs to outcomes is straightforward; and results can be seen in many cases in a relatively short period. Many communicable disease programs have dedicated workers and facilities, although most still rely on the rest of the health system. All of the AIDS projects have faced the challenge that the ultimate outcome for HIV prevention—HIV incidence—is difficult to observe and rarely measured (though the behaviors that spread it can be). Success in stopping the spread of HIV also depends on reaching marginalized, high-risk individuals, which can be technically and politically difficult.

Africa Region AIDS projects have more complex designs than other projects.

While there are specific characteristics of HIV prevention and control that present challenges, what sets the Africa Region AIDS projects apart from the other communicable disease projects is their relatively more complex design. As the findings of chapter 2 indicate, complexity of design in low-capacity settings is a strong predictor of weak performance. The large number of implementers in both government and civil society make the Africa MAP projects highly complex. A demand-driven design with so many actors makes it more difficult to assess coverage and quality of key activities. Beyond this, while other communicable disease programs are often run from long-existing directorates within the Ministry of Health,

Simplification of project design is easily within the control of the Bank and borrowers.

the Africa Region AIDS projects have generally relied on newly created and inexperienced institutions, separate from the Ministry. Finally, many were prepared in an emergency mode; the

investment in M&E and "learning by doing" in these projects (which was supposed to be 5–10 percent of costs) has not been realized, and the large number of implementers would challenge any M&E system. Most of the completed AIDS projects in Africa have been unable to establish a clear results chain linking outputs to outcomes or to address systematically the key drivers of the epidemic, although the latter is a weakness of most AIDS projects in other Regions.

Simplifying the design of HIV/AIDS projects is under the control of the Bank and borrowers. While it is difficult to change capacity in the short run, and some of the inherent difficulties confronting HIV/AIDS cannot be fixed, HIV/AIDS programs do not require an overly complex design. The relatively more successful AIDS projects in Argentina, Brazil, and India, in settings with greater capacity, still do not have project designs as complex as those in Africa. Findings and lessons from Bank support for HIV/AIDS projects were evaluated by IEG in 2005, with recommendations that remain relevant to support in all Regions (box 3.2).

Notwithstanding the accomplishments of many of these communicable disease projects:

- ***M&E has been weaker than for other HNP projects, even though the results chain is theoretically easier to construct than for projects that address broad health issues.*** Only one in five closed communicable disease projects had at least substantial M&E, compared with a third in the rest of the HNP portfolio.[13] An example of this paradox can be seen in malaria control. While the number of bednets distributed or treated with insecticides is generally available, none of the seven completed projects supporting malaria control could provide data on actual bednet use, and only one had data on bednet ownership (the endpoint only). The low capacity, weak institutions, and lack of M&E have led to governance problems in a number of these projects, both in Africa and India.[14]

- ***There is little evidence to confirm that the poor—however defined—have dispro-***

portionately benefited from communicable disease control within countries. Even when the poor are at greater risk, the literature suggests that the non-poor have greater access to information and services, which makes it more likely that they will benefit (Gwatkin, Wagstaff, and Yazbeck 2005). Without data on the socioeconomic distribution of benefits, it cannot be assumed that the incidence of disease control outcomes is pro-poor, particularly for HIV/AIDS, which in many developing countries does not disproportionately affect the poor. There are equity dimensions to some of the programs—such as in the distribution of free bednets or malaria drugs and access to subsidized antiretroviral treatment—that are rarely studied.

- *Very few Bank projects have attempted to calculate the actual costs or effectiveness of interventions as implemented in the field as a basis for improving performance.* A case in point is the Egypt Schistosomiasis Control Project. One of the objectives was to strengthen the capacity to periodically assess the cost-effectiveness of the program and to adjust the strategy accordingly (IEG 2008c). However, most studies were not carried out. Recent economic and sector work on AIDS treatment in Thailand and India points to tradeoffs in cost-effectiveness and sustainability of AIDS treatment programs under varying assumptions (Over and others 2004; Revenga and others 2006). Yet this key information is not available for low-income Africa, which has the greatest HIV burden and the fewest resources. Only two public expenditure reviews (PERs) issued in Africa since 2000 have discussed the costs and sustainability of AIDS programs, including the long-run cost of providing antiretroviral therapy to patients.[15]

Synergy Between Communicable Disease Programs and the Health System

The 2007 HNP strategy calls for synergy between efforts to strengthen health systems and the focus on priority disease results in low-income countries, noting that a well-functioning health system is also essential for the success of these programs.[16] This is clearly borne out in the experience of support for communicable disease control: health

---

Box 3.2: Recommendations of IEG's 2005 Evaluation of World Bank Support for AIDS Control Remain Relevant

Committing to Results: Improving the Effectiveness of HIV/AIDS Assistance (IEG 2005a) evaluated the World Bank's country-level HIV/AIDS support through mid-2004. It pointed to three main avenues for improving performance:

- Help governments to be more strategic and selective and to prioritize activities that will have the greatest impact on the epidemic.
- Strengthen national institutions for managing and implementing the long-run response, particularly ministries of health.
- Improve the local evidence base for decision making through improved M&E.

Source: IEG 2005a.

---

system problems with the procurement and distribution of pharmaceuticals and the understaffing or low performance of fixed facilities for treatment and immunizations also affect the efficacy of communicable disease control programs. Yet it also could be said that a well-functioning health system depends on effective communicable disease control, because prevention of communicable diseases is often low cost and reduces demand for more expensive treatment, freeing resources for other conditions.

In a number of countries, the Bank's support has strengthened the health system by building capacity in national disease control programs. In Cambodia, for example, the Disease Control and Health Development Project (1996–2002) strengthened health infrastructure and decentralized health management, while financing complementary disease control programs for malaria, TB, and HIV/AIDS. Prior to the project, international donors were operating communicable disease interventions outside the framework of government, and capacity was weak. The project funded the government communicable disease programs, enabling the Ministry of Health to fulfill its mandate, while integrating the disease control programs into the health system at the provincial and district levels. Bank support for multiple dis-

In many countries, the Bank has strengthened the health system by building capacity in national disease control programs.

ease and endemic disease projects has generally sought to improve communicable disease surveillance and cross-cutting disease-control functions, such as health promotion and laboratory service, to improve efficiency.

However, the monitoring systems for communicable disease programs often exist in parallel to, and are not well linked to, government management information systems (MIS). This can lead to duplication and inhibit sharing of data between agencies. However, weaknesses in the overall health MIS can shake the confidence of communicable disease control managers, who need timely information for a rapid response, and such weaknesses can lead them to maintain separate monitoring systems, as in Ghana (IEG 2007d). This creates, in turn, a heavy burden at the district and service levels, which are required to supply information through multiple, overlapping systems (IEG 2007d). The problem has been overcome in Eritrea, where the National Malaria Control Program maintained a parallel data collection system, and it was reported to the MIS with little delay.

As support to systemwide reforms continues to expand, there is a risk that the capacity that has been built in disease control will be lost.

As the Bank and donors enhance their support to systemwide reforms and sectorwide approaches, there is a risk that the capacity that has been built in many disease control programs will be lost. The first health SWAp in Bangladesh included plans to integrate the National TB Program (NTP) into the approach, yet neglected to include the NTP or any TB indicators in the logframe (IEG 2006b). Support for Ghana's health SWAp provided districts with increased financing to carry out communicable disease activities. But the districts often did not prioritize communicable disease interventions, assuming that central-level units would continue to support them (IEG 2007d). In Egypt, the success of investments in schistosomiasis control has not been sustained by the Health Reform Project that supported these activities as part of an integrated basic package (IEG 2008c). In Malawi, there is a concern that the much-needed emphasis on a functioning health system pursued

The large amount of donor funds earmarked for specific diseases in small countries may be creating distortions in the rest of the health sector.

by the health SWAp maintain the technical strength of disease programs as an important element (Elmendorf and Nankhuni forthcoming).

While the World Bank was among the first to step up to increase dramatically HIV/AIDS resources to Africa (fiscal 2001–02), there are signs that the high level of earmarked disease funds may be creating distortions in the rest of the health system. Only about one in five freestanding AIDS projects is in a country with more than 50 million people; a third are for countries with fewer than 5 million people, and half of those are for countries with populations of less than 1 million. In many cases, the Bank is not the only donor—the Global Fund and PEPFAR, in addition to bilateral funds, are also often providing earmarked funding to a specific disease (Martin 2009). In these cases, there is a risk of a huge imbalance between investment in communicable diseases (including AIDS and any other earmarked program) and investment in the rest of the health system. A recent study calculated that HIV/AIDS funding represented from 33 to 45 percent of total public and donor health expenditures in four African countries.[17] The 2007 PER for Malawi reported that HIV/AIDS accounts for as much as 60 percent of health expenditures (World Bank 2007f, p. 89).

The problem of distortions created by earmarking of external assistance is unlikely to be extensive enough in the large countries receiving Bank support for AIDS, TB, malaria, or other endemic diseases (such as Bangladesh, Brazil, China, or India) to create such difficulties. But two problems arise with relatively large shares of money earmarked for disease in the context of a small country. First, the large funds in a small program relative to the needs of the rest of the system can pull scarce resources—such as nurses or doctors, who are in short supply—from elsewhere in the health system and reduce services elsewhere in the system.[18] Second, as the availability of IDA money and Bank supervision resources are constrained, it is very likely that there is competition between freestanding communicable disease projects and projects that support the entire health system in small countries. A case in point is Malawi: because of constraints in the availability of Bank budget for supervision, IDA funds were available for the health SWAp or the AIDS SWAp, but not for both. The Bank opted to drop support for the health SWAp and continue support for HIV/AIDS, despite the large share of earmarked funds as a percentage of overall health expenditure (Elmendorf and Nankhuni forthcoming). Despite these risks, the Bank has continued to approve new HIV/AIDS projects in small countries that receive a lot of other earmarked foreign aid.

In sum, the past decade has seen an enormous increase in the share and absolute amount of World Bank support for communicable disease control, most of which has been for HIV/AIDS. Communicable disease projects other than for AIDS are more likely to be in large countries, perform better than the rest of the HNP portfolio, and are generally somewhat less complex. The HIV/AIDS projects are almost all multisectoral and involve multiple public sector entities and diverse segments of civil society, in addition to dealing with a highly stigmatized disease. Furthermore, most are in Sub-Saharan Africa, and many are in smaller countries with a large donor presence. The complexity of the support and low capacity have resulted in lower outcomes. M&E has been inadequate for most communicable disease support, there is little evidence that the poor have disproportionately benefitted, and the actual cost-effectiveness of interventions as implemented has rarely been calculated. There are signs that the high level of earmarked disease funds may be creating distortions in the health systems of some small countries.

Reforming Health Systems

There is no internationally accepted model of how a health system should function; the specific activities or policy content of health reform are context-specific. Generally, however, reform programs are about fundamental changes in structure, incentives, and allocation of resources. Improved efficiency of health care delivery, coupled with improvements in health status and reduction in inequities, is often at the core of health reform programs. Health reform is thus distinct from efforts to improve outcomes by increasing inputs—money, training, salaries, facilities, and materials—although increasing inputs

can be, and has been, used to leverage and support reforms.

About a third of all World Bank HNP projects approved from fiscal 1997 to 2006 had an objective to reform or restructure the health system. These included objectives involving health finance, health insurance, decentralization, or regulation of or enhancing the role of the private sector in service delivery.[19] Implicitly if not explicitly, most of these projects aimed to improve the efficiency of the health system.[20] The share of approved projects with health reform objectives has declined by nearly half over time—from 45 percent of approved projects during fiscal 1997–2001 to only 26 percent in fiscal 2002–06 (figure 3.3).[21] The share has declined in all Regions except South Asia, and in Latin America and the Caribbean and Africa the decline is statistically significant.[22]

About a third of Bank HNP projects had health system reform or restructuring as an objective.

Health reform projects are concentrated in middle-income countries. Three-quarters of all health reform projects were in middle-income countries and half of all HNP projects in middle-income countries over the decade had health reform objectives, compared with only 18 percent of all projects in low-income countries. Health reform is an objective in about half of the projects in lower-middle-income countries and in 63 percent of the projects in upper-middle-income countries. About two-thirds of the HNP portfolio in Europe and Central Asia and the Middle East and North Africa is comprised of health reform projects, as is 43 percent of projects in Latin America and the Caribbean.

Health reform projects are concentrated in middle-income countries.

Health reform projects have somewhat lower outcomes than do projects without reform objectives in middle-income countries, although this difference is not statistically significant. Seventy-one percent of closed projects with health reform objectives in middle-income countries had satisfactory outcomes, compared with 86 percent of HNP projects with other objectives (table 3.1). The borrower's performance is also slightly lower for health reform projects.

They have somewhat lower outcomes than do projects without reform objectives.

Figure 3.3: The Share of HNP Project Approvals with Health Reform Objectives Has Declined in Middle-Income Countries and in Most Regions

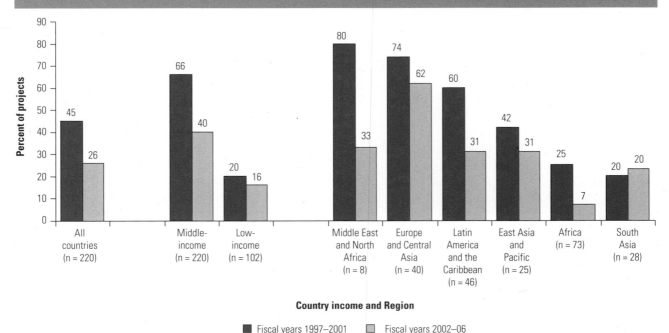

Source: IEG portfolio review.

Note: The decline in share of health reform projects overall and in middle-income countries is statistically significant at p < .01, and the decline in Latin America and the Caribbean and in Africa at p < .05. Eight Regional projects are excluded from the tabulation by country income.

Table 3.1: Outcomes and Bank Performance Are Lower for Health Reform Projects than for Other HNP Projects in Middle-Income Countries

IEG rating–satisfactory	Health reform projects (n = 29)	Other HNP projects (n = 14)
Outcome	71	86
Bank performance	69[a]	93[a]
Borrower performance	72	79

Source: IEG portfolio review.

Note: In low-income countries there are only 8 completed health reform projects that were approved during fiscal 1997–2006 and 37 other completed HNP projects. Both outcome and Bank performance are substantially higher for health reform projects than for other projects in low-income countries, but these differences are not statistically significant because of the small sample. Borrower performance is similar for the two groups.

a. The difference between health reform and other HNP projects is weakly significant at p = .08.

Bank performance for health reform projects in middle-income countries is substantially and significantly lower than for HNP projects with other objectives. The Bank's performance—including quality at entry (preparation) and supervision—was satisfactory in only 69 percent of health reform projects, compared with 93 percent of other HNP projects. IEG reviews of Implementation Completion Reports (ICRs) found the following factors associated with good Bank performance:

- A design based on strong sector work[23]
- Thorough institutional and stakeholder analysis[24]
- Use of local experts, consultation with stakeholders, good communication, and full ownership of the reforms[25]
- Creative use of other instruments to backstop reforms[26]
- Strong and active dialogue with government throughout implementation.

Poor Bank performance was often linked to weaknesses in these same areas, as well as inadequate institutional analysis or risk mitigation plans, overoptimism about capacity or political commitment, project complexity, and the failure to restructure projects that are performing poorly.[27]

Health care reform usually takes place over an extended period, beginning with the reforms with the least political opposition and quickest gains, and often proceeding in fits and starts. This means that the efficacy of the support for the later-stage, more difficult activities is not yet tested in many instances. However, the varying experience of the countries where IEG has conducted in-depth fieldwork highlights some of the achievements, shortcomings, and lessons to date. Health reforms are often linked to more general civil service and administrative reforms across all sectors; the obstacles to public sector reforms are in many ways similar to those for health reforms (box 3.3).

The Bank supported health system reforms in the Kyrgyz Republic, Peru, and Egypt that shared some common elements, with different outcomes. In all three countries, the reform strategy called, first, for improving access to and quality of primary health care, which would disproportionately help the poor and reduce the demand for inpatient care, and for setting up output-based reimbursements, before attempting more politically controversial and technically challenging reforms, such as rationalizing hospitals and public sector contracting with the private sector or reimbursements with the private sector to deliver services. Implementation and results on improved efficiency were uneven, although health status nevertheless continued to improve in all three countries. Only in the Kyrgyz Republic, however, is there evidence of efficiency gains and any plausible link of health outcomes to any of the reforms.[28]

In the **Kyrgyz Republic,** the Bank and other donors supported implementation of a home-grown reform agenda:

- Set up an institution to serve as a single payer for health insurance.
- Separate the financing of health care from health care delivery.

Bank performance in health reform projects is lower than for HNP projects with other objectives.

Box 3.3: Shared Themes: Public Sector and Health Systems Reform

The obstacles to many health system reforms are similar to those blocking improvement in public administration more generally, as are the measures to overcome them. The recent IEG evaluation, *Public Sector Reform: What Works and Why?* (IEG 2008f) found that activities aimed at strengthened financial management and tax administration were far more effective than those focused on civil service and administrative improvements. Ministries of finance tended to strongly support this type of reform, which was usually underpinned by extensive technical analysis, and often generated quickly observable results, expressed in terms of clear public expenditure and financial accountability indicators. The World Bank's expertise in these issues is widely recognized.

In contrast, measures affecting personnel policies, including downsizing, pay decompression, and merit-based reforms were particularly unsuccessful. They often failed because of lack of political commitment, discontinuities in leadership, politicians' resistance to measures diluting their control over patronage, and union opposition. The World Bank's analytical tools are less developed in these fields and, more fundamentally, there is a "lack of consensus around the 'right' civil service model for developing countries, or indeed for developed countries." (IEG 2008f, p. 54) Basic data are often lacking, and political leaders may not be able to identify tangible benefits. Almost identical language could be used to describe health sector reforms entailing changes in organization and personnel policies.

Public Sector Reform nevertheless identified six factors associated with comparatively successful administrative reforms: good analysis and diagnosis; pragmatic opportunism in selecting reforms; realistic expectations; appropriate lending packages (usually including technical assistance); tangible indicators of success; and effective donor coordination. Successful major health reform programs, as in the Kyrgyz Republic, feature similar characteristics.

Source: IEG 2008f.

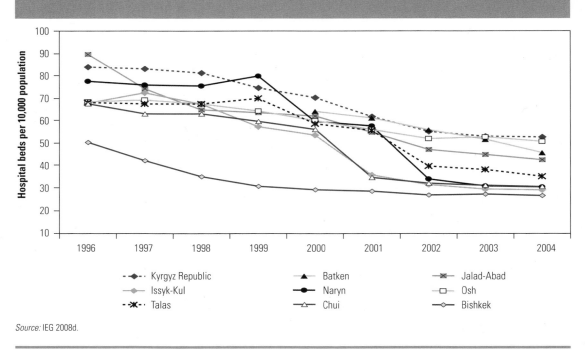

Figure 3.4: Excess Inpatient Bed Capacity Declined across the Kyrgyz Republic

Legend:
- - ◆ - - Kyrgyz Republic
- ◆ Issyk-Kul
- - ✱ - - Talas
- ▲ Batken
- ● Naryn
- △ Chui
- ✖ Jalad-Abad
- □ Osh
- ◇ Bishkek

Source: IEG 2008d.

- Use output-based financing that pays for services delivered, rather than line budgets.
- Increase autonomy for health facilities in budget allocations.
- Reduce excess inpatient capacity.
- Adopt a guaranteed package of services.
- Create a new type of family practice that reduces resort to specialists, provides more cost-effective primary health care on an outpatient basis, and serves as a gatekeeper for referrals to higher and more specialized facilities.

The share of the population covered by the Mandatory Health Insurance Fund rose from 25 to 85 percent and excess inpatient capacity was significantly reduced (figure 3.4). Hospitals used their remaining capacity more efficiently, and the quantity and quality of outpatient services increased. By 2005, almost 99 percent of the population had access to primary health care, and the share of government health spending on that care had risen from 11 to 25 percent. Hemorrhagic insult among patients with high blood pressure in one region dropped by three-quarters.

Yet, despite Bank intervention and policy dialogue at key moments, political opponents still managed to block the restructuring of tertiary hospitals in the two major cities. Private payments remained a significant share of health spending. The finance ministry reallocated the savings from improved health sector efficiency to other activities, dampening the enthusiasm of health reformers. Since then, the government has met all commitments to increase public financing of health. However, low pay scales have led to outmigration of family physicians, jeopardizing the achievements of the reforms.

In **Peru,** the World Bank and Inter-American Development Bank support to the government's reform program saw a huge expansion in access to a package of basic services among the poor through the Integrated Health Insurance (SIS) program, despite significant political changes over the period.[29] Adopted nationwide in 2002, the SIS reimburses Ministry of Health care providers for the variable costs of the use of services by its beneficiaries, increasing the incentives for efficiency. In addition, support was provided to expand and improve the quality of community-managed health facilities, organized under a quasi-private management scheme in which the community participates. However, the SIS still does not reimburse private providers or other public providers and there are no major new revenues for the system. The extent to which hospital costs have been reduced is unclear, and ESSALUD, the entity providing insurance to formal sector workers and their families,[30] has resisted reforms that would separate funding from service delivery and that would provide better coordination with the Ministry of Health.

In *Egypt,* the Bank, the U.S. Agency for International Development (USAID), and the European Commission have supported a health reform program over the past decade, with uneven ownership by key government players. There has been progress in strengthening primary health care and family services and defining a basic package of primary health care and public health services for universal coverage. However, efforts to transform the Health Insurance Organization into a single-payer plan and to separate finance from health delivery have met opposition from the Ministry of Health and Population and other entities that want to retain control over finance. Rationalization of hospitals has not occurred and the system remains highly fragmented, with nearly two dozen different public or parastatal entities providing and financing health care, as well as overuse of and excess capacity in expensive tertiary care.

The most pervasive lesson from the Bank's experience with health reform is that failure to fully assess the political economy of reform and to prepare a proactive plan to address this issue can considerably diminish prospects for success. One source of political economy risk is that reforms with high-level support will be abandoned with a change in government. Among the five countries that undertook health reform and were studied in-depth by IEG, four experienced changes in leadership with the potential to affect the reform agenda (Bangladesh, Egypt, the Kyrgyz Republic, and Peru[31]). Given the long period over which reforms to health systems typically take place, the starting assumption

should be that there *will* certainly be a change in government or in leadership of the sector that can affect the ownership of and commitment to reform. This underscores the importance of generating evidence that reforms work, so they can transcend a single administration, and of enlisting key stakeholders in the system who are vested in the reforms and likely to remain in place.

The impact of reforms on the interests and incentives of key stakeholders also constitutes a significant political economy risk. Health reform projects create winners and losers; it is important that their interests be understood from the outset. High-level commitment is no guarantee that key stakeholders in the health system or the general public will go along with a reform; stakeholders who have a role in implementing any reform can simply not cooperate. The general public may perceive that a reduction in excess hospital capacity is reducing their access to health care. Even within an institution, the interests and incentives may vary according to whether the person is a manager or delivers services. The Kyrgyz health reform experience was an exception in this regard. It was based on a reform strategy that was totally owned by a group of reformers in the Ministry of Health and a considerable prior analysis and a strategy for navigating the winners and losers. Even then, Bishkek and Osh, the two wealthiest regions, remain outside the reforms of tertiary care. The experiences of Bangladesh, Egypt, and Russia are more typical (box 3.4).

Failure to assess the political economy of reform and to plan to address it can diminish prospects for success.

The political risks and the risk of complexity—two of the issues found to be most critical in the case studies—are often missing in the risk analysis for health reform projects. Review of the risk analysis of the appraisal documents for closed health reform projects approved since fiscal 1997 found that only 59 percent cited risks of a change in government commitment to reforms (following turnover in ministry staff or elections of top leadership), and only 43 percent pointed to the risk that specific stakeholders—physicians, hospital managers, patients, managers of decentralized facilities—would be

---

Box 3.4: Consequences of Inadequate Stakeholder Analysis

The Bangladesh Health and Population Program (1998–2005), which involved many donors in a sectorwide operation, sought to merge the Health and Family Planning Directorates within the Ministry of Health and Family Welfare, starting from the subdistrict level and moving downward, a reform to improve efficiency. While some family planning workers were pleased to become regular public employees through this reform, mid-level workers feared that their jobs would be abolished and took their case to the Supreme Court. The government won the lawsuit, but the implementation of the reform had been delayed and unification was reversed by a new government. Other proposed reforms in the project were tainted by association.

In Egypt, there was high-level commitment and participatory analytic work from the Minister of Health and Population for health reforms in the mid-1990s, but the incentives of nearly two dozen other public and parastatal providers of health care were not taken into account. The ministry would have lost control over financial resources with a single payer arrangement; it therefore welcomed investment in primary health care, but resisted reforming the Health Insurance Organization. The insurance reforms were subsequently dropped from the Health Reform Project, while expansion of family health services continued.

The Russia Health Reform Pilot Project (1997–2004) aimed to make changes in two regions. It was to introduce output-driven, cost-conscious provider payment mechanisms, accompanied by information-based quality assurance, and to reorient health care by strengthening primary and outpatient care, centered on a network of family physicians, and reducing inpatient care services. The new models were not uniformly implemented; where introduced, they coexisted with the old and had little staying power. Family practitioners were trained, their offices equipped, and a standard Russian family medicine curriculum developed, but obstetrics, gynecology, and maternal and child health were excluded because of the influence of specialists in those fields.

Sources: IEG 2006b, 2007f; Gonzalez-Rosetti forthcoming.

Political risks and complexity are often missing in the risk analysis of health reform projects. resistant to or undermine the reforms. The risk of excessive complexity was mentioned in only 22 percent of the appraisal documents. Overall, only a third of projects with health reform objectives were assessed at appraisal as having substantial or high risks.[32]

To have a chance at success, both the political economy risks and complexity need to be taken into account and planned for in health reform operations. The projects reviewed for this evaluation have used a number of strategies to deal with these issues:

- ***Institutional and stakeholder analyses*** are essential during the design of the reforms and to inform decisions during implementation about when to intervene and when not to. Stakeholder consultations can help to flag possible resistance and solutions.
- ***Information and outreach*** to all stakeholders and the public to explain the reforms, the benefits, and how they will be affected.

- ***Sequencing of reforms***, so that some constituencies win up front, before the more difficult choices—on hospital rationalization, for example—must be decided. Four of the five case studies on health reform followed a deliberately sequenced approach, whereby the first step was to improve access to and quality of outpatient and primary health care, while in most cases introducing changes in the payment system.[33] This is also a strategy for avoiding complexity, a big problem in health reform projects.
- ***Piloting reforms*** in specific geographic areas to demonstrate their feasibility and efficacy before they are expanded. The Issyk-Kul region of the Kyrgyz Republic piloted most reforms, sponsored by USAID, generating interest in other regions.
- ***Creating new institutions,*** like the Mandatory Health Insurance Fund in Kyrgyz and the SIS in Peru, can often result in less resistance than attempting to reform existing ones—such as ESSALUD and the health care units of the armed forces and the national police in Peru or

---

Box 3.5: Programmatic Lending Maintained Momentum on Health Reform

Kyrgyz Republic

Governance Structural Adjustment Credit (2003). The objectives of the project were to improve the transparency and responsiveness of the public sector and enhance the ability of external stakeholders to hold it accountable, and to increase efficiency, effectiveness, and accountability within the public sector. The operation supported ongoing reforms to improve service delivery in health.

Sources: IEG 2008d, 2009b.

Peru

Programmatic Social Reform Projects I–IV (2001–04). The objectives of this series of projects were to improve the antipoverty focus of public expenditure, increase the access of the poor to quality health and education services, and enhance the transparency of social programs, while empowering beneficiaries in their design and implementation. They supported health reform objectives, including trying to promote the reform of ESSALUD.

---

the Health Insurance Organization in Egypt, which was eventually dropped from the project.

- *Complementary programmatic lending with the finance ministry* has helped sometimes to maintain momentum when implementation of reforms through health sector investments has flagged, as in the Kyrgyz Republic and Peru (box 3.5). The implementation of health reform may be piecemeal, but the Bank can help ensure support that extends beyond a specific project. The Programmatic Social Reform Projects in Peru were effective in maintaining the reform agenda, despite the political cycle.

Eliciting the participation of stakeholders can be important for ownership of reforms, but it is still necessary to prioritize. In Bangladesh, there was wide stakeholder participation in defining the Essential Service Package, with the 1993 *World Development Report* as background. However, the final package was a wish list that was not prioritized, was not technically and financially feasible, and was not based on Bangladesh-specific data.[34] The Russia Health Reform Pilot project identified two pilot regions based on their indicated interests. This strengthened ownership, but each region proposed many different reform activities, increasing complexity and the likelihood of incomplete reforms. Further, the project involved multiple layers of government and a large number of separate health and health policy challenges.[35]

Reforms based on careful prior analytic work and evidence relevant to the country in question hold a greater chance of success, but analytic work does not ensure success. The reform projects in Peru[36] and the Kyrgyz Republic[37] both benefited from extensive Bank-sponsored analytic work that helped to ensure that the reform agenda was technically sound and encouraged ownership by the technical stakeholders. In Egypt, analytic work sponsored by the Bank and USAID included stakeholder and institutional analyses. However, in the case of Egypt, this could not compensate for the absence of a local reform team with the willingness, technical capacity, and political support to lead the process.[38]

M&E are critical for implementing and monitoring health reforms and for demonstrating impact, but the record of Bank-supported health reform projects in actually evaluating pilot activities is weak. There was no evaluation design for the activities piloted in the Russia Health Reform Pilot Project; there was no basis for decisions for wider replication. Nor was there any evaluation design for the health reforms supported in specific regions of Peru. Strong and consistent M&E is important—first, for understanding whether the proposed reforms will work, given that they involve changing the incentives for both providers and patients. Thus, most of the projects first launch reforms in pilot regions. Second, based on these

Stakeholder participation can be important, but it is still necessary to prioritize.

results, successful reforms can be expanded more broadly. Evaluation of pilot reforms and rapid dissemination of results can also demonstrate to skeptics that the reforms are feasible, weakening political resistance. The lessons of USAID's pilot reform activities in the Issyk-Kul region of the Kyrgyz Republic were fully incorporated into the design of the first Health Reform Project, and the demonstration effect of that region encouraged other regions to accelerate reforms. As discussed in chapter 2, however, the Bank's record of ensuring that pilot and reform projects include rigorous evaluation is weak.

M&E are critical in health reform projects.

To summarize, about a third of Bank projects support health reform objectives, mainly in middle-income countries. The share of projects with health reform objectives has been in decline. The outcomes of health reform projects and the Bank's performance are lower than for other HNP projects. This is an area with a lot of risk—political and technical—but nevertheless highly relevant. Many lessons have been learned. Two of the most important of these, which should affect future performance, are the need to carefully assess the political risks beforehand—including the interests and incentives of key stakeholders—and to try to minimize complexity.

Sectorwide Approaches

In 1995, the World Bank defined and promoted a new approach to lending to address chronic problems in implementing health projects. These problems included insufficient local ownership and commitment; the lack of any noticeable trickle-down effect from some projects; low sustainability of benefits after initial implementation; confusion and dissipation of effort caused by the approaches supported by different donors; excessive expatriate technical assistance personnel; the weakening of government capacity by the proliferation of donor-financed project units; and unsatisfactory results from some adjustment operations in the allocation of public expenditure (Harrold and others 1995). The term *sector investment program* was coined, encompassing six principles of sound project development that supported a "broad sector ap-

The Sectorwide Approach, or SWAp, was developed between 1995 and 1997; the Bank was a major proponent.

proach to lending." A sector investment program had to be:

- Sectorwide in scope, covering all current and capital expenditures
- Based on a clear sector strategy and policy framework
- Run by local stakeholders, including government, direct beneficiaries, and representatives of the private sector
- Adopted and financed by all main donors
- Based in common implementation arrangements among all financiers
- Reliant on local capacity, rather than on technical assistance, for implementation.

Two years later this approach was relabeled a "Sectorwide Approach," or SWAp, at a meeting of donor agencies (box 3.6), but the principles remained the same.[39] The anticipated benefits from the approach included: greater country ownership and leadership in managing health support; improved coordination and oversight of the technical and financial inputs of all partners; strengthened country capacities and systems for strategic sector management, fiduciary functions, and implementation arrangements;

Box 3.6: Genesis of the Sectorwide Approach in Health: An International Consensus

During the 1990s, the concept of a programwide approach was discussed at a forum on health sector reform chaired by WHO with the active participation of Ghana, Zambia, and other partners. This led to the first meeting of several countries and development partners to discuss the approach in 1997.

Cohosted by the Danish Ministry of Foreign Affairs and the World Bank, the meeting coined the term "sectorwide approach" and reached a consensus on two follow-up actions: (a) to commission a SWAp guide for the health sector and (b) to create an Inter-Agency Group to foster learning and promotion of SWAps, with WHO as the chair and with the active participation of partners and developing countries.

Source: Vaillancourt forthcoming.

reduced transaction costs; more efficient use of development assistance; more reliable support for the health sector strategy; and greater sustainability of health programs. Ultimately, the approach, through its support of national health policies and programs, was to contribute to improvements in health sector performance and sustained improvements in people's health.[40]

The SWAp concept represented a fundamental change in the focus, relationship, and behavior of development partners and government—a reform in the relationship between government and development partners and among the partners. The specific health policies and programs supported by this approach depend on the content of the national sector strategy, which varies greatly across countries. World Bank and other donor support for a SWAp can be financed in a number of different ways—through parallel project-specific financing,[41] pooled financing,[42] general budget support to the finance ministry, or a combination of these.

Between fiscal 1997 and 2006, the World Bank approved 28 HNP projects supporting health SWAps in 22 countries.[43] Thus, in the decade following the launch of the approach, about 13 percent of all approved HNP projects supported a SWAp. The World Bank project approvals came in two spurts—immediately after the 1997 meeting, followed by a two-year pause, and then more projects approved in fiscal years 2003–06 (figure 3.5). Two-thirds of the projects that supported health SWAps were in Sub-Saharan Africa. Support for health SWAps is mainly found in low-income countries, accounting for nearly a quarter of HNP projects approved in those countries, compared with only 6 percent of those in lower-middle-income countries, and none in upper-middle-income countries.[44] In 71 percent of the projects, Bank resources were pooled with those of government and other donors.[45]

The assessment of the Bank's support for health SWAps addresses three questions. First, were the benefits of the *approach* realized, in terms of better donor harmonization and coordination, reduced transaction costs, capacity

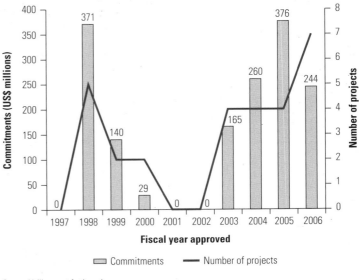

Figure 3.5: After an Initial Spurt, Growth in World Bank Support for Health SWAps Resumed after 2002

Source: Vaillancourt forthcoming.

building, and so forth? Second, were the objectives of the *health strategies* supported by government and development partners achieved? Third, in what ways did channeling support through a SWAp affect the efficacy of the Bank's support, including its ability to conduct policy dialogue? A desk-based portfolio review of all Bank-supported SWAps approved in fiscal 1997–2006, including 11 completed operations, and fieldwork in five countries (table 3.2) serve as a basis to answer these questions.

Benefits of the Approach

The objectives, anticipated benefits, and specific mechanisms of the SWAp approach are not clearly articulated and often not discussed in the Bank's project appraisal documents. These documents usually deal with the substance of health programs and policies. There tend to be a lot of process indicators that implicitly convey what the objectives of anticipated benefits were, and they are generally consistent with the SWAp features described in the literature.

Over the period fiscal 1997–2006, the Bank approved support for 28 health SWAps in 22 countries.

The objectives, anticipated benefits, and specific mechanisms of the SWAp approach are not clearly articulated and often are not discussed in appraisal documents.

Table 3.2: HNP Projects Supporting Health SWAps in IEG Country Cases or Project Evaluations

Country	Project
Bangladesh	Health and Population Program (1998–2005)
	HNP Sector Program (2005–10)
Ghana	Health Sector Support (1997–2002)
	Health Sector Support II (2003–07)
Kyrgyz Republic	Health and Social Protection (2005–11)
Nepal	Health Sector Program (2004–10)
Malawi	Multisectoral AIDS (2003–08)
	Health Sector Support (2004–08)

Source: World Bank data.

Note: In all five countries, World Bank SWAp support was pooled.

Country capacity in the health sector has been strengthened through the approach.

Country capacity has been strengthened in the areas of sector planning, budgeting, management, and fiduciary systems. Resources are used to finance an explicit Program of Work linked to the national strategy; annual or semi-annual joint review meetings of national and external partners are held for planning, programming, budgeting, resource allocation, and monitoring of progress in implementation and achievement of objectives. Governments have been enabled to exercise greater leadership in directing the use of development partner resources and conducting and coordinating the dialogue.

The performance of SWAps in reducing transaction costs cannot be assessed because they have not been monitored.

- In the *Kyrgyz Republic*, the SWAp has resulted in greater delegation of planning and decision making to staff at the levels of department head and below within the central ministry, and from central to decentralized levels. Fiduciary strengthening in the health sector has begun to influence the overall governance of the country.[46]

- In *Bangladesh*, line directors prepare annual operational plans and budgets, and all funding is on budget,[47] in contrast with the previous arrangement of disparate, multiple projects managed by project directors who would bypass line managers. All national procurement is now handled by government, where previously it was provided by, among others, UN agencies.

- In *Nepal,* the SWAp has helped to consolidate and coordinate dispersed donor assistance. Budgeting and financial processes within the SWAp account for government, pooled, and nonpooled resources, but attempts to improve financial management under the SWAp have encountered some obstacles that are governmentwide and difficult to address (Shaw forthcoming).

- Government capacity for procurement and financial management in *Ghana* was developed at central, regional, and district levels, enabling the consolidated management of the public budget and pooled financing. However, spending is not always consistent with sector priorities and the poverty focus articulated in the Program of Work. Nor is spending routinely monitored or allocations adjusted to achieve greatest impact.

- In *Malawi*, however, health stewardship and governance is weak, aside from the structured arrangements for cooperation with development partners. The use of government fiduciary systems in the health SWAp was ruled out; World Bank policies and procedures are followed for all pooled funding, and the Bank issues no-objections on the use of all pooled funds. Donors have continued project financing outside of the pool.[48] In contrast, the HIV/AIDS SWAp enjoys a higher level of confidence of donors, due in part to the stronger capacity of AIDS institutions, compared with the Ministry of Health—a result of the ability of the HIV/AIDS SWAp to attract the best people, including those from the Ministry.

Weaknesses persist in the design of M&E and in the use of country M&E systems. All of the countries supported have instituted periodic joint reviews of health-sector performance using a common set of indicators, with data generated increasingly from the countries' health management information systems. However, with the exception of Kyrgyz, the national strategies and programs are not underpinned by a well-developed M&E framework. For the most part, the results chain of the strategies and programs is not fully articulated. In Ghana, for example, the M&E plan, strategy, methodology, roles, and responsibilities were not articulated at the outset; the 20 indicators were largely process indicators and had only a modest overlap with indicators for measuring health sector performance and outcomes. In Senegal and other countries, baseline data were outdated or missing. Duplication of M&E and reporting has been reduced in Nepal and the health management information system is of good quality and reliable, but information and systems are scattered, making it difficult to assemble a coherent picture of the evolution of outputs and how they relate to outcomes.[49]

The performance of SWAps in reducing transaction costs—a major anticipated benefit of the approach—cannot be assessed in any country because they have not been monitored. In fieldwork, IEG was unable to compile any data measuring transaction costs before and after adoption of a SWAp, for the government or for donors. Nor do there appear to be any studies of staff time allocations across tasks in government or by the development partners before and after adoption of a SWAp. Efficiency gains were mentioned in interviews with public sector officials, citing the reduction in the number of individual donors, missions, and projects; the reduction in reporting requirements; and the consolidation of M&E as good steps. However, high transaction costs were mentioned in association with the time and expense of preparing for joint review meetings.

The allocation of time of development partner staff since the launch of the approach is not regarded as entirely efficient. Some partners continue to micromanage, while in other cases there is a mismatch between the partner's skills (for example, generalists or health experts) and the needs of the SWAp (financial management, M&E, among others). World Bank supervision costs for the Bangladesh SWAp were one-third of pre-SWAp levels because fewer Bank staff and more partners went on joint missions. In contrast, in the Kyrgyz Republic, Bank supervision costs are reported to be very high because of the high transaction costs of collaborating and communicating with other partners, oversight of procurement and financial management, and investments in capacity building.

HNP Outcomes under Health SWAps

There are countries where progress is being made both in achieving the objectives of the SWAp approach and in improving HNP outcomes. The Tanzania health SWAp, supported by the Health Sector Development Project, was favorably evaluated by a joint external evaluation financed by the international donor community and had satisfactory outcomes (COWI, Gilroy, and EPOS 2007). Health outcomes continue to improve in Nepal, although it is not clear whether they should be attributed to health policy, the SWAp, both, or neither.

There has been progress in achieving the objectives of the SWAp approach and improving HNP outcomes in several countries.

However, achieving the objectives of the approach has not always ensured better health outcomes. The implementation and efficacy of the policies supported by the approach are key. For example, during the 10 years of Ghana's health SWAp, despite the increased use of country systems and better harmonization and coordination of donors, there were no improvements in health status indicators (figure 3.6), nor were there significant improvements in health sector performance, such as assisted deliveries, that might have contributed to better outcomes. Inefficiencies in the health sector persist because of duplication and rivalry between the Ministry of Health and the Ghana Health Service, an issue that the development partners and government have not been able to resolve. Substantial investment in the SWAp process, suboptimal allocation of resources,[50] inadequate flows of funds to the districts, and failure to resolve key impediments to service delivery were all factors affecting performance in Ghana. Only 4 of the 11 closed projects supporting health SWAps had satisfactory outcomes in terms of achieving their relevant program objectives.

Achieving better health outcomes, however, depends on the implementation and efficacy of the policies supported by the approach.

The approach can have adverse effects on outcomes in the short run: setting up a SWAp can be disruptive, diverting time and energy from the achievement of results. There is evidence from Bangladesh, Ethiopia, Ghana, Mali, and Senegal that in the short run,

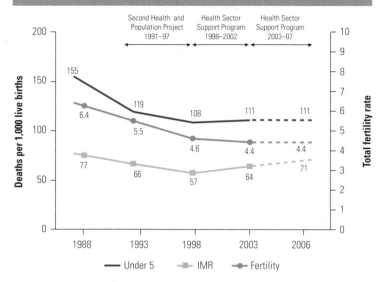

Figure 3.6: Neither Mortality nor Fertility Declined during the 10 Years of Ghana's Health SWAp

Sources for 1988–2003: Ghana Demographic and Health Surveys.

Sources for 2006: Multiple Indicator Cluster Survey for 2007 (for under 5 and infant mortality); Population Reference Bureau (for fertility).

Note: The mortality rates are averaged over the five years preceding the Ghana Demographic and Health Surveys (GDHS). The fertility rates for GDHS 1988, 1993, and 1998 are averaged over the five years preceding the surveys, while the fertility rates for GDHS 2003 and the Multiple Indicator Cluster Survey for 2006 are averaged over the three years preceding the surveys.

Setting up a SWAp can divert time and energies from delivering on substance.

the process can take priority over results. In Bangladesh, despite the long history of working with a consortium of donors, there was disruption with the formal adoption of a SWAp. However, in Kyrgyz there was a longstanding and productive working relationship among experts in government and between government experts and the donors' trust, and the SWAp formalized what was already happening. Beyond the short-run disruption, it is difficult to tell whether the improved coordination, ownership, and other reforms in foreign aid introduced by the SWAp have had any long-run impact on the quality or efficacy of health programs. This remains a hypothesis.

SWAPs often supported overly ambitious programs that exceeded the capacity of government to implement.

SWAps have often supported overly ambitious programs of work, involving many complex reforms and activities that exceed government implementation capacity. Ex-

amples of the types of activities found in the programs of work of countries such as Ethiopia, Mauritania, Senegal, and Tanzania include: delivery of a basic package of essential health services; reorganization and decentralization of services; redefining the role of the central Ministry of Health; contracting with the nongovernmental sectors; hospital reform; new supply- and demand-side service delivery mechanisms; health financing; and cost-sharing. All of these are in addition to the challenging capacity building and reforms in development partner relationships inherent in a SWAp. Guidance for reasonable sequencing and implementation that would make such reforms feasible is often absent. The result is that not everything gets done, the higher-priority interventions are neglected, and outcomes are below expectations.

Impact of the Approach on the Bank's Effectiveness

In the operations that IEG studied, the Bank has often been instrumental in getting other development partners to pool resources; the donors who pool generally have a seat at the table in the policy dialogue (Vaillancourt forthcoming). The Bank has played a crucial role in supporting national capacities and systems for financial management, procurement, and other fiduciary aspects of the SWAps within the health sector.

The Bank has not withdrawn from policy dialogue under the SWAp, but there is a risk that consensus decisions among development partners and government will inhibit strategic choices and the setting of priorities, areas in which the Bank has often provided valued support to improve the efficacy of health policy. The SWAp implies ceding leadership and decision making to government and reducing the bilateral relationship with government in favor of collaborative partnerships with development partners. But the partners collectively may not have the will to intervene. In Ghana, for example, the partners were unsuccessful in pressing the government to address duplication of services between the Ministry of Health and the Ghana Health Services, although inaction in reform is likely one reason for stalled health results. They may also merely continue to press for their own priorities within the SWAp. Aides-memoire for joint review meetings often represent an amalgam of the priorities of each of the participating development partners.

There is often not a clear understanding _beforehand_ of the decision-making rules among individual development partners and between the partners and the government, in the event that the government reverses or does not act on agreed-upon policy. This leads to ambiguity with respect to how the Bank should act. In the case of Bangladesh, the development partners were split on how to react to the government's decision not to merge family planning and health services within the Ministry of Health and Family Welfare in the face of political pressure. The partners were divided on the appropriate response; the Bank, supported by some of the partners, temporarily stopped disbursements, trying to force something that was not politically feasible, an action that was shortly reversed. In contrast, in Nepal, a politically driven policy decision was made to provide free basic care to all that would have serious repercussions on health finance. In response, the Bank and other partners are supporting analytical work to document the cost and equity implications of the new policy, as a contribution to the Ministry of Health strategy on sustainable financing.

For most of the SWAps studied by this evaluation, the rules for resolving disagreements are still somewhat ambiguous, which does have implications for the efficacy of the Bank's support and its ability to engage government and the partners on critical policy issues that have not achieved a consensus. Memoranda of understanding remain too general and have not provided the guidance needed during times of fundamental disagreement on policy.

Participation in SWAps has not meant a withdrawal from policy dialogue.

To summarize, SWAps implicitly have two types of objectives—those of the approach, and those of the program supported by the approach. Certain anticipated benefits of the approach supported by the Bank are being realized—strengthened country sector capacity to plan budgeting, management, and fiduciary systems, and greater country leadership in setting the direction of the sector—but weaknesses persist in M&E of the approach and the programs. One major anticipated benefit of the approach—reduced transaction costs—has not been systematically monitored, but field visits suggest that transaction costs in some instances remain high. The rules for resolving differences among donors and between donors and government are not well articulated and have led to friction in some cases and a lack of prioritization. To date, there is little evidence that the approach by itself has had additional positive impacts on the effectiveness of the overall sectoral program and policies. Even while adopting these reforms in working relationships, it is important for the program to support the right things, that it be properly implemented, and that the focus on results be maintained.

But there often is not a clear understanding of the decision-making rules among the partners and between the partners and the government.

Chapter 4

Evaluation Highlights

- The CAS has helped identify the key sectors that affect HNP, but has not brought those other sectors to bear on HNP outcomes, nor has it documented or monitored their contributions.
- The efficacy of multisectoral HNP projects hinges on prioritizing sectors in the face of limited implementation capacity and ensuring strong coordination of activities.
- The potential for Bank support for water supply and sanitation and transport to contribute to health outcomes and the health MDGs is great, but the incentives to deliver health results and a poverty focus are weak.
- Results are more likely when the health objectives are made explicit and when targets and monitorable indicators are included for retrofitted health components.

Girls from Kuje village in Abuja, Nigeria, demonstrate how to wash hands with soap and clean water.
Photo courtesy of UNICEF Nigeria/2006/Moses.

The Contribution of Other Sectors to Health, Nutrition, and Population Outcomes

Recognizing that it takes more than health services to improve HNP outcomes, the 2007 HNP strategy calls for leveraging interventions in other sectors to deliver results.[1] One of the five strategic directions of the strategy is to strengthen Bank capacity to advise countries on an intersectoral approach to HNP results. The proposed vehicle for coordinating sectors to maximize impact on health outcomes is the CAS.

This chapter seeks to inform implementation of the HNP strategy by assessing, first, to what extent have CASs actually been used as a vehicle for achieving multisectoral synergies to improve HNP outcomes? Second, what has been the experience of multisectoral HNP lending operations—that is, HNP projects that engage multiple sectors in a single operation—in improving HNP outcomes? Finally, what has been the contribution of lending in other sectors—in particular, water supply and sanitation and transport—in achieving health benefits?

Intersectoral Approaches in Country Assistance Strategies

The CAS is the business plan that guides World Bank Group activities in a member country engaged in borrowing or is receiving grant funding. Management and the Board use the CAS to review and guide the Bank Group's country programs and to judge the impact of its work. IEG reviewed 137 CASs approved between fiscal 1997 and 2006 with respect to their use as an instrument to ensure that actions from other sectors are brought to bear on HNP outcomes.[2]

Over the past decade, the CAS has fallen short of its promise of coordinating and bringing to bear the actions of multiple sectors on HNP outcomes. Three-quarters of CASs acknowledged the contribution of other sectors to HNP outcomes, and about half proposed a multisectoral lending strategy for HNP (figure 4.1).[3] Water supply and sanitation was the sector most often cited as having an impact on HNP outcomes, followed by education and the environment. The two main multisectoral lending strategies to improve health outcomes involved, first, financing projects in sectors that are complementary to health (41 percent of CASs), and, second, financing multisectoral HNP projects that tied the actions of many sectors into a single lending operation (18 percent of CASs).[4] Most of the CASs proposing multisectoral HNP projects planned a multisectoral HIV/AIDS project (12 percent of CASs). However, almost none of the CASs that incorporated complementary lending by other sectors proposed any specific HNP targets or common management arrangements, or explained what form of coordination with the HNP sector was envisaged.[5]

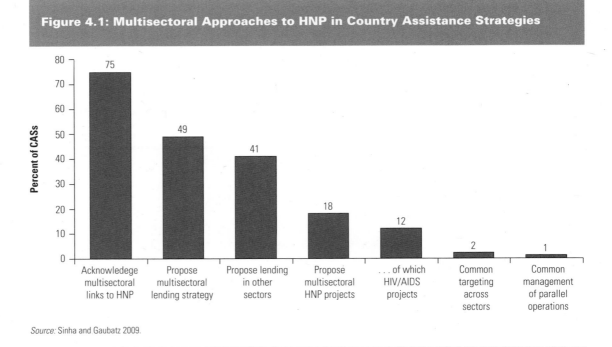

Figure 4.1: Multisectoral Approaches to HNP in Country Assistance Strategies

Source: Sinha and Gaubatz 2009.

Though three-quarters of CASs acknowledged the contribution of other sectors to HNP outcomes, almost none included coordinated, complementary lending by other sectors.

There was little evidence in the CAS Completion Reports (CASCRs) that multisectoral collaboration or tracking of outcomes arose from the multisectoral approaches. Eighteen of the 19 completed CASs for which a completion report had been written had proposed a multisectoral approach to HNP outcomes. While in most cases the proposed lending was wholly or partly implemented, there was little mention in the completion reports of the results of health components in the complementary lending, and in most of these the health components were dropped. Only in one CAS, for Mali (fiscal 2004), were health indicators tracked—in that case to assess the impact of safe water on cholera incidence. It was unclear in any of the CASCRs whether collaboration across sectors occurred to achieve HNP outcomes. Even in Mali, the CASCR commented that sectoral staff worked independently, which was attributed to insufficient incentives to work in cross-sectoral teams.

This lack of intersectoral coordination in most of the CASs completed to date does not detract from the fact that investments in other sectors can have important impacts on HNP outcomes, even without coordination. This was shown in IEG's evaluation of maternal and child health outcomes in Bangladesh (IEG 2005b). That study concluded that improvements in access to safe water accounted for a quarter of the decline in stunting, and that increased levels of female secondary education supported by the Bank had an impact on reducing infant and child mortality that was independent of health programs. The 2007 HNP strategy points to the potential of better coordination and synergy through the CAS, beyond what might have been achieved without such coordination.

Multisectoral Health, Nutrition, and Population Lending

One strategy for bringing to bear the contribution of other sectors to HNP outcomes is through assigning responsibility for those contributions in a single multisectoral lending operation. This section reviews in greater depth the rationale and performance of the multisectoral part of the HNP-managed lending portfolio, drawing on the results from IEG's in-depth portfolio review of projects approved from fiscal 1997 to 2006.

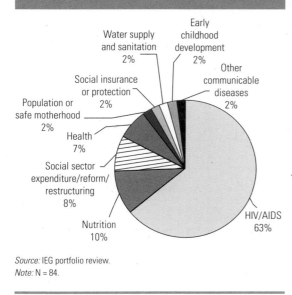

Figure 4.2: Two-Thirds of Multisectoral HNP Projects Involve HIV/AIDS

Source: IEG portfolio review.
Note: N = 84.

More than a third of the HNP-managed projects approved between fiscal 1997 and 2006 (38 percent) were managed or implemented by more than one ministry or agency in the borrowing country. Nearly two-thirds of multisectoral projects were HIV/AIDS projects; the remaining third included projects in nutrition, health (multisectoral components), water supply and sanitation, early childhood development and multisectoral social sector lending, (figure 4.2). Compared with the rest of the HNP portfolio, multisectoral projects were more likely to have objectives to improve health or nutrition status or to change behavior. They were less likely to have objectives of improving the access to or quality of health care, reforming or decentralizing the health system, or to have poverty-targeted objectives.

The share of HNP multisectoral projects doubled in 10 years, from a quarter to nearly half of all projects. This increase is attributable to a growing number of multisectoral HIV/AIDS projects. The share of non-HIV multisectoral projects has remained constant, at 14 percent, while the share of multisectoral HIV projects tripled, from 11 to 35 percent (figure 4.3). Multisectoral projects are more common in low-income countries (45 per-

cent of all HNP projects) than in middle-income countries (35 percent). Regionally, more than half of projects in Africa, a third in East Asia and Latin America, and a quarter in South Asia are multisectoral (figure 4.4). Multisectoral HIV/AIDS projects comprised 45 percent of all HNP projects approved in Africa, while about a third of all projects approved in East Asia were non-AIDS multisectoral projects.

The main rationale for involving several sectors in managing or implementing these projects is their complementarity in producing health outcomes. The choice of sectors is based on the perceived or demonstrated comparative advantages in relation to the outcome in question. Early child development, for example, may involve both learning opportunities and proper health and nutrition. Nutrition objectives may require inputs from health, agriculture, or even industry (in the case of salt iodization). There are many examples of collaboration between the education and health ministries to promote health education in the schools. In projects featuring social sector expenditure reform, health

More than a third of HNP-managed projects were managed or implemented by more than one ministry or agency.

Figure 4.3: Multisectoral HIV/AIDS Lending Accounts for All of the Increase in Multisectoral HNP Lending

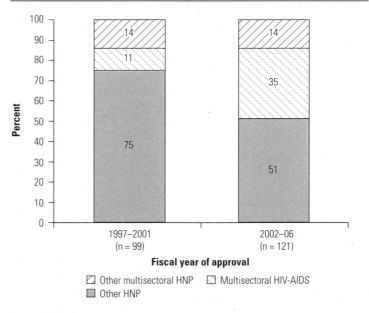

Source: IEG portfolio review.

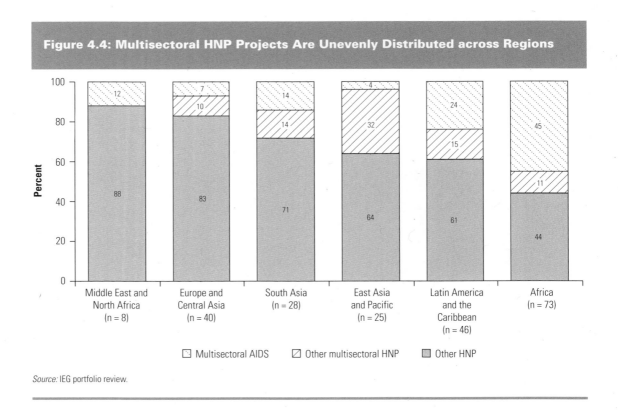

Figure 4.4: Multisectoral HNP Projects Are Unevenly Distributed across Regions

☐ Multisectoral AIDS ☑ Other multisectoral HNP ☐ Other HNP

Source: IEG portfolio review.

The share of HNP multisectoral projects doubled in 10 years because of the growing number of HIV/AIDS projects. is bundled with other sectors facing similar expenditure problems for reasons of efficiency. Some health support is multisectoral because more than one key ministry is involved in health care delivery or reform—the Ministry of Health and the social security agency, for example. In these instances, there may or may not be any implied synergy; the multisectoral operation may simply be packaging activities for separate entities, intending to work in parallel.

There are two distinct justifications for multisectoral design offered for HIV/AIDS projects. The first is based on the notion of sectoral expertise and comparative advantage to address an issue—for example, enlisting the Ministry of Defense for HIV/AIDS prevention in the military, the Ministry of Justice for HIV/AIDS in prisons, the Ministry of Education for HIV/AIDS education in the schools, and the Ministry of Social Welfare to care for orphans. This is similar to the argument for other multisectoral projects, and achieving the objective would require generating working relationships and intersectoral collaboration between these agencies and the Ministry of Health. The second rationale is essentially mobilization: because HIV/AIDS affects all sectors of the economy, all sectors must be involved in its prevention and mitigation.[6] This rationale leads to the involvement of large numbers of ministries and public agencies, irrespective of their sectoral mandate or expertise, with or without the collaboration of the Ministry of Health.

Most HIV/AIDS projects were managed by recently established multisectoral institutions without long experience in cross-ministerial coordination.[7] Nearly two-thirds of multisectoral projects not pertaining to HIV/AIDS are managed entirely or partly by the Ministry of Health, while two-thirds of multisectoral HIV/AIDS projects are managed by an entity under the president or prime minister, or by the Ministries of Finance, Economy, or Planning (table 4.1). Only 36 percent of multisectoral AIDS projects rely on Ministry management exclusively, or in collaboration with another ministry. The Ministry is explicitly identi-

Table 4.1: Distribution of Multisectoral HNP Projects by Management and Implementation Arrangements

Multisectoral management or implementation	Total		HIV/AIDS		Non-AIDS	
	Number	Percent	Number	Percent	Number	Percent
Managed by an entity directly under the president or prime minister and implemented by the Ministry of Health and/or other sectors	31	(37)	**30**	**(57)**	1	(3)
Managed by the Ministry of Health but implemented by other sectors	29	(35)	16	(30)	**13**	**(42)**
Managed by the Ministry of Finance, Economy, or Planning but implemented by the Ministry of Health or other sectors	11	(13)	4	(8)	7	(23)
Managed and implemented by more than one ministry (one of which is the Ministry of Health)	9	(11)	3	(6)	6	(19)
Managed by another ministry, implemented by the Ministry of Health	4	(5)	0	(0)	4	(13)
Total	84	(100)	53	(100)	31	(100)

Source: IEG portfolio review.

Note: For the types of non-AIDS projects, consult figure 4.2.

fied as at least one of the implementing agencies in project design documents in all of the multisectoral HNP projects and all but eight of the multisectoral HIV/AIDS projects.

Multisectoral projects are more demanding of institutions and require a greater degree of coordination. In 90 percent of the multisectoral projects, at least one implementing agency—and as many as six—was explicitly identified, and in most cases the activities that the agencies were accountable for were clearly spelled out.[8] The multisectoral HIV/AIDS projects had fewer assigned implementing agencies (1.3 agencies, on average) than did the other multisectoral HNP projects (2.8 agencies, on average), but this is deceptive.

More than half of multisectoral projects also had a demand-driven element at the ministerial level: ministries not explicitly identified beforehand can submit funding proposals to achieve the project's overall objectives. Some of the PADs estimate the total number of ministries or agencies that will likely be involved, with a range of from 1 to 20. For eight HIV/AIDS projects, there were no assigned implementation agencies; all multisectoral implementation came from the demand-driven component.

Taking into account both the explicitly identified implementing agencies and the anticipated number involved in demand-driven ministerial components, multisectoral HIV/AIDS projects had twice as many implementing agencies (about 6, ranging from 0 to 20), as did other multisectoral HNP projects (about 3, ranging from 1 to 6; figure 4.5). Yet even this is an understatement. A third of the HIV/ AIDS projects with demand-driven components did not set a maximum number of implementing agencies; the ultimate number and their activities are determined during implementation.

The ability to deal with this complexity was often weak. Among the closed projects, ineffective multisectoral coordination was cited as a contributing factor to low outcomes in 10 unsatisfactory projects, while effective multisectoral coordination was cited as contributing to 2 satis-

Most non-AIDS multisectoral projects are managed by the Ministry of Health; most multisectoral AIDS projects are managed by coordinating agencies under the president or prime minister.

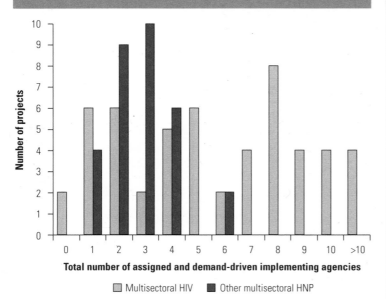

Figure 4.5: Distribution of Multisectoral HNP Projects by the Number of Assigned and Demand-Driven Implementing Agencies

Total number of assigned and demand-driven implementing agencies

Number of projects

■ Multisectoral HIV   ■ Other multisectoral HNP

Source: IEG portfolio review.

Box 4.1: Quality-at-Entry for Multisectoral Projects Is Weak

In 2008, the Bank's Quality Assurance Group (QAG) issued an assessment of *quality at entry* of the lending portfolio approved in fiscal 2006–07, highlighting results for multisectoral projects. QAG's conclusions were based on a review of a sample of 10 development policy operations and 10 investment projects Bank-wide. The report expressed the following concerns about the outcomes of multisectoral projects:

- Excessive complexity and overly ambitious objectives
- Weak institutional capacity
- Lack of readiness of the first year's program for implementation
- Task teams lacking adequate technical expertise and global experience
- Fragmented managerial guidance because of the multisectoral nature of the projects.

Source: World Bank 2008b.

factory projects (both in nutrition).[9] The Bank's Quality Assurance Group (QAG) recently expressed concerns with respect to quality at entry for multisectoral projects Bank-wide, across all sectors (box 4.1). Evidence from IEG field assessments of multisectoral projects in Eritrea and Ghana contrasts a project design that encouraged intersectoral collaboration with the Ministry of Health with one that mobilized a large number of actors with less Ministry oversight and collaboration (box 4.2).

The lower performance of HIV/AIDS projects drove down the outcomes of multisectoral projects as a group.

Multisectoral projects had lower outcomes than did other HNP projects, but this is mainly because of the lower performance of HIV/ AIDS projects. Fewer than half of the multisectoral projects approved and completed during fiscal 1997–2006 had satisfactory outcomes, compared with about two-thirds of single-sector projects (figure 4.6).[10] Bank and borrower performance were also lower for multisectoral HNP projects, although the difference for borrower performance is not statistically significant. However, the performance of non-AIDS multisectoral projects was similar to that of single-sector HNP projects, while the multisectoral HIV/AIDS projects performed at a much lower level. *Both* types of multisectoral HNP projects had lower institutional development impact (IDI) than other HNP projects: only 43 percent of projects had substantial or high IDI, compared with 61 percent for single-sector HNP projects.[11]

In sum, multisectoral projects are inherently more demanding, and their share in the HNP portfolio has doubled, almost wholly due to the increase in HIV/AIDS project approvals. Multisectoral HNP projects with objectives other than HIV/AIDS perform at levels similar to projects in the rest of the HNP portfolio, but multisectoral HIV/AIDS projects do not. The large number of sectors involved, the lack of specificity in design documents about the roles and responsibilities of each participating sector, the relatively new institutions asked to manage the complex design, and the other factors that bring about lower performance in the Africa Region likely all contribute to lower outcomes for these projects.

Box 4.2: Greater Selectivity in Sectoral Participation Can Improve Multisectoral Performance

Experience from two communicable disease projects suggests that the complexity and efficacy of multisectoral projects can be improved by enlisting a smaller number of priority sectors and by stronger collaboration with the Ministry of Health.

In Eritrea, for example, the HIV/AIDS, Malaria, STD, and TB (HAMSET) Control Project engaged a limited group of priority ministries with a direct stake or comparative advantage in preventing and treating the HAMSET diseases—health, education, defense, transport, and labor and human welfare—under the leadership of the Ministry of Health and built on past collaboration. While the project nevertheless challenged the Ministry, by avoiding creation of new institutions, scarce human re-

sources were conserved, duplication avoided, and complexity reduced.[a]

In contrast, the Ghana AIDS Response Project (GARFUND) was managed by a newly formed Ghana AIDS Commission under the president and financed at least 16 non-health ministries and public agencies, in addition to research institutions, regional coordinating councils, district assemblies, parliamentarians, traditional councils, and chiefs. The National AIDS Control Program (NACP) in the Ministry of Health retained responsibility only for implementing activities falling within a very narrow mandate. As a consequence, "GARFUND subprojects continued to suffer from poor technical quality and inadequate public health content."[b]

Sources: IEG 2007c, 2009a.

a. The project nevertheless remained highly complex, addressing four diseases, the zoba-level line ministries, and a community-driven component.

b. IEG 2007c, p. 32.

Health in the Lending Portfolios of Other Sectors

Since 1997, the World Bank has committed $5.0 billion in the form of 350 HNP components of projects managed by other sectors. In contrast to the part of the portfolio managed by the HNP sector, which is relatively flat, approval of projects in other sectors with HNP components is growing, while the size of the components is relatively small—amounting to only 30 percent of all HNP commitments since 1997 (figure 4.7). This part of the portfolio has grown steadily and steeply since 1988 and reflects lending for social funds,[12] initiated in fiscal 1989, and of poverty reduction support credits (PRSCs), begun in fiscal 2001. Until 2001, almost all projects with HNP components were investment projects; since then, the majority have been development policy lending.[13] The efficacy of these HNP components is not easily assessed unless they reflect explicit objectives for which the projects are accountable. IEG evaluated social funds in 2002,[14] and an ongoing evaluation of PRSCs will look at the adequacy of these instruments for achieving HNP results (box 4.3).

This section examines in greater depth the extent to which lending in two key sectors—water sup-

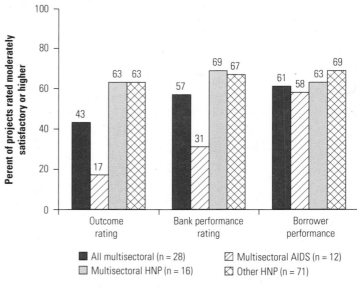

Figure 4.6: Multisectoral Projects Had Lower Performance than Other HNP Projects

Percent of projects rated moderately satisfactory or higher

Outcome rating: 43, 17, 63, 63
Bank performance rating: 57, 31, 69, 67
Borrower performance: 61, 58, 63, 69

■ All multisectoral (n = 28)   ▨ Multisectoral AIDS (n = 12)
▨ Multisectoral HNP (n = 16)   ⊠ Other HNP (n = 71)

Source: IEG portfolio review.

ply and sanitation and transport—has been used to improve HNP outcomes. The selection of these two sectors for evaluation is illustrative, because there are many others with large, demonstrated

Figure 4.7: Approval of HNP Components Managed by Other Sectors Has Grown Steadily Since 1988, though the Commitment per Project Is Small

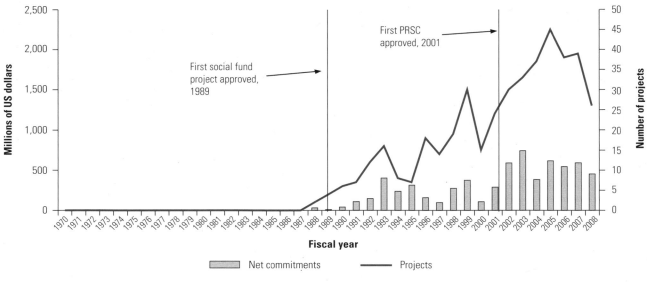

Source: World Bank data.

Note: The commitment for the entire project is attributed to the fiscal year of approval.

Box 4.3: Poverty Reduction Support Credits: Multisectoral Development Policy Lending in Support of HNP

Since 2001 there has been a steady climb in approvals of Poverty Reduction Support Credits (PRSCs), which are programmatic development policy operations intended to support certain IDA countries as they implement a national Poverty Reduction Strategy (PRS). PRSCs may include simultaneous policy actions in several sectors aligned with the Strategy and do not necessarily seek to exploit cross-sectoral synergies to produce HNP outcomes. They are typically implemented in a series of three to four single-tranche operations.

As of the end of fiscal 2008, 87 individual PRSC operations had been approved, of which 83 percent had a health policy measure. According to an ongoing IEG evaluation of PRSCs to be delivered in 2009, the five top HNP issues addressed were:

- Improved access and utilization of health care
- Improved efficiency and accountability of resource use
- Improved health outcomes

- Enhanced service delivery
- Improved sectoral management and regulation.

These are largely similar to the objectives of HNP-managed investment projects. PRSCs are sometimes used to address sectoral policy issues that require attention and support beyond a specific sector (for example, by the Ministry of Finance or prime minister) and can be used to enhance the dialogue between the line ministry and the Ministry of Finance. While HNP investment project approvals are essentially flat, demand for PRSCs has been growing.

The forthcoming PRSC evaluation will assess, among other issues, the effectiveness of the PRSC in promoting sector dialogue and achieving results in sectors delivering services (HNP, education, and water supply) under varying country conditions; the extent to which outputs and outcomes are actually tracked; and the extent to which there have been sectoral investment or technical assistance projects working in tandem with PRSCs.

impacts on HNP outcomes, such as education and social protection, the latter being key to the sector's objective of reducing the impoverishing effects of illness.

The evidence base for this section is an in-depth review of all 117 water supply and sanitation projects and 229 transport projects approved from fiscal 1997 to 2006. The review examined the extent to which the projects cited potential health benefits (or risks, in the case of transport) in project design documents; included explicit objectives to improve health (or mitigate health risks); proposed and implemented environmental improvements that could plausibly provide health benefits; and targeted services and health or behavioral outcomes to the poor.[15] For the closed projects—26 for water supply and sanitation and 105 for transport—it assessed the extent to which expected health benefits or objectives have been measured, achieved, and can be attributed to the activities implemented.

Water Supply and Sanitation

Extensive evidence has emerged supporting the potential effectiveness of improvements in water supply and sanitation infrastructure and hygiene behaviors on health outcomes in developing countries, particularly on the incidence of diarrheal and other water-related diseases.[16] Diarrheal diseases accounted for an estimated 1.6–2.1 million deaths annually between 1990 and 2000 and remain among the top five preventable killers of children under five in developing countries (Keutsch and others 2006). There is a strong correlation between unhygienic conditions in poor households and communities and the frequency and severity of diarrheal episodes. Water supply and sanitation was the sector most frequently cited in CASs as having potential benefits for health.

While water supply and sanitation interventions *can* have an impact on diarrheal and other water-related diseases, the research literature shows that these benefits cannot be *assumed*. The number of high-quality studies demonstrating impact is small, and meta-evaluations of impact studies of water

supply and sanitation interventions show high variability in the findings (Overbey 2008; IEG 2008i). For example, one synthesis of findings across 10 relatively rigorous studies of the impact of improved hygiene found a median reduction of 33 percent in diarrhea episodes, but the reduction ranged from 11 to 89 percent (Huttly and others 1997; see also studies reviewed in IEG 2008i). The variability in impacts is brought about by variations in the technology; the extent to which interventions were actually implemented; pre-intervention levels of pathogens, sanitation, water quality and quantity, and hygiene behavior; and the socioeconomic status and culture of the beneficiaries. In short, the effectiveness of an intervention depends critically on contextual factors, local conditions and pathogens, and technology. There is little conclusive evidence on the extent to which water supply, sanitation, and hygiene interventions are complements or substitutes in producing health benefits; few studies have tested each separately and in combination in the same setting.

Even when water supply and sanitation interventions generate health benefits *on average*, the benefits do not necessarily reach the poor. Few studies measure the benefits of water supply and sanitation improvements on the health of the poorest beneficiaries; most measure average impacts. The handful of studies that have examined the distribution of health benefits show that one cannot assume that the poor are helped. An analysis in rural India, for example, found a positive association between expanding piped water and a reduction in the prevalence and duration of diarrhea in the lowest two quintiles only if there was a woman with more than a primary education in the household (Jalan and Ravallion 2003).

Recognition by the Bank's water supply and sanitation sector of the potential contribution of water and sanitation interventions to

Over the fiscal 1997–2006 period, the Bank committed $5 billion to 350 HNP components in projects managed by other sectors.

Water supply and sanitation interventions can have an impact on waterborne diseases, but those benefits cannot be assumed.

Even when water supply and sanitation interventions do generate health benefits, those benefits do not necessarily reach the poor.

Box 4.4: Health Has Been Featured in World Bank Water Supply and Sanitation Strategies Since 1993

The first World Bank water supply strategy to recognize health benefits of water supply and sanitation investments was the 1993 policy paper, *Water Resources Management: A World Bank Policy Paper* (World Bank 1993b). It emphasized the potential health benefits of clean water supply and better hygiene, particularly in reducing the incidence of diarrheal diseases. It also advocated public health education on the safe handling of water to change hygiene behaviors and improve health outcomes, especially among the poor.

The 1993 policy paper led to the Bank's involvement in an increasing number of international partnerships such as the Global Water Partnership and World Water Council, both formed in 1996, and the World Bank–United Nations Development Program Water and Sanitation Partnership. However, the comprehensive principles at the heart of the strategy, including those that particularly affect health outcomes, initially were not widely adopted in Bank water-related projects (IEG 2002a). Initiatives specifically related to sanitation, hygiene, and health became

more common after 2000, following the World Water Forum and adoption of the MDGs.

The World Bank Group's Program for Water Supply and Sanitation was adopted in 2004 with objectives and priorities similar to those of the overarching water strategy issued 10 years earlier. It acknowledged the critical relationship between better sanitation and hygiene and improved health outcomes, noting that the health benefits from water supply and sanitation investments depend on a "three-pronged strategy: (i) access to sufficient quantities of water; (ii) sanitary disposal of excreta; and (iii) sound hygiene practices." Improving health outcomes was recognized as one of five "cross-cutting operational, policy, and institutional priorities" requiring both investment in water supply and sanitation infrastructure and behavioral change. The strategy also advocated targeting interventions to the poor as an institutional priority. The Sanitation, Hygiene and Wastewater Advisory Service was created in 2004, and a health specialist was hired for the program in 2005.

Source: Overbey 2008.

---

health outcomes dates back to 1993, when it introduced its first comprehensive strategy for water resources (box 4.4). Over the decade from fiscal 1997 to 2006, the World Bank committed more than $7.2 billion in resources to 117 new water supply and sanitation projects worldwide that were managed by the water supply and sanitation sector.

Eighty-nine percent of the 117 water supply and sanitation projects approved from fiscal 1997 to 2006 financed infrastructure that plausibly could improve health. These included interventions to improve water supply, sewerage, wastewater treatment, solid waste management and water quality and to construct latrines or toilets or handwashing facilities (figure 4.8). According to project design documents, only 28 percent of these projects targeted infrastructure to the poor.

While half of all water supply and sanitation projects cited potential

Though half of all water supply and sanitation projects cited potential health benefits as justification for the investment, only 10 percent had an objective to improve health.

health benefits to justify the investment, only 1 in 10 had an objective to improve health for which it was accountable. Even fewer—only 3 percent of all approved projects—had an objective to improve health outcomes among the poor. Thus, the primary objectives underlying the water supply and sanitation lending portfolio are expanding services, increasing the efficiency of utilities, and reducing economic costs and the time it takes to fetch water—not producing health benefits or ensuring that those benefits reach the poor.

Accountability for health outcomes in the water supply and sanitation lending program appears to be declining. Projects approved from fiscal 2002 to 2006 are *less* likely to have been justified by health benefits, to have explicit health objectives, or to plan to collect health indicators than projects approved in the preceding five years (figure 4.9). They are also less likely to target behavior change, which is critical in transforming water supply and sanitation infrastructure improvements into sustainable health

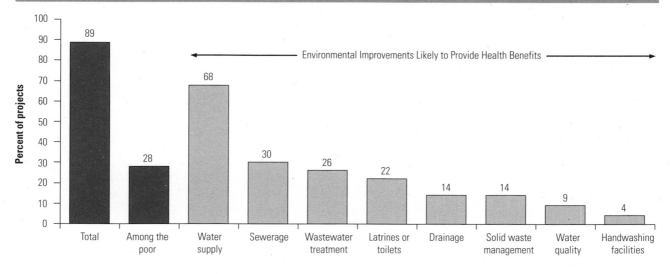

Figure 4.8: A Large Percentage of Water Supply and Sanitation Projects Invested in Environmental Improvements That Could Boost Health Outcomes

Source: Overbey 2008.

Note: N = 117. Categories are not mutually exclusive, because a project may include more than one intervention.

gains. Interviews with water supply and sanitation staff indicate that since 2000 the sector has focused largely on the MDG of improving access to safe water.

The actual health benefits of water supply and sanitation investments as implemented remain obscure. Among the 26 projects approved from fiscal 1997 to 2006 that have closed and for which there were completion reports, only four documented a change in health outcomes, all of them positive. Those with explicit health objectives were more likely to collect health outcome data than were projects without the objectives or indicators, though the sample is small.[17] Among the projects that showed improvement in health outcomes, there was no indication in project documents of specific collaboration within the country or the Bank between people in the water supply and sanitation and HNP sectors.

Four water supply and sanitation projects measured positive health outcomes, but attribution of the improvements to water sup-

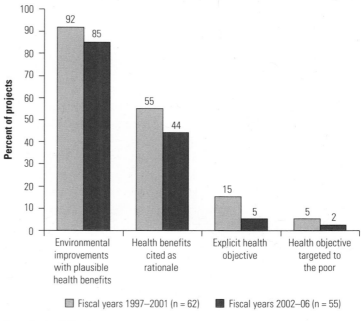

Figure 4.9: The Share of Water Supply and Sanitation Projects with a Health Perspective Has Declined

☐ Fiscal years 1997–2001 (n = 62)   ■ Fiscal years 2002–06 (n = 55)

Source: Overbey 2008.

The actual delivery of health benefits by water supply and sanitation projects is unclear; only a few have documented positive health outcomes.

Transport investments can have both positive and negative health impacts.

ply and sanitation interventions was weak. The extent to which infrastructure improvements have been carried out is generally well documented. However, poor sanitation and hygiene behavior can wipe out any potential health benefits. Few of the projects measured these behavioral indicators, which would offer greater confidence in interpreting the outcomes. Further, the completion reports do not account for the effects of other factors—such as rainfall, better health facilities, or successful health campaigns—on health outcomes, a point made by the project staff in the case of Madagascar.

None of the completed projects measured health outcomes separately for poor and non-poor project beneficiaries. The Nepal Rural Water Supply and Sanitation Project had an explicit health objective and was targeted to rural areas, which are apt to be poor (box 4.5). However, the project primarily helped communities along or near main roads, while the really poor tend to live in more remote areas. The follow-on project is now targeting those remote areas.

Transport

Transport investments can produce important health benefits in terms of improved access to health care, including access to emergency obstetric care, and better distribution of drugs, blood, and other medical supplies. Moreover, better access to markets can lead to greater household income and better nutrition and health. But the impact of better access to health care depends on context: it will not result in better health if the health facility offers bad care, for example.

Better transport can also have detrimental impacts on the environment and on human health. Every year, 1.2 million people die in road accidents worldwide (over 3,000 per day), and as many as 50 million more people are injured, some suffering permanent disabilities (WHO 2004). Eighty percent of the deaths and 90 percent of the losses from road traffic injuries occur in low- and middle-income countries.[18] While traffic accidents, injuries, fatalities, and noise have long been considered negative externalities, recent evidence suggests that there are direct effects of transport-induced air pollutants on mortality and respiratory disease. WHO estimates that sus-

---

Box 4.5: Better Hygiene Behavior through Rural Water Supply and Sanitation in Nepal

The Nepal Rural Water Supply and Sanitation (RWSS) Project (1996–2003) had an objective to "deliver sustainable health and hygiene benefits to the rural population through improvement in water supply and sanitation facilities."

Building on a previous pilot, the project created a semi-autonomous RWSS Fund Development Board to finance infrastructure. Support from nongovernmental organizations helped communities implement sustainable schemes. There was apparently no formal or informal collaboration between the scheme and the health sector—either in Nepal or within the World Bank. The RWSS project built capacity in rural villages to maintain water supply and sanitation investments, provided funds for infrastructure that was cofinanced by communities, and extended hygiene education to improve health outcomes. Good sanitation practices

were reinforced through community grants for latrines sufficient to cover 25 percent of the total beneficiary population at a rate of 750 rupees per household. The community then on-lent this to individual households at an agreed rate of interest for 6 to 12 months.

Between 2000 and 2002, the share of residents in project areas who used tap stands rose from 18 to 91 percent, and the share using a latrine rose from 24 to 64 percent.[a] The share of respondents (mostly women) who reported washing their hands after defecation rose from 65 to 88 percent, and the percent washing hands before cooking from 58 to 81 percent. However, there were fewer behavioral improvements in the most remote and poorer areas of western and far-western Nepal, and the impact of better hygiene on health status could not be confirmed except by a reduction in self-reported water-related diseases.

Source: IEG forthcoming.

a. The project was implemented in four "batches" at different times. These results are from Batch III. Similar results were observed for Batch IV.

Box 4.6: Health and Transport in the World Bank's Sector Strategies

Sustainable Transport: Priorities for Policy Reform (1996) accorded a higher priority to moving people than vehicles, ensuring greater transport safety, and minimizing adverse health effects. It recommended benchmarked safety programs, adoption of cleaner fuels, and systematic estimation of the impact of transport programs on safety and air pollution. It also highlighted three areas where the Bank could improve its advice and reduce the accident rate: the separation of motor vehicles from pedestrians and nonmotorized traffic; improvements in driver behavior through better education, regulation, and enforcement; and introduction of geometric road designs that take into account the large number of vulnerable road users in developing countries.

Cities on the Move (2002) advocated the development of a national road accident data collection and analysis capability. It maintained that accident frequency and severity can be reduced by improved road design and traffic management. It also recognized that poor people are the most vulnerable to the effects of air pollution, and that little is known about the environmental impact of urban transport. A road safety specialist was appointed to the transport anchor, and collaborative work with WHO was launched. In 2004, WHO and the World Bank jointly published the

World Report on Road Traffic Injury Prevention (WHO and World Bank 2004), which highlighted the growing public health burden of road deaths and injuries in low- and middle-income countries. The World Bank contribution was a collaborative effort by staff in the HNP and transport sectors.

HIV/AIDS interventions are a priority for the transport sector because the risk of contracting and spreading HIV at transport construction sites is high, and because people engaged in transport are at high risk of spreading HIV along transport corridors. *Intensifying Action against HIV/AIDS in Africa* (1999) committed to mainstreaming HIV into other sectors, including transport. The 2005 *Global HIV/AIDS Program of Action* committed to including HIV/ AIDS activities in all Bank-funded construction contracts, in all new transport projects in India and Africa, and in all ongoing Africa transport projects at mid-term. This approach has been incorporated into the recent Transport Business Strategy (2008), which is designed to strengthen transport sector capacity and institutions engaged with HIV/AIDS prevention strategies. The 2008 Business Strategy also commits to make roads safer, including support for governments to develop and implement "strategies, policies, institutions, infrastructure design, vehicle and driver regulations, and enforcement mechanisms."

Sources: Freeman and Mathur 2008; World Bank 2005c, 2008f.

pended particulate matter leads to the premature death of over 500,000 people each year (WHO 2002). Other potential health risks of transport investments include water pollution, disease transmission, and reduced physical activity, raising the risks of heart ailments, cancer, and diabetes.

Several strategy documents have helped shape the Bank's approach to health in relation to the transport sector since 1996 (box 4.6). From fiscal 1997 to 2006, the World Bank committed nearly $28 billion to 229 new projects managed by the transport sector. The main health-related transport interventions included: elimination of hazardous locations by rehabilitation or upgrading; improvements in road traffic management, bus priority, and risk behavior (such as traffic signals, lane markings, pedestrian crossings, traffic calming, seatbelt and helmet usage); emissions controls; and public health interventions concerning the movement of

people along transport corridors or traveling by air (for HIV/AIDS and other communicable disease).

About a quarter of transport sector-managed projects in the review period had an objective to improve health outcomes or mitigate a health risk. About one in five projects had a road safety objective; other objectives having to do with institutional capacity and reducing accidents and "black spots" (hazardous road locations) on roadways were related to road safety (figure 4.10). Only a handful had objectives related to aviation or waterway safety, HIV/AIDS prevention, or improved air quality.[19] However, nearly half of the projects had a health component (46 percent); almost all of the components were about transport safety (42 percent of all projects), with the next most common components for HIV/AIDS prevention (8 percent) and air quality (4 percent).

About a quarter of transport projects included an objective to improve health outcomes or mitigate health risks, but about half had a health component.

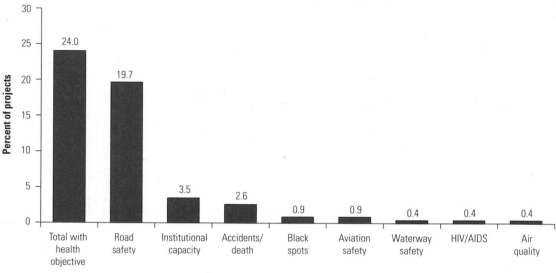

Figure 4.10: The Majority of Health-Related Objectives in Transport Projects Are for Road Safety

Source: Freeman and Mathur 2008.

While the share of approved transport projects with health objectives has been stable, *the share with health components has increased dramatically over time—from 36 percent in 1997–2001 to 59 percent in 2002–06.* Almost all of this increase can be attributed to transport safety (rising from 33 to 52 percent), and almost all of that to road safety. The share of projects with HIV/AIDS components at appraisal also rose, from 3 to 15 percent. The increase in transport projects with health components was particularly evident in middle-income countries, South Asia, Europe and Central Asia, Latin America, and Africa (figure 4.11).

The share of transport projects with health components has increased dramatically.

One in four transport projects planned to collect health *outcome* indicators, but only 5 percent planned to collect health *output* or *behavioral* indicators that would help to link the projects' activities with health outcomes. The road safety outcome indicators included the number of accidents, injuries, and fatalities and accident, injury,

Projects with health objectives are more likely to plan and collect health indicators than those without the objectives.

and fatality rates. *None of the projects proposed to collect health outcome data specifically for the poor.*

Among the 105 closed transport projects, a quarter (28 projects) had explicit health objectives or financed components with potential health benefits. All of the planned road safety, waterway, and port safety components were at least partly implemented. However, more HIV/AIDS components were implemented than had been planned at the time that the projects were designed, which is consistent with the efforts by the health and transport sectors to "retrofit" HIV/AIDS components into ongoing transport projects.

Closed projects with explicit health objectives were far more likely to plan and to collect health indicators than were projects with health components but no explicit objective (figure 4.12). Two-thirds or more of transport projects with explicit health objectives collected health outcome data, compared with only a fifth of projects without them. All 15 closed transport projects that measured health outcomes

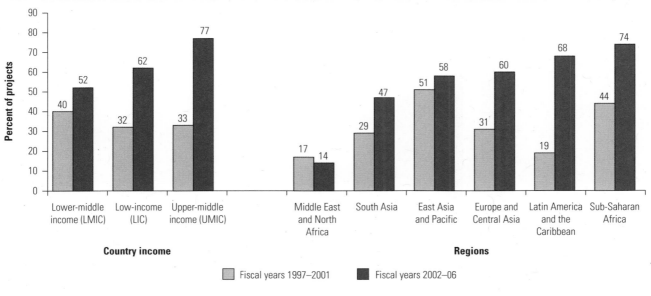

Figure 4.11: The Share of Transport Projects with Health Components Has Increased Sharply

Source: Freeman and Mathur 2008.

---

were related to transport safety, and in all but one, the indicators showed an improvement. Reductions in fatalities per 10,000 vehicles have been documented for projects in several countries (figure 4.13).

None of the small number of closed transport projects with HIV/AIDS components collected data on health outcomes, so the effectiveness of these activities is unknown.[20] A recent update on the implementation of the Bank's *Global HIV/AIDS Program of Action* notes that more than half of the projects in the active transport lending portfolio include HIV/AIDS activities, most of them added after the project was approved. The experience in the rest of the transport portfolio suggests that health indicators are rarely collected in the absence of an explicit objective.

The link between transport safety improvements and project outputs was often weak. Outputs were not well documented, other factors that might have affected the accident rate were not considered, behavioral and other intermediate variables (such as seatbelt use and accidents by

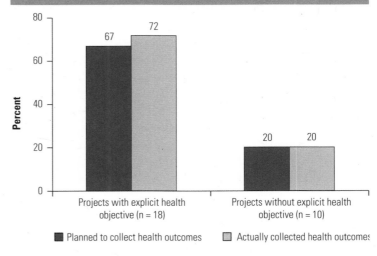

Figure 4.12: Projects with Explicit Health Objectives Are More Likely to Measure Health Outcomes

Source: Freeman and Mathur 2008.

cause) were not measured, and the health outcome data were often not specific to the areas covered by project interventions. It is thus difficult to identify the share of the reductions in fatalities and ac-

Figure 4.13: Reduction in Fatalities per 10,000 Vehicles in Closed Transport Projects

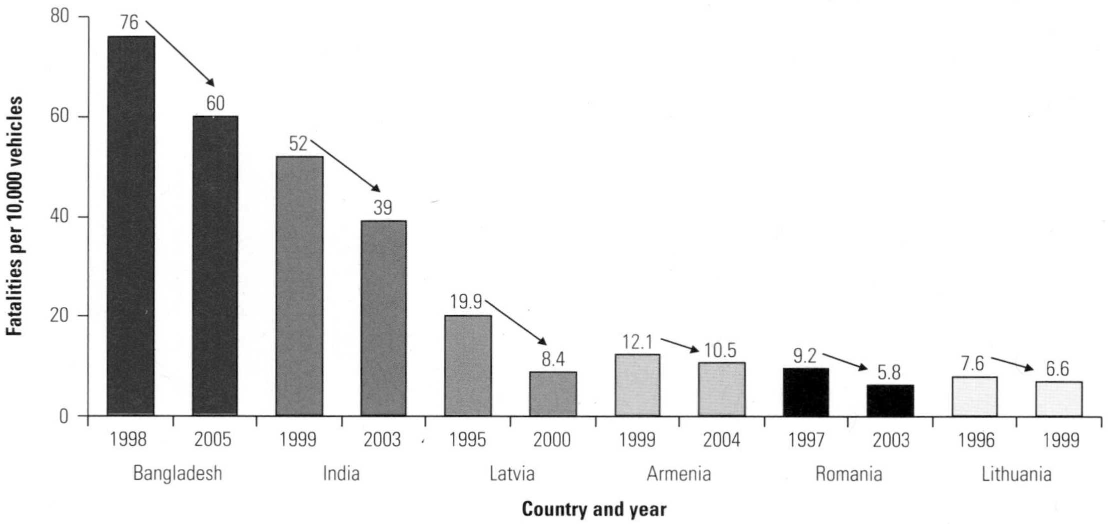

Source: Freeman and Mathur 2008, table 5.12.

cidents observed in so many of the projects that arise from traffic safety programs (box 4.7).

In summary, CASs invoke the language of synergies and health benefits to justify the lending portfolio, but lending activities in complementary sectors generally proceed independently of each other. While it is likely that investments in other sectors are contributing to HNP outcomes, these benefits are not well documented, and attempts to coordinate or monitor the contribution of Bank support for complementary sectors in producing health outcomes are rare.[21] Multisectoral HNP projects can produce results if the degree of complexity can be minimized by prioritizing the sectors, keeping the number manageable in relation to country coordinating capacity, and ensuring that collaborating agencies have clearly defined roles and responsibilities.

There is great potential for improving HNP outcomes by enlisting both the water supply and

None of the projects with HIV/AIDS components collected data on health outcomes.

sanitation and transport sectors in a more systematic and effective way. However, it is important to remember that the main objectives of support in these other sectors are not for health. It would make sense to assess beforehand, case-by-case, the expected costs and benefits at the margin of incorporating explicit health objectives. One could argue, however, in the case of transport, that there are always potential negative externalities of road projects, so road safety objectives might be relevant in virtually all cases. In the case of water supply and sanitation, it is important that the sector recognize that its responsibility for achieving the MDGs is not limited to improved access to safe water, but also includes contributing to the health and nutrition goals. Incentives to deliver HNP outcomes are improved in both water supply and sanitation and transport projects if the health objectives are made explicit. There is virtually no accountability for the results of retrofitted health components—this is something that needs to be addressed. Attempts to ensure that the health benefits reach the poor are rare.

Box 4.7: What Accounts for Fewer Road Fatalities in Romania?

The Romania Roads II Project had two health objectives—to improve road safety and reduce lead emissions. Road safety activities included reducing accident "black spots" and launching a 10-year Safety Action Plan, which involved public education to deter speeding; wear seat belts; use child restraint devices; and reduce driving under the influence of alcohol, medication, and drugs. The modernizing, safer national vehicle fleet would also likely have contributed to fewer accidents. The accident rate nationally declined, even as the number of registered cars rose by a quarter (see figure, below). The road safety activities reached their height in 2002–03 with the launch of a "Year of Traffic Safety."

Yet, the accident rate was already in decline even before the launch of the program. Engineering improvements to the first 1,000 kilometers of roads under the previous project, Roads I, is a possible contributory factor; rising fuel prices and a difficult economic climate might also have led to less driving or driving shorter distances, even as the vehicle fleet increased. The failure to account for factors affecting the accident rate—such as seatbelt use, sales of child restraining devices, and the number of drug and alcohol-related accidents—makes it difficult to understand the contribution of road safety activities to the reduction in traffic fatalities.

Road Fatalities Began to Decline in Romania Long Before Safety Interventions Were Launched

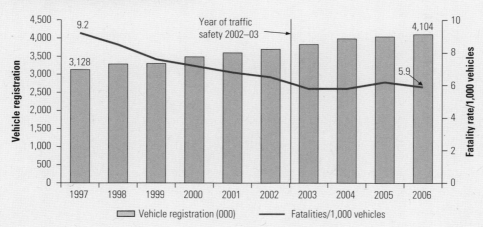

Source: IEG 2008g.

Chapter 5

Evaluation Highlights

- The health sector is relatively new to IFC and its investments are small and geographically scattered.
- The early projects did not perform well, but performance has improved and lessons learned led to the 2002 strategy.
- Support for public-private partnerships has expanded, especially through Advisory Services.
- Greater diversity in the portfolio would improve the social impact of IFC's investments.
- Health sector activities and responsibilities in IFC are segmented and linked to different departments, implying a need for internal coordination.
- Closer collaboration with the World Bank on regulatory issues would improve the climate for expanding IFC investments and Advisory Services.

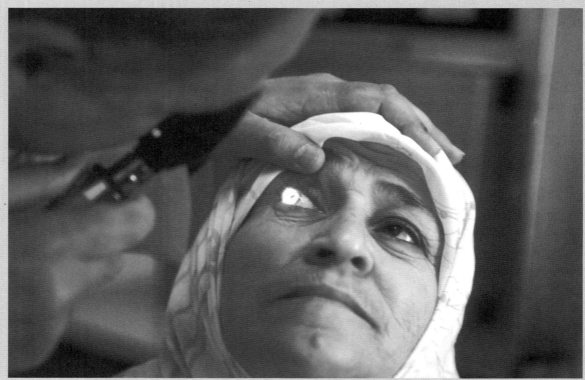

Woman receives a health exam in Beirut, Lebanon. Photo by Alan Gignoux, courtesy of the World Bank Photo Library.

IFC's Health Strategy and Operations

Health is a relatively new area to IFC. Until the early 1990s, it had only a few, sporadic health projects and no health department or specialized health staff. Between 1997 and 2007, IFC approved only 54 investment projects in the health sector, with total new commitments of about $580 million; health investments represented only 2 percent of total IFC projects and commitments (appendix D). During the same period, Advisory Services projects on health were approved for a total of $23.67 million.

This chapter reviews the evolution of IFC's approach to investments in the private health sector, examines trends in the content and efficacy of the portfolios of investments and Advisory Services since 1997, and assesses the design and implementation of its 2002 health strategy up to the present. While it is possible to review the characteristics of the health investment portfolio since 2002, most of the investments launched since then are not sufficiently mature to evaluate their efficacy.

Evolution of IFC's Approach to Private Investment in Health

Following adoption by the World Bank of its 1997 HNP strategy, IFC planted the seeds for development of a health strategy with the formation of a Health Care Best Practice Group in February 1998 (figure 5.1). The Group was to analyze potential investments in health and to share and leverage knowledge about the health care industry that was developing across IFC departments (IFC 2002, p. 24).

In 1999, the Health Care Best Practice Group issued "Investing in Private Health Care: A Note on Strategic Directions for IFC," which highlighted the potential contribution of IFC health investments to improving health outcomes for people in developing countries, particularly among the poor (IFC Health Care Best Practice Group 1999). First, such investments were expected to provide private health services and finance to low- and middle-income patients in the event that public health systems failed to reach them with quality care. Second, in countries where private investment not only complements but also competes with public sector health services, investment in private health care was expected to alleviate the burden on over-stretched public resources and improve the efficiency of the health sector more generally. In the long run, this was expected to enhance health care for the entire population, including the poor. Third, private facilities were expected to set aside beds and services for poor clients.

IFC subsequently adopted a *frontier country strategy* to steer resources toward underserved sectors in high-risk or low-income countries (IFC 1998). Health care, including investments in private clinics, hospitals, and health care management, was considered a frontier sector, and priority was assigned to the social sectors more generally.

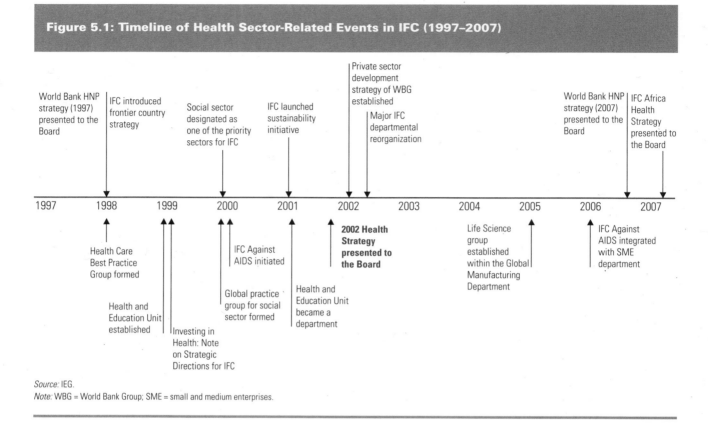

Figure 5.1: Timeline of Health Sector-Related Events in IFC (1997–2007)

Source: IEG.

Note: WBG = World Bank Group; SME = small and medium enterprises.

In April 2000, IFC established the Global Practice Group for the Social Sectors, which became IFC's Health and Education Department in September 2001.

The 2002 strategy "Investing in Private Health Care: Strategic Directions for IFC" was the first IFC health strategy presented to the Board of Directors. The goals for the sector were broadly defined: to improve health outcomes, protect the population from the impoverishing effects of ill health, and enhance performance of health services (IFC 2002, p. 3). The strategy had two sets of objectives (see chapter 1, table 1.2). The *business objectives* were similar to those of any other IFC investment: "financing should be provided in situations where other investors are not prepared to invest; the investment should encourage private resource flows through a demonstration effect; investments should be made only in financially viable

IFC's first Board-approved strategy was issued in 2002; it planned to continue to invest in hospitals but to diversify into other areas as well.

operations; and managerial and financial value added should be provided where necessary" (IFC 2002, p. 32). The *developmental objectives* sought to ensure that IFC investments would contribute to institutional and systemic capacity building and promote efficiency and innovation within the sector, while improving health security and expanding financial protection against the impoverishing effects of ill health (IFC 2002, p. 4).

Under the 2002 strategy, IFC planned to continue to invest in the hospital sector but to diversify its portfolio. Hence, it focused more on private health insurance to benefit the lower-middle and middle classes in countries without universal risk pooling; support for supplementary insurance; investment in pharmaceutical production, medical device manufacture, and biotechnology; and greater investments in the education and training of health workers (IFC 2002 p. 7). The strategy proposed six follow-up actions to implement the new investment strategy: develop instruments for small projects; increase efforts to reach the poor; enhance promotional activities; strengthen collaborative efforts and leverage existing knowledge; deepen collaboration with other multilateral financial institutions; and develop an M&E framework for IFC investments in the health sector (IFC 2002, p. 37).

The 2002 strategy took into account both the internal and external environments of the health sector. Internally, it considered the relative newness of health investments to IFC. Externally, three issues were considered (IFC 2002, pp. 6–19). First, demographics were changing; health expenditures were increasing; there were advances in medical technology and practice, information, and biotechnology; and changes in consumer behavior and expectations were increasing inequity. Second, global trends pointed to a significant and expanding role for the private sector, particularly as a partner with the public sector in the provision of health care. Many governments were rethinking the roles of public and private agents in the health sector and were beginning to turn to market instruments to enhance the efficiency and quality of health care provision. Third, the strategy acknowledged the World Bank Group mission of reducing poverty and promoting economic growth and the role of the private sector for growth and poverty reduction (IFC 2002, p. 21).

The strategy subscribes to and supports the goals of the Bank's 1997 HNP strategy (IFC 2002, p. 20). The IFC strategy identifies the different roles of the World Bank and IFC, recognizes their potential complementarity, and advocates closer collaboration.[1] IFC clearly recognized that while it has the mandate, the growing staff capacity, and the instruments to address directly private sector financing, the staff of the Bank's Human Development Network have the relevant sector knowledge and the mandate to inform and lead policy dialogue with country authorities and to support needed changes through the development and financing of public sector operations (IFC 2002, p. 41). Moreover, the strategy includes a specific subobjective that health investments should support the Bank's health sector objectives. It mentions that discussions with Bank col-

leagues through the appraisal process are vital and aim at deriving a meaningfully integrated approach between IFC and the Bank—one that should maximize the benefits to clients and to both organizations (IFC 2002, p. 23).

The strategy did not specify targets, estimate the resources needed for implementation, or put in place M&E arrangements. Goals for the sector were defined broadly, and a strategic investment approach that would maximize IFC's impact and role in the health sector was not defined. There was no estimate of the resources required to implement the strategy. The strategy proposed to refine the evaluation framework and to develop a set of baseline indicators that would adequately measure IFC's health sector objectives. However, the strategy itself provided no indicators.

Since 2004,[2] addressing the regulatory, financing, and implementation constraints to private sector investment in infrastructure, health, and education has been one of IFC's five strategic priorities. For the health sector, IFC's corporate strategy aimed to:

- Facilitate public-private partnerships (PPPs).
- Provide input and advice on regulatory improvements.
- Provide innovative financing, advice, and project development activities with local private players, such as expanding the use of local currency and taking new approaches to financing small health facilities.
- Develop cooperative programs with the World Bank (IBRD and IDA) to address sectorwide constraints comprehensively.

IFC's strategy in the health sector is continuing to evolve. The Health and Education Department's strategy is moving away from top-tier bricks-and-mortar projects to focus on repeat investments with strategic clients with broad reach, South-South investments in large, for-profit providers, and in local clients' operating networks of hospitals. The Life Sciences strategy is to em-

The strategy supports the goals of the Bank's 1997 HNP strategy.

It did not specify targets, estimate resources needed for implementation, or establish M&E arrangements.

phasize innovation through new products to address unmet needs and neglected diseases, and broader access to medicines through production of generics with high quality standards. IFC is extending its partnership with private foundations in the area of health.[3] In 2007, IFC adopted a strategy to improve private financing and provision of health services in Sub-Saharan Africa, partnering with other institutions such as the Bill and Melinda Gates Foundation, with the objective of mobilizing up to $1 billion over five years in investment and Advisory Services to boost health care in the Region. Because this strategy has only recently been launched, it is not a focus of this analysis.

IFC's Investment Portfolio in Health

Between fiscal 1997 and 2007, IFC approved 54 investment projects in the health sector, with total new commitments[4] of about $580 million. The average investment in individual health projects was therefore small—only about $11 million. Health investments represented only 2 percent of total IFC projects and commitments for the period. The majority of the projects have been in hospitals, pharmaceuticals, and biotechnology (table 5.1). IFC had only one project each in medical equipment manufacture, medical equipment leasing, medical training, and health payment processing.[5]

Over fiscal 1997–2007, IFC approved 54 investments in the health sector with $580 million in commitments.

Trends in IFC Health Investments

The health investment portfolio grew unevenly over the fiscal 1997–2007 period. New investment commitments were stable between 1997 and 2002, but after the establishment of the Health and Education Department in 2001 and introduction of the 2002 strategy, the number of new projects and commitment volume actually dropped. Investment growth then surged from 2005 onward (figure 1.3, chapter 1). This is consistent with a pattern observed in the dynamics of other industries in IFC where newly established departments first go through a consolidation phase, sorting out portfolio issues and developing strategies and standards for investments, before embarking on an expansion phase.

For the purposes of evaluation, IFC project approvals can be divided into three periods: (a) committed projects approved before fiscal 2000, prior to the issuance of any strategic documents about IFC and health; (b) committed projects approved from fiscal 2000 to 2002, when the Department of Health and Education was established and the Board was presented with a formal strategy for the sector; and (c) committed projects approved from fiscal 2003 onward. The analysis of the first period is only illustrative, since no strategic directions were in place. The second period is short, but it has been used to assess whether any of the ideas of the 1999 Strategic Note

Table 5.1: IFC Health Investments by Type of Investment and Period

	Type of investment				Total projects	Total net commitments	
	Hospitals	Pharmaceuticals	Laboratory	Other[a]		$US million	(Percent)
Projects by fiscal year of approval							
1997–99	8	2	—	1	11	70	(12.1)
2000–02	7	4	3	—	14	140	(24.1)
2003–07	14	11	1	3	29	370	(63.8)
Total	29	17	4	4	54		
(Percent)	(53.7)	(31.5)	(7.4)	(7.4)	(100)		
Net commitments							
Total	298	197	41	44		580	(100.0)
(Percent)	(51.3)	(34.0)	(7.0)	(7.7)		(100.0)	

Source: IEG data.

a. Medical equipment leasing, medical training, medical equipment manufacture, and provider of medical payment transactions services.

Table 5.2: Geographic Distribution of IFC Projects by Period

Period (fiscal years)	Africa	Asia	Europe and Central Asia	Latin America and Caribbean	Middle East and North Africa
1997–99	0	2	3	6	0
2000–02	0	5	3	5	1
2003–07	2	13	8	4	2
Total	2	20	14	15	3

Source: IEG data.

were implemented. It is too early to assess the projects in the third period.

Hospitals have continued to be the most significant type of investment, but the share of hospital projects has decreased from almost 80 percent in the first period to around 50 percent in the later periods (table 5.1).[6] The notable increase in life science projects in the third period reflects the efforts of the specialized Life Sciences Group in 2005.

Although the number of projects and net commitments expanded in life sciences, IFC did not expand operations in private insurance as the strategy intended.[7] To date, IFC has not financed a freestanding insurance project, though it has invested in some prepayment arrangements. The lack of proper regulatory frameworks in countries, weak IFC focus and experience in the subsector, and the lack of institutional arrangements required to promote these investments (such as regulatory regimes) contributed to the gap.

Health projects have been concentrated in three Regions—Asia, Latin America and the Caribbean, and Europe and Central Asia. These Regions account for 89 percent of the projects in the sector. This distribution follows the general pattern of IFC's portfolio as a whole. However, the distribution of commitments indicates that Asia has a much larger share in the health portfolio.

Geographically, IFC health sector operations did not experience increased diversi-fication until after fiscal 2002 (table 5.2). Before 1999, IFC's health projects were concentrated in Latin America and the Caribbean. The only health-related operations in Africa were those in the Africa Enterprise Fund (AEF).[8] The distribution evened out across Regions from fiscal 2000 to 2002. Then, from fiscal 2003 to 2007, IFC committed to health projects in Africa for the first time and substantially expanded its operations in Asia and Europe and Central Asia. The net commitment volume followed a similar geographic distribution pattern.

IFC's health investments are concentrated in middle-income countries. This, too, largely mirrors the pattern in IFC's overall investment portfolio. But there is a larger concentration of health investments in low-risk countries and a slightly larger concentration in nonfrontier countries (middle-income countries not at high risk). These results could be explained by IFC's greater experience working in low-risk countries where the environment for business is favorable. However, health itself was considered a frontier sector in 1998 (IFC 1998) because the operations were new and risky. Data for the corporation as a whole show a relatively more even distribution.

Efficacy of IFC's Investment Operations in Health

IEG's evaluation framework for assessing the efficacy of IFC operations focuses on both IFC's investment outcome[9] and project-level develop-

Investments are concentrated in middle-income countries and hospitals continue to account for the largest share of investment.

Although investment in life sciences expanded, it did not grow in private insurance as the strategy intended.

IFC investments did not diversify geographically until after 2002.

Table 5.3: Profitability of IFC Health and Pharmaceutical Investments

Period (fiscal years)	Health projects' profitability (percent)		Pharmaceutical projects' profitability (percent)	
	Excluding unrealized capital gains	Including unrealized capital gains	Excluding unrealized capital gains	Including unrealized capital gains
1997–99	−51.0	−48.0	−3.4	−2.4
2000–02	−8.6	−6.7	−13.0	−14.5
2003–07	−2.2	−0.4	11.6	33.3

Source: IEG data, based on IFC's accounting of operational income and expenditure by project. The data reflect the profit and loss calculation of all projects active during each financial reporting year.

ment outcome, based on methodology consistent with the Multilateral Development Bank's Good Practice Standards for Evaluation of Private Sector Projects (MDB, ECG, and WGPSE 2006, p. 2). The development outcome of projects is based on four development dimensions—project business success, economic sustainability, environmental and social effects, and private sector development impact—relative to what would have occurred without the project, and compared against established benchmarks as well as stated objectives.[10]

The early health investments, including in pharmaceuticals, were highly unprofitable.

IFC's health investment results between fiscal years 1997 and 2002, including pharmaceuticals, were highly unprofitable (table 5.3). The financial losses, minus 51 percent in profitability for health in the first period and minus 13 percent for pharmaceuticals in the second period, indicate that these lines of business were a significant cost to IFC, a situation that was not sustainable. In the subsequent periods, IFC contained its losses. More recently, pharmaceutical businesses have started to contribute to IFC's bottom line, and the profitability of health operations has been improving.

In fiscal years 1997–99, both investment and development outcomes were low.

The evaluation assessed the results of projects that reached *early operating maturity*. This occurs when the project has been substantially completed and has generated at least 18 months of operating revenues

for the company, and when IFC has received at least one set of audited annual financial statements that cover at least 12 months of operating revenues (MDB, ECG, and WGPSE 2006, p. 2). This usually happens about five years after project approval. **Thus, only projects in the first and second periods meet early operating maturity criteria and will be fully assessed below, while projects of the third, most recent, period will be included selectively, based on the extent to which particular effects could be discerned at this stage.**

In the first period (fiscal years 1997–99), investment and development outcomes were both low. Only 18 percent of health projects (2 out of 11) achieved both a high development rating and high investment return (figure 5.2), compared with 48 percent for all IFC investments. About two-thirds of projects in the first period were referred to the Department of Special Operations—a dedicated team that handles projects in distress—for workout, restructuring, rescheduling, and recovery. The reasons for these referrals included long delays in completing projects, negative influence of sponsors' other lines of business, difficulties in increasing the number of new patients served, the impact of financial crises in certain regions, and delays in obtaining regulatory clearances. The experience also reflects IFC's weakness in screening and structuring health sector deals owing to a lack of sector-related experience during the period. Frequently, IFC provided foreign exchange–denominated loans to clients, but this approach was not appropriate to the business, which generates revenues mainly in local currencies.

In many cases these early poor-performing operations resulted in: complete failure of the business and bankruptcy of the sponsor company, followed by sale of the project company to a third party; early termination of investment funds, because of poor ramp-up of the investment portfolio; abandonment of the project construction; or illiquidity, when a company ran out of cash from operations in other countries. Other projects with low development outcomes included hospitals with large underutilization of facilities and heavy financial losses in early years. Although some of the businesses are still operational, the financial and economic returns were lower than the benchmarks. Pharmaceutical projects with low development outcomes failed to achieve export market penetration, which was the original project objective and critical for their business growth. They also encountered policy obstacles (price controls, collection problems with state health funds). Lessons from hospital projects in the first period are summarized in box 5.1. The projects with low development outcomes tended to confirm the perception of the health sector as high risk, and thus had negative demonstration effects.

In contrast, nearly three-quarters of projects approved in the second period (10 out of 14 projects, fiscal 2000–02) had high development outcomes and a high investment return, substantially better than the rest of IFC portfolio (figure 5.3). Only 4 projects were rated low in development outcome. One was a complete business failure, and the company has been liquidated. Two were hospitals that had lower-than-expected patient admittance and struggled to ramp up revenues. Both are operational and expect to be sustainable, though with a lower return to financiers than anticipated. The fourth, a pharmaceutical project, decided to drop investments in research and development of new drugs following pessimistic market views of blockbuster drugs,[11] and to cut back on employment. Although 3 of the 10 projects with high development outcomes showed business results below the benchmark, all met or exceeded economic benefit benchmarks and contributed positively to private sector development. Between the first and second periods, performance improved in all four dimensions of development and investment outcomes (figure 5.3).

IFC hospital projects offer several potential benefits to governments. First, to the ex-

Nearly three-quarters of the projects in the second period had high development outcomes and high investment return—better than the rest of the IFC portfolio.

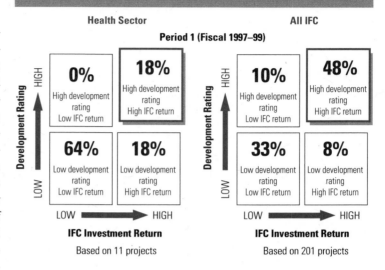

Figure 5.2: IFC Development and Investment Outcomes in Two Periods

Health Sector — All IFC

Period 1 (Fiscal 1997–99)

Health Sector — Development Rating (HIGH/LOW) vs. IFC Investment Return (LOW→HIGH):
- 0% High development rating, Low IFC return
- 18% High development rating, High IFC return
- 64% Low development rating, Low IFC return
- 18% Low development rating, High IFC return

Based on 11 projects

All IFC — Development Rating (HIGH/LOW) vs. IFC Investment Return (LOW→HIGH):
- 10% High development rating, Low IFC return
- 48% High development rating, High IFC return
- 33% Low development rating, Low IFC return
- 8% Low development rating, High IFC return

Based on 201 projects

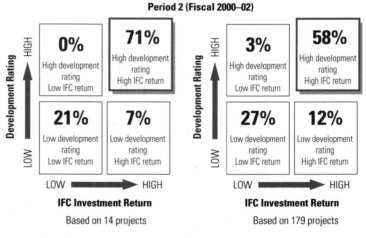

Period 2 (Fiscal 2000–02)

Health Sector — Development Rating (HIGH/LOW) vs. IFC Investment Return (LOW→HIGH):
- 0% High development rating, Low IFC return
- 71% High development rating, High IFC return
- 21% Low development rating, Low IFC return
- 7% Low development rating, High IFC return

Based on 14 projects

All IFC — Development Rating (HIGH/LOW) vs. IFC Investment Return (LOW→HIGH):
- 3% High development rating, Low IFC return
- 58% High development rating, High IFC return
- 27% Low development rating, Low IFC return
- 12% Low development rating, High IFC return

Based on 179 projects

Source: IEG data.

Box 5.1: Early Hospital Investments Provided Important Lessons

1. Sponsors of hospital projects may not be focused on the bottom line.

Hospital projects sponsored by doctors are unique—the sponsors invest in and work in the facilities they build, and trade-offs are always necessary. Doctors may not expect financial returns (especially from equities), but they may prioritize access to facilities for more lucrative practices. Professional management in financial control is necessary. IFC must insist that measures be put in place to control expenditures during the construction phase as well as during operations.

2. Just because people are sick, that does not mean they will go to a new hospital.

Competitively positioning a health care project in the local market is difficult. To be successful, a project must establish that the quality of service provided justifies its higher cost. If a hospital charges too much, potential clients will find other options for critical care. At the time of appraisal for a new health care project, IFC should carefully review the market plan.

3. IFC should expect conflicting interests in health care projects among stakeholders and plan accordingly.

Managing the relationships among doctors, sponsors, managers, contractors, technical partners, and others is complex, and conflicts are bound to arise. IFC should review the procedures for dispute resolution at appraisal and monitor them during implementation and operation. It is particularly important that such procedures include ways to deal with cash shortfalls. IFC has experienced difficulty with different project structures, including 50–50 joint ventures, single sponsors, and multiple sponsors. The strengths and weaknesses of the proposed structure should be reviewed carefully at appraisal, and weaknesses should be mitigated.

4. IFC should be cautious in providing loans denominated in foreign currencies.

Because health care services usually generate revenues in local currency, providing foreign currency loans increases project risk. In countries vulnerable to capital flight, IFC should consider mechanisms to provide local currency loans. If this is not possible, it should consider either providing guarantees to local banks that supply local currency loans or establishing a hedging mechanism at secure, global banks.

Source: IEG analysis of ELRN data.

Figure 5.3: IFC Evaluation Results Show Substantial Improvement in the Second Period

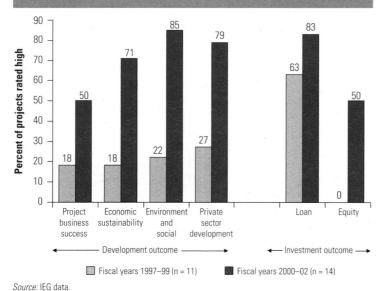

Source: IEG data.

tent that they attract patients among the non-poor, private hospitals can reduce the burden on public hospitals so that they can focus on the needs of the poor. Second, the projects may introduce services not previously available, increase capacity, or improve hospital management. For example, a project in the Philippines was the first major tertiary hospital built in the capital city in 25 years. Third, projects supported by IFC often have state-of-the-art technology and equipment that are out of the reach of governments.

Managers of client medical institutions in Argentina and the Philippines reported that state-of-the-art facilities in the country attracted doctors that had established successful careers in medical institutions in Europe and the United States. Four out of seven IFC projects appeared to attract doctors back to their native countries to practice. However, some facilities experienced difficulties in retaining quality nurses. Training for medical employees was observed in projects with both high and low development outcome. Furthermore, three of them have formal arrangements with universities or medical schools to accept internships or continuing education for doctors in their facilities.

Many hospitals supported by IFC have addressed governance issues in the private health sector. IFC projects in Eastern Europe introduced the posting of fees that doctors are charging, with the objective of reducing informal payments. Other projects have introduced some control of doctors' side practices outside the institutions. More generally, IFC requires financial and environmental reporting that prompts client hospitals to improve their management practices, which in turn can bring forth better decision making.

IFC's Advisory Services in Health

Trends in IFC Advisory Services for Health

IFC's Advisory Services projects have worked to address the regulatory, financing, and implementation constraints to private investment in the health sector.[12] Between fiscal years 1997 and 2007, 36 advisory projects in health were approved for a total of $18.48 million, excluding HIV/AIDS projects. The largest number

of such projects was for studies related to investment project preparation and follow-up (table 5.4). This is consistent with the need to address IFC's lack of knowledge about the best way to do business in health.

Advisory Services resources for public-private partnerships comprise the largest share of total funding and have shown the largest increase over the study period (box 5.2). From fiscal 2003 onward, Advisory Services have increasingly worked with governments to encourage public-private partnerships in the form of seminars and advice on design and implementation of IFC investment projects (table 5.4). Public-private partnerships can be effective for expanding IFC's reach, but they have been difficult to implement because it is the government that decides which partnership model would be the most appropriate. The decision also depends on the government's capacity to regulate and effectively control the quality of health care delivery. This is important for the success of the partnership, because after the agreement is signed, there are economic incentives to reduce the provision of services or their quality. Fur-

Projects for public-private partnerships make up the largest share of Advisory Services funding and project approvals.

Managers of two client hospitals reported that upgraded facilities helped attract doctors with successful careers in Europe and the United States.

Many hospitals supported by IFC have addressed governance issues.

Table 5.4: IFC Advisory Services in Health (1997–2007)						
Time period (fiscal years)	Assistance to investment clients	Retail[a]	Public-private partnerships	Studies	IFC Against AIDS	Total
Projects						
1997–99	5			4		9
2000–02	3		1	7		11
2003–07	2	2	9	3		16
Total	10	2	10	14	n.a.[b]	36
Commitments						
Total (US$ million)	1.02	0.45	12.51	4.50	5.19	23.67
(Percent)	(4)	(2)	(53)	(19)	(22)	(100)

Source: IEG.

a. Retail refers to IFC's direct assistance to nongovernmental organization/grassroots business entities through its Advisory Services window.

b. HIV/AIDS activities, carried out by IFC Against AIDS, were not recorded in the centralized database until recently, and historical project-specific data are not able to be mapped out against the other Advisory Services operations at this time.

Box 5.2: What Are Public-Private Partnerships in Health?

A public-private partnership in health is any joint program or project that involves collaboration between the public and private sectors, including contracting between the public sector (government or development agencies) and private providers to offer health services and goods and/or private financing to support health infrastructure. Governments worldwide are developing such partnerships in health to manage increased demand for health services and fiscal constraints. Private participation in public hospitals is sought to improve efficiency, reduce costs, and transfer operational risk.

Public-private partnerships can take many forms with different degrees of private sector responsibility and risk. They are differentiated by whether the private sector manages medical services, owns or leases the facility, employs the staff, or finances and manages capital investments.

IFC Against AIDS was initiated to get businesses involved in the fight against the disease through risk management and workplace programs.

thermore, public consensus is needed because, in practice, opposition can arise over the fairness of privatization and health care cost increases. The other challenge for IFC has been to find private investors willing to participate in these partnerships. To meet these challenges, IFC emphasized Advisory Service operations to governments.

The Regional distribution of Advisory Services funds differs from that of investment projects. Africa accounted for 38 percent of the total funding, Europe and Central Asia for 28 percent, while Asia accounted for only 6 percent. The significance of IFC funding for Advisory Services in Africa is explained by *IFC Against AIDS*, as well as by a $3.2 million study (almost 14 percent of total funding) to analyze opportunities for private health investments in Africa, which also shaped the new IFC Business of Health in Africa initiative.

A new system for evaluating IFC Advisory Services has been piloted, but only 10 advisory operations in the health sector have been evaluated.

IFC Against AIDS, a corporate initiative, was initiated in 2000 as a response to the identification of the HIV/AIDS epidemic as a critical obstacle for sustained competitiveness of enterprises (cost increases, productivity drops, and losses of experienced personnel) in regions where the disease is more prevalent. The aim of the initiative is to get businesses involved in the fight against HIV/AIDS through risk management and implementation of workplace programs in countries where IFC operates. The program is detailed and assessed in box 5.3.

Efficacy of Advisory Services

IFC is rolling out a new system for evaluating its Advisory Services operations. Under this system, Project Completion Reports (PCRs) will be prepared by IFC staff, cleared by IFC management, and reviewed for quality of content by IEG. This system assesses *development effectiveness* across five dimensions: strategic relevance, efficiency, outputs, outcomes, and impacts. It also rates Advisory Services on the *role and contribution of IFC*, which reflects the extent to which IFC brought additionality or some special contribution to the project. The system has been implemented on a pilot basis on 293 operations that closed in 2004–06. Of these, 10 are in the health sector.

Inferences about the performance of Advisory Services in health are constrained by the small sample of evaluated health projects and considerable data gaps. Among the small group of health Advisory Services that was evaluated, ratings on some of the dimensions were not available. For example, only 2 PCRs had valid judgments on the dimension of impact achievement (in both cases, negative), while the results of the other 8 projects were either inconclusive or it was too early to tell at the time of project completion (table 5.5). The overall development effectiveness for Advisory Service health projects is based on only 6 projects.[13] Projects rated high include public-private partnerships (see box 5.4 for a successful example) and studies for the introduction of health insurance. The six Advisory Services projects in health that were rated on outcome achievement performed below those in the rest of IFC: only a third had high outcome achievement (meeting expected outcomes or better), compared with 71 percent of projects in other IFC sectors. The cost-effectiveness of the health projects was also lower.

Box 5.3: *IFC Against AIDS:* A Preliminary Assessment

IFC initiated its *IFC Against AIDS* program in 2000. Its mission is to protect people and profitability by being a risk-management partner, HIV/AIDS expert, and catalyst for action. The program has three objectives: to prevent new infections, to deal with or manage existing infections, and to mitigate the effect of HIV on the company itself. The biggest beneficiaries of the initiative have been companies in Africa, but IFC has been trying to expand to other Regions and countries as well (China and Russia). Except for one operation conducted by the Private Enterprise Partnership for Africa (PEP-Africa), all *IFC Against AIDS* work is directly related to IFC investments.

Completion Reports have been issued for *IFC Against AIDS* program components, with the following findings:

- The program objective has been relevant and aligns with the strategic directions and priorities of IFC. It takes advantage of IFC's position with private sector clients and links their corporate risk management issues to the social agenda. By targeting workers, *IFC Against AIDS* is able to work with the adult population, which is difficult to reach by traditional health awareness campaigns (IFC 2006, p. 27).

- The program has developed products and services, tools, and publications to implement HIV/AIDS policies and training programs in businesses. As of January 2008, the program had reached 88,000 employees and over 628,000 people in nearby communities (IFC 2008). In Africa, the program engaged in activities ranging from large seminars to assisting individual firms (large companies and small and medium enterprises) as well as nongovernmental organizations. In India, it worked with four client companies (covering about 20 sites nationally) to proactively address HIV/AIDS in the workplace, clinical facilities,

and communities at risk. IFC prepared and disseminated studies on Occupational Health and HIV/AIDS Perceptions in Russia and a briefing book on HIV/AIDS in China.

- *IFC Against AIDS* often relies on other departments/operations to reach potential clients. Since it is targeted to IFC clients, close cooperation across IFC was critical. However, in a joint project with the Africa Project Development Facility (APDF, predecessor of PEP-Africa), the training program lost momentum because of IFC organizational changes and shifting strategic priorities. Similarly, *IFC Against AIDS* encountered a problem about the selection criteria of the small and medium enterprises, which were opportunistic and resulted in the inclusion of some businesses that were not linked to IFC activities.

- The project in China only delivered a handbook after nearly two years of implementation. Although the project seems to have been in support of business development aligned with IFC's value added on the AIDS agenda, IFC appears to have dropped the project after the business development mission to the country. IFC did not achieve the two goals—increased involvement of private enterprises in the fight against HIV/AIDS by being a risk-management partner to clients, and being supportive of IFC's business development by providing value-added services and contributing to IFC's brand.

Since 2006, *IFC Against AIDS* has incorporated a broader approach that also considers tuberculosis, malaria, and maternal health. Although it has been in operation for seven years, *IFC Against AIDS* has not been subject to a systematic outcome and impact assessment of the whole program. In December 2007, IFC launched a comprehensive external evaluation of the program.

Source: IEG review of Project Completion Reports.

IFC has also started to assist social enterprises that are directly serving rural and poor people. Among these is the Sustainable Health Enterprise Foundation in Kenya, a microfranchise network of outlets that extend affordable health care and medicines to rural areas, which includes community pharmacies and community-based clinics that employ certified nurses. IFC's Grassroots Business Initiative helped the network to become autonomous by providing capital loans to partially support the organization's efforts to improve its operational performance and franchise management. Another example is GNRC community pharmacy outlets in northeast India. The Advisory Service project was to transform community "medi-shops" into retail pharmacies delivering not just medicines, but also health planning and counseling. This was done with a partnership between IFC and GNRC Hospital, with IFC providing advice on business operations.

IFC has started to assist social enterprises that directly serve rural and poor people.

Table 5.5: Percentage of Health and IFC Projects Rated High, PCR Pilots 1 and 2

Main ratings and dimensions	Health sector projects		IFC overall (percent)
	Percent	Number of projects	
Development effectiveness	33	6	69
Strategic relevance	80	10	89
Efficiency	33	9	72
Output	60	10	84
Outcome	33	6	71
Impact	0	2	57
IFC role and contributions	78	9	87

Source: IEG data.

Box 5.4: Outpatient Dialysis Services in Romania—A Successful Advisory Services Public-Private Partnership in Health

Between 2003 and 2005, Romania privatized dialysis services. Previously, inpatient and outpatient dialysis services were provided in about 40 public hospitals. Dialysis supplies were purchased by the National Health Insurance Fund (NHIF), and the equipment was purchased by the government and allocated to the hospitals. Funding difficulties and increasing demand for services had created a backlog of patients, and the facilities needed to be upgraded and expanded.

IFC's Advisory Services helped the government: (i) revise and update national dialysis standards and practices and prepare legislation, including harmonization with European Union clinical guidelines; (ii) establish regional survey reporting of dialysis cost and prices; (iii) conduct cost analysis of dialysis; and (iv) create model tender documents.

The partnership was structured as a contract for dialysis services between the government and private service providers, who became owners. The Ministry of Health set prices, and the private operators were required to re-equip the facilities and provide about 200,000 outpatients a year with dialysis treatments at quality and service standards comparable to those of the Eu-

ropean Union. The individual contracts, totaling €20 million per year, could be extended if the operator constructed a new facility within 18 months. All public patients were to receive free treatment, and the operators were to be reimbursed by the NHIF under specified fee schedules.

The Advisory Services project introduced transparency into government procurement processes. In 2004, NHIF conducted simultaneous tenders for eight dialysis centers, with strict pre-qualification criteria to ensure participation of experienced providers. Bidders were restricted to winning two centers to limit market concentration. Winning bidders were selected based on highest investment commitments. The average investment commitment in a center was $2 million, which was realized within 18 months after awarding the contracts. NHIF did not have to finance the modernization from public funds and there were significant operational cost savings to NHIF (estimated at about $4 million). The project improved patient services at lower cost to the national health system. The quality of services and patient satisfaction increased at lower cost because of the new standards, improved equipment and facilities, and more efficient organizational structure.

Sources: IEG review of Project Completion Report; Nikolic and Maikisch 2006; Maikisch 2007.

IFC's Institutional Arrangements for the Health Sector

The activities and responsibilities in IFC related to the health sector are fragmented and linked to different departments, placing a premium on coordination across units. While health facilities and service providers are the responsibility of the Health and Education Department, the industries related to the health sector—pharmaceuticals, medical supplies, and medical equipment—are all the responsibility of the Global Manufacturing and Services Department (CGM), under its Life Sciences Group. However, that group also handles investments in products, such as biotechnology, cosmetics, and nutritional products.[14] Advisory Services are the result of the work of different units across IFC: the Infrastructure Advisory Department, Small and Medium Enterprise Department, and numerous Regional facilities, as well as Regional departments and the Health and Education Department. Beyond this, other IFC units implement health-related projects with varying degrees of specialization.

IFC's organizational structure is broadly in line with the traditional organization of the health sector, but recent developments in the sector pose challenges to this structure. Historically, there has been a clear separation in the industry between the main players—manufacturers and health providers. However, the health care market is becoming more integrated. The boundaries between statutory and private health insurance are becoming blurred; payers and providers are coming together in integrated health care provision and e-health; and the industry and health insurance companies are developing joint business models.[15] These developments require more integrated approaches to business development and client service in IFC's health sector. Many of IFC's potential clients are operating in both pharmaceutical and service provision, and these two are complementary in addressing health outcomes. In IFC, groups dealing with health are part of different departments, and incentives differ and have inhibited response to business opportunities and implementation of cross-sectoral initiatives.

The Health and Education Department is small—until recently the smallest of IFC's investment operations departments. The Department averaged 19 full-time/full-year professional staff between 2001 and 2005.[16] The number of staff increased by 42 percent, to 27, from 2006 to 2007. Investment officers in the department are not specialized and cover both the health and education sectors. Between 2001 and 2008, 56 percent of the department's staff time was spent on health sector activities. Originally, the Life Sciences Group within the Global Manufacturing and Services Department had a sector leader, five investment officers, and two analysts. By 2007, another investment officer and a life sciences specialist joined the group.

Health sector activities and responsibilities in IFC are segmented and linked to different departments, implying a need for coordination.

IFC's activities have tended to complement World Bank Group operations, but efforts to collaborate and pursue synergies have not been consistent. IFC's support to expand the production of vaccines and to improve access to medicine for diseases such as malaria in East Africa had strong complementarities with World Bank HNP strategies and operations. In a few cases, IFC projects followed from the World Bank's support in sector policy reform, with intensive collaboration between the two institutions. For example, a hospital investment in Argentina was developed in close collaboration with the World Bank and sequenced with World Bank projects.[17] However, efforts to exploit synergies as outlined in the sector strategies have not been consistent. In July 2008, for example, IFC's Health and Education Department pointed out that "one possible barrier to working together is a lack of knowledge and understanding of the strategy and processes of the IBRD and IFC" and called for a dialogue with its colleagues from the World Bank in order to "begin a more focused dialogue." The institutional fragmentation of health across several units at IFC also inhibits greater collaboration with World Bank staff.

IFC's health activities have tended to complement Bank operations, but efforts to collaborate and pursue synergies have been inconsistent.

Given that most of IFC's operations in the health sector are in middle-income countries, coordination with the World Bank in the health sector faces the same inhibitors identified by IEG's study on middle-income countries. These include incompatible timelines for projects, differences in organizational culture, and staff concerns that their time can neither be easily allocated to cooperation nor recognized in performance assessments (IEG 2007b, p. 63). This is further complicated for health by the asymmetry in the size of IFC interventions relative to

Bank operations. Although collaboration at the operational level turns out to be impractical, there is recognition that collaboration to develop the appropriate environment (policy level) for private investment would be beneficial. World Bank assistance in creating the regulatory environment for private sector operations could help to attract private investment by establishing appropriate incentives to invest (eliminating the constraint of lag of regulation in the sector).

Collaboration has been more situational than systematic; IFC's investments rarely feature in joint CASs.

Collaboration between the World Bank and IFC in health has been situational rather than systematic. Currently, IFC's investment officers are communicating with the World Bank's health sector experts during project appraisal. Advisory Services for public-private partnerships, which naturally involve government entities, have active communication within the World Bank Group, but there is a limit because of the ethical guidelines concerning the actual and perceived conflicts of interest. However, those interactions depend on the initiative of particular people and are driven by transactions. **There is no systematic avenue of collaboration between the two institutions in developing IFC strategies in health.** Because of

IFC's projects are small in scale and geographically scattered, limiting the overall impact.

IFC's opportunistic approach in identifying health investment in most countries, its health sector operations rarely feature in the Bank-IFC joint CASs.[18]

Social Impacts of IFC Health Investments

The 2002 strategy did not specify approaches to address poverty, though it recognized the need to assess the potential for private participation in health. IFC strategies for health investment have limited direct references to poverty. The 1999 Note on Strategic Directions, for example, highlighted the potential of IFC health investments to improve health outcomes across the entire population and among the poor (IFC Health Care Best Practice Group 1999). In the implementation of the 2002 health strategy, IFC aimed to diversify its portfolio to indirectly promote access to health care services for poor people by improving access to and quality of health services for the lower-middle and middle class (IFC

2002, p. 39) and by working with not-for-profit institutions (IFC 2002, p. 5). Then, in a 2007 briefing to the Board of Directors, the Department of Health and Education stated that its projects and role were changing, and that it had begun to focus on clients serving lower-income populations (IFC 2007d, p. 18). The Life Science Group, for its part, has identified three strategic areas where it can contribute to the fight against diseases that disproportionately affect poor people in developing countries (IFC 2007c): the production of generic pharmaceuticals, innovation and research to help discover technologies or treatments for diseases that affect poor people, and neglected diseases that affect people in developing countries.

IFC's investments in health services, mainly hospitals, have benefited primarily upper- and middle-income people at the "top of the pyramid" (IFC 2007a; IFC and WRI 2007). Among the 12 hospitals in the third period for which information is available, 3 were mainly targeted to expatriates and 6 were aimed at high- and middle-income populations. Among the evaluated hospitals, only 1 had a confirmed linkage with a public insurance scheme that paid for treatment of complicated cases referred to public hospitals. In other cases, links to public insurance funds helped private diagnostics and laboratory service providers to serve people's needs, irrespective of income level, as observed in two evaluated projects. Freestanding facilities can be successful and provide some desired development outcomes, but linkages to other institutional arrangements, such as insurance, are necessary to meet the health needs of a wider population. Among the evaluated projects in the first two periods, only three had such features.

All of IFC's clients in the hospital sector have some initiatives that directly target underserved populations. In addition, some clients provide free or reduced-price access to health care. Others target patients with health insurance coverage (often through employers), which allows hospitals to reach a much wider population as well as the middle class. IFC's client hospitals and clinics also typically have or contribute to dedicated foundations for charitable activities and community programs that target the poor and disadvantaged. Contributions normally account for 1 to 5 percent of their income. However, IFC's additionality in this area is very limited—many clients were involved in charitable activities even before IFC investment. In June 2008, IFC and the World Bank engaged in a project that seeks to help improve maternal care among some of Yemen's poorest people. This project uses output-based aid to reach the poor. New opportunities also are arising within the recent IFC *Business of Health in Africa* initiative.

IFC's life sciences interventions, particularly in pharmaceuticals, have the potential for broader reach and for more direct benefits to the poor. Household surveys throughout the developing world have shown that pharmaceuticals account for more than half of all health spending by people in the lowest income groups (Hammond and others 2007). Thus, investments by IFC in pharmaceutical projects that reduce the costs of drugs and improve quality control have great potential for helping the poor.

The majority of the pharmaceutical projects financed by IFC have resulted in significant declines in the price of generic drugs, enhancing affordability. Four of the six evaluated projects in pharmaceuticals involve production of generic drugs. The introduction of generic drugs in Mexico in 1999 resulted in a 30 percent decline in prices, and in Brazil, generic products cost an average of 40 percent less than brand-name products (Homedes, Ugalde, and Forns 2005, p. 695). Some projects, especially in China and India, are concentrated on the domestic markets and use local inputs. Since IFC promotes Good Manufacturing Practices and other international standards necessary for many export markets, some of the generic drugs are exported to neighboring countries. Only one project

had confirmed success in penetrating export markets with certification from the regulatory authority. One project had an objective to establish a research and development facility in a pharmaceutical company. However, as the sponsor company's business objectives shifted away from proprietary drug production because of the competitive pressure from international producers as well as strategic shifts toward generic drug production to the U.S. market, the company reduced its research and development functions, which resulted in fewer jobs for local scientists and lab technicians. This demonstrates the high-risk nature of research and development in drug production.

In summary, the health sector is still relatively new to IFC, and the approach to investment has remained largely a matter of seizing opportunities rather than developing them within a clear strategic framework. IFC's investments in the health sector are still small and geographically scattered. There were marked improvements in the performance of the small health investment portfolio, mainly in hospitals, and important lessons were learned leading up to the 2002 strategy. The expansion of public-private partnerships supported through Advisory Services has been an important development with potential to contribute to improved efficiency of the health sector of developing countries. Greater diversification of the portfolio, particularly toward pharmaceuticals and health insurance, would improve the social impact of the health investment portfolio and bring it more in line with the objectives of the 2002 strategy and the mandate of the World Bank Group. Closer collaboration with the World Bank on private sector regulatory issues with respect to the health and pharmaceutical sectors would improve the climate for expanding IFC health investment and Advisory Services.

The IFC strategy did not specify approaches to address poverty, and its investments in health services have primarily benefited upper- and middle-income people.

IFC's pharmaceutical investments have the potential for broader reach and more direct benefit for the poor.

Chapter 6

A woman and children pose after taking part in a health survey in Bukoba, Tanzania. Fertility and maternal mortality remain extremely high in most of Sub-Saharan Africa.
Photo courtesy of Martha Ainsworth.

Conclusions and Recommendations

The global aid architecture in health has changed over the past decade with the adoption of international goals and a major expansion of the levels and sources of development assistance, particularly for low-income countries. The World Bank Group's support for health, nutrition, and population has been sustained over the decade, but it is now a smaller share of global HNP assistance.

The mandate of the World Bank Group is to promote poverty reduction and economic growth in developing countries. Poor health is both a cause and consequence of poverty and an impediment to economic growth. This evaluation has pointed to some important accomplishments of the World Bank's HNP support to countries, often in difficult settings, and its contribution in helping build government capacity to manage the sector. The latter is important for improving aid effectiveness more generally, given the increasing reliance of the international community on government systems. The evaluation has also found improving performance in IFC's health portfolio and important lessons learned in this small but expanding sector.

The fieldwork for this evaluation also points to areas where the World Bank and IFC continue to add value (box 6.1). The results are a reminder that the value added by the World Bank Group is not measured solely by the magnitude of its support, and that its actual comparative advantage or that of any other development partner depends not only on its institutional assets, but also on the country context, health needs, and the activities of others.

Looking forward, the developments in the international aid architecture for health over the past decade and the increased levels of assistance from other sources present both opportunities and challenges for the World Bank Group. In the context of the *Paris Declaration on Aid Effectiveness*, the Bank has an opportunity to leverage its experience to help governments strengthen their capacity to manage effectively their own resources as well as the new donor funding being channeled through government. While the Bank's resources are now a smaller share of global development assistance for health, the Bank nevertheless continues to bring key institutional assets to the table: long-term, sustained engagement in the sector; experience in many countries with similar issues; a history of support for building country capacity for implementing social sector investments; sustained large-scale financing; strong links to the Ministry of Finance, which can be critically important both in leveraging reforms and in improving the dialogue between the ministries of health and finance; and a country approach in which HNP support is part of a portfolio of activities in many sectors, some of them with potential complementary contributions to health outcomes. These are assets that the Bank can continue to bring to bear on making health systems work better and to ensure that health benefits reach the poor.

Box 6.1: Evolving Value Added of the World Bank Group in HNP

Field interviews for this evaluation point to major areas in which the World Bank's policy dialogue, analytic work, technical advice, and lending have added value to HNP in countries.

In *Peru*, officials valued highly the Bank's ability to mobilize financial and human resources and connect technical assistance with financial services; its experience with health reforms in countries with similar conditions; its poverty focus, underscored by highly effective analytic work providing an "outsider's" perspective; its long-term relationship, which has helped to maintain a medium-term agenda and dialogue on health in the face of high turnover in the sector; and its institutional culture, which has emphasized outcome-oriented projects, efficiency, and transparency in the allocation of resources.

In the *Kyrgyz Republic*, the Bank played a leadership role, mediating conflicts among the donors and using its leverage to keep health reform on the political agenda in the face of strong opposition. It built institutional capacity over time in the Ministry of Health, was able to intervene to work out implementation details, and provided capacity-building inputs for public sector fiduciary management. The country would have implemented health reforms even without the Bank, but respondents felt that progress would have been more limited geographically and institutionally, resources would have been used less efficiently, and there would have been less focus on improving access for the poor.

In *Nepal*, the Bank brought value added with its poverty focus, analytic work, and living standards surveys focusing on the health of the poor. It helped to strengthen national capacity to lead and manage donor funds and provided technical assistance for monitoring social sector expenditures and for financial management in support of the SWAp. Without the Bank, there would have been less financing of civil works and training of village health

workers, a weaker poverty focus, and less attention to public expenditures and expenditure frameworks. Other donors likely would not have participated in the SWAp without the Bank's involvement.

In *Malawi,* the Bank's value added took the form of leadership on procurement and financial management in support of the health SWAp and individual operations; increased knowledge through analytic work, exchange of experience, facilitating access to expertise, and an attempt to maintain the focus on outcomes; and its convening power and strong links with the sectoral and macro level.

The proposed health interventions likely would have occurred in *Eritrea* even without the Bank's involvement, but not on the same scale. The Bank's engagement brought credibility and eventual support from others in the international community, built the institutional capacity of the Ministry of Health, and highlighted the need to focus both on the supply of health care and on community demands, and on both hardware and software.

Respondents also expressed views on the "additionality" of IFC's health support. Often IFC was the only source of long-term finance (loan and equity) where private investments in the health sector were considered risky and local banks did not have experience in financing the sector. A pharmaceutical business in China emphasized that IFC's value added was not so much its financial contribution, but the value of its "stamp of approval" in environmental and social standards, which provides a level of comfort to the other investors. Another company said that IFC's association with the World Bank Group, a public entity, facilitated public-private partnerships with local authorities. A third client valued IFC's role as an honest broker between stakeholders, including government and regulatory agencies, to increase visibility and bring strategic partners to the project.

Sources: IEG 2009a, 2009b, 2008d; Shaw forthcoming; Elmendorf and Nankhuni forthcoming.

The evaluation has also revealed substantial challenges for the future. About a third of the Bank's HNP support is not performing well, and there has been no sign of improvement. Contributing factors are the increasing complexity of HNP operations, particularly in Africa but also in support of health reform to middle-income countries; inadequate risk assessment and mitigation; and weak M&E. The Bank has underinvested in support to reduce high fertility and malnutrition

among the poor. The performance of IFC's health investments has improved markedly, but the program has been less successful in expanding investment in activities that both make business sense and are likely to yield broader benefits for the poor. Accountability for results has been weak—both the accountability of Bank- and IFC-supported projects for ensuring that results have actually reached the poor, and the accountability of the projects supported by the Bank's non-health sectors, such as water supply and sanitation and transport, for demonstrating the health benefits of their investments.

The expansion of external assistance for health also featured a large increase in resources earmarked for specific infectious diseases or other programs within the health sector. Many of these previously attracted insufficient attention. To the extent that large amounts of earmarked support have the potential to adversely distort resources within the health systems of small countries to the detriment of other critical services for the poor, the Bank needs to consider, on a case-by-case basis, whether additional earmarked funds of its own for some of the same programs are appropriate and cost-effective in improving health, nutrition, and population outcomes, given possible alternative investments elsewhere in the health system.

In short, the new international aid architecture has provided the World Bank Group with opportunities to improve health outcomes among the poor, to prevent poverty due to illness, and to improve the efficiency and efficacy of health systems. By improving their performance and maintaining focus on these core objectives, the Bank Group has the potential to contribute not only to meeting the Millennium Development Goals but also to ensuring that the poor benefit and that the benefits will be sustained.

Recommendations

The following recommendations for the World Bank and IFC are offered to help improve the implementation and impact of their respective HNP strategies and further the mandate of poverty reduction and economic growth in the context of the new aid architecture:

1. **Intensify efforts to improve the performance of the World Bank's health, nutrition, and population support.**

   - Match project design to country context and capacity and reduce the complexity of projects in low-capacity settings through

greater selectivity, prioritization, and sequencing of activities, particularly in Sub-Saharan Africa.
   - Thoroughly and carefully assess the risks of proposed HNP support and strategies to mitigate them, particularly the political risks and the interests of different stakeholders, and how they will be addressed.
   - Phase reforms to maximize the probability of success.
   - Undertake thorough institutional analysis, including an assessment of alternatives, as an input into more realistic project design.
   - Support intensified supervision in the field by the Bank and the borrower to ensure that civil works, equipment, and other outputs have been delivered as specified, are functioning, and are being maintained.

2. **Renew the commitment to health, nutrition, and population outcomes among the poor.**

   The World Bank should:

   - Boost *population* and *family planning* and other support in the form of analytic work, policy dialogue, and financing to high-fertility countries and countries with pockets of high fertility.
   - Incorporate the poverty dimension into project objectives to increase accountability for health, nutrition, and population outcomes among the poor.
   - Increase support to reduce *malnutrition* among the poor, whether originating in the HNP sector or other sectors.
   - Monitor health, nutrition, and population outcomes among the poor, however defined.
   - Bring the health and nutrition of the poor and the links between high fertility, poor health, and poverty back into poverty assessments in countries where they have been neglected.

   IFC should:

   - Expand support for innovative approaches and viable business models that demonstrate private sector solutions to improve the health of the poor, including expansion of investments in low-cost generic drugs and technologies that address health problems of the poor.

○ Assess the external and internal constraints to achieving broad social impacts in the sector.

3. **Strengthen the World Bank Group's ability to help countries to improve the efficiency of health systems.** Improving the efficiency of **health** systems may only indirectly produce health benefits, but it is a valid objective in its own right, contributing to more sustainable financing and economic growth. Health reform projects address structural inefficiencies, are inherently politicized, and thus are risky. However, they are nevertheless worth pursuing if deemed relevant and a high priority of government.

The World Bank should:

○ Better define the efficiency objectives of its support and how efficiency improvements will be improved and monitored.

○ Carefully assess decisions to finance additional earmarked communicable disease activities in countries where other donors are contributing large amounts of earmarked disease funding and additional funds could result in distortions in allocations and inefficiencies in the rest of the health system.

○ Support improved health information systems and more frequent and vigorous evaluation of specific reforms or program innovations to provide timely information for improving efficiency and efficacy.

IFC should:

○ Support public-private partnerships through Advisory Services to government and industry and through its investments, and expand investments in health insurance.

○ Improve collaboration and joint sector work with the World Bank, leveraging Bank sec-

tor dialogue on regulatory frameworks for health to engage new private actors with value added to the sector, and more systematically coordinate with the Bank's policy interventions regarding private sector participation in health.

4. **Enhance the contribution of support from other sectors to health, nutrition, and population outcomes.**

The World Bank should:

○ When the benefits are potentially great in relation to the marginal costs, incorporate health objectives into nonhealth projects, for which they are accountable.

○ Improve the complementarity of investment operations in health and other sectors to achieve health, nutrition, and population outcomes, particularly between health and water supply and sanitation.

○ Prioritize sectoral participation in multisectoral HNP projects according to the comparative advantages and institutional mandates to reduce complexity.

○ Identify new incentives for Bank staff to work cross-sectorally for improving health, nutrition, and population outcomes.

○ Develop mechanisms to ensure that the implementation and results for small HNP components retrofitted into projects are properly documented and evaluated.

IFC should:

○ Improve incentives and institutional mechanisms for an integrated approach to health issues across units in IFC dealing with health, including the way that IFC is organized.

5. **Implement the results agenda and improve governance by boosting investment in and incentives for evaluation.** Weak M&E is a constraint to achieving the results focus and governance agenda of the Bank's new HNP strategy and inhibits the results orientation of IFC.

The World Bank should:

- Create new incentives for M&E, for both the Bank and the borrower, linked to the project approval process and the midterm review. This would include requirements for baseline data, explicit evaluation designs for pilot activities in project appraisal documents, and periodic evaluation of main project activities as a management tool.

IFC should:

- Enhance its results orientation by developing clearly specified baseline indicators and an evaluation framework that adequately measure IFC's health sector objectives and results.

Appendixes

An auxiliary nurse midwife speaking to slum dwellers about contraception and other sexual health matters in India. Photo by John Isaac, courtesy of the World Bank Photo Library.

APPENDIX A: WORLD BANK GROUP HNP TIMELINE

Appendix A: World Bank Group HNP Timeline

Year	World Bank group events	HNP sector events	HNP publications and strategies	HNP partnerships and commitments
1952	Economic Survey mission to Jamaica to study the country's development requirements considers the effects of rapid population growth. (March) (1)	Concern over the impact of population growth on development is discussed at Seventh Annual Meetings in Mexico City. Chairman of the Board of Governors argues that the World Bank is well placed to combine sound banking principles with creative efforts to address population growth issues. (September) (1)		
1956	IFC is established as an institution of the World Bank Group to promote sustainable private sector investment in developing countries.			
1961	World Bank begins lending for water supply and sanitation projects. (2)			
1964		The first IFC investment in pharmaceuticals, "Huhtamaki-Yhtyma Oy" of Finland, is approved.		
1968	Robert McNamara becomes World Bank President. (April) (1) McNamara calls for governments to develop strategies to control population growth. He admits that there is no alternative to the World Bank's involvement in "this crisis." (October) (1)	Economics Department's Special Studies Division is reorganized to create a Population Studies Division headed by E.K. Hawkins. (3) Population Projects Department is established under the Office of the Director of Projects. (November) (4) K. Kanagaratnam is asked and accepts the post as head of the Population Projects Department; however, he is unable to start immediately, and in the interim George C. Zaidan becomes the first division chief of the new department. (3)		

1969		McNamara calls for emphasis on population planning, educational advances, and agricultural growth in his Annual Meetings address. He highlights the need for development in nutrition, water supply, and literacy. (September) (1)
1970	World Bank/WHO Cooperative Program is established to address water supply, waste disposal, and storm drainage. (September) (1)	First population loan is approved for $2 million to support Jamaica's family planning program. (June) (1)
1971		In his Annual Meeting address, McNamara emphasizes the importance of addressing the basic problems affecting the daily lives of people in developing countries, including nutrition, employment, and income distribution, among others. He describes malnutrition as a major barrier to human development. (September) (1)
1972	World Bank participates in an advisory capacity in WHO's Special Program of Research Development and Training in Human Reproduction (HRP). (7)	*Possible Bank Actions on Malnutrition Problems* is released. It is influential in calling attention to the Bank's role in addressing malnutrition. (January) (5*) *Sectoral Programs and Policies Paper* includes recommendations on population policies. It points to the economic effects of population growth in developing countries, describes the Bank's efforts to assist member countries to reduce population growth rates, and outlines its future program in population assistance. (March) (6*) A Bank-wide reorganization creates a senior vice president of operations with five Regional vice presidents and a vice president for project staff. (August) (1)
1973	World Bank convenes Meeting of Onchocersiasis Control Program in Paris with WHO, the U.N. Food and Agriculture Organization (FAO), the United Nations Development Program (UNDP). The purpose of the meeting is to formulate a strategy to fight river blindness. (June) (1)	A nutrition policy paper makes the case for investment in nutrition and proposes that the Bank "assume a more active and direct role in nutrition." (8*) The Board of Executive Directors approves McNamara's proposal for the Bank to take the lead in mobilizing international funds for an onchocersiasis (river blindness) control program. (May) (1) McNamara uses his address at the Annual Meetings to emphasize the need to incorporate population planning into development strategies. (September) (1)

(Table continues next page)

Appendix A: World Bank Group HNP Timeline (continued)

Year	World Bank group events	HNP sector events	HNP publications and strategies	HNP partnerships and commitments
1974		Funds to cover the first year of the Onchocersiasis (river blindness) Control Program are mobilized. (March) (1)	Population Policies and Economic Development analyzes the impact of population growth on the fight against poverty. (August) (9*)	WHO, FAO, UNDP and the World Bank implement the Onchocersiasis Control Program (OCP), which is endorsed by the seven governments of West Africa, the countries most affected by the disease. (March) (1)
1975			1975 Health Sector Policy Paper is published. As the first formal HNP policy statement, it establishes that lending will be only for family planning and population. (10*)	World Bank cosponsors the Tropical Research Program along with WHO, UNICEF, and UNDP to coordinate a global effort to combat diseases that affect the poor and disadvantaged through research and development, and training and strengthening. (1)
1976		First loan in nutrition, $19 million to Brazil, is approved. (June) (1)		
1977				World Bank helps to found and becomes a member of the UN Subcommittee on Nutrition (SCN). (11)
1979		The Population, Health, and Nutrition Department (PHN) is established. The Bank approves a policy to consider funding freestanding health projects and health components of other projects. (July) (2) John R. Evans appointed PHN Department Director. (12)		World Bank and UNDP initiate the UNDP-World Bank Water and Sanitation Program (WSP) to analyze cost-effective strategies and technologies to bring clean water to the poor. (1)
1980	WDR 1980: Poverty and Human Development highlights the importance of the health sector, education, and social protection to alleviate poverty. Part of the report describes the role of human development programs, its effects on productivity and population growth. (August) (13*)		1980 Health Sector Policy Paper commits the Bank to direct lending in the health sector. The strategy focuses on the need for basic health services, especially in rural areas, and describes the links between the health sector, poverty alleviation, and family planning. (14*)	

1981	First loan to expand basic health services is made to Tunisia. (15) The first IFC investment in hospitals, the Dr. Simo Milosevic Institute located on the Mediterranean coast of Yugoslavia (now Montenegro), for a medical rehabilitation facility is approved. (1a)		
1983	John N. North becomes Director of the PHN Department. (12)		World Bank partners with The Rockefeller Foundation, UNDP, UNICEF, and WHO to establish the Task Force for Child Survival and Development, a campaign to achieve the goal of universal child immunization by 1990. (1)
1984	*WDR 1984: Population and Development* emphasizes the role of governments to reduce mortality and fertility. (16*) Research Department launches the first Bank-sponsored Living Standards Measurement Survey in Côte D'Ivoire. LSMSs are multi-topic household surveys capable of linking the level and distribution of welfare at the household level to health care decisions, the availability and quality of health services, and HNP outcomes. (17)		
1985	Frederick Sai appointed Senior Population Adviser. (18)		
1986	Barber Conable is appointed as the Bank's 7th President. (July) (1) A Poverty Task Force composed of senior staff is established to review the Bank's work and propose new activities. (19)		*Poverty and Hunger: Issues and Options for Food Security in Developing Countries* argues that food insecurity is caused mainly by poor people's lack of purchasing power. It asserts that the role for international donors is to provide assistance to develop and financing to support improved policies to reduce food insecurity, as well as addressing international trade factors that contribute to food insecurity. (20)

(Table continues next page)

Appendix A: World Bank Group HNP Timeline *(continued)*

Year	World Bank group events	HNP sector events	HNP publications and strategies	HNP partnerships and commitments
1987	President Conable announces an internal reorganization to be completed by September. (May) (1)	PHN becomes a division of the Population and Human Resources (PHR) Department. Technical departments, including PHN units, are created within each region, and country departments are created within Regions, combining the functions formerly divided between programs and projects departments. (21) Ann O. Hamilton is appointed PHR Department Director. (12) Dean T. Jamison is appointed Chief Manager of PHN Division. (12)	*Financing Health Services in Developing Countries: An Agenda for Reform* argues that government expenditures should shift toward providing health services for the poor. The policy study addresses themes of inefficient public spending on health care and recurrent cost financing. (May) (22*)	World Bank cosponsors the Safe Motherhood Conference in Nairobi, Kenya. The Bank pledges to take specific steps to address issues affecting women, and the Safe Motherhood Initiative is launched. (February) (1)
1988		First freestanding AIDS project is approved in Zaire. This is also the first approved freestanding Bank project for a single disease. (21) Anthony Measham becomes PHN Chief Manager. (12)	*Acquired Immunodeficiency Syndrome (AIDS): The Bank's Agenda for Action* is prepared by the Africa Technical Department. It was not formally adopted by the Bank management as a strategy but released as a working paper. (23*)	World Bank becomes a funder of the WHO's HRP. (24)
1989	The IDA Debt Reduction Facility is established to reduce the stock of debt owed to commercial creditors by IDA-only countries. (August) (1) Bank finances the first freestanding nongovernmental organization-implemented project for grassroots development in Togo. (19) First social fund project is approved. (1)		*Sub-Saharan Africa: From Crisis to Sustainable Development* calls for a doubling of expenditure on human resource development: food security, primary education, and health care. (November) (25*)	
1990	The IBRD approves the largest loan at this point in its history (nominal terms) to Mexico to support a debt-reduction program, and the Debt-Reduction Facility for IDA-only countries undertakes its first operation in Bolivia. (19)	Steven Sinding becomes Senior Population Adviser. (26)		

1991	Lewis T. Preston is appointed as the 8th president of the World Bank. (September) (21)		World Bank joins with UNDP, UNICEF, WHO, and Rotary International to form the Children's Vaccine Initiative (CVI). CVI's goal is to vaccinate every child in the world against viral and bacterial diseases. (27)
1992	A report of the Task Force on Portfolio Management (the "Wapenhans Report") is transmitted to the Executive Directors and is a major factor in the Bank's impetus to redouble its efforts toward effective implementation of lending projects. (1)	Bank issues a statement that abortion is an issue countries themselves must address and denies advocating the legalization of abortion in Latin America. (March) (1) The first health-related advisory service project is approved by IFC for the Thailand Bumrungrad Hospital.	World Bank participates in International Conference on Nutrition in Rome. (December) (15)
1993	*WDR 1993: Investing in Health* evaluates the roles of governments and markets in health, as well as ownership and financing arrangements to improve health and reach the poor. It introduces the disability-adjusted life year (DALY) to calculate the Global Burden of Disease, and argues that the international community must commit to addressing health issues. (June) (27*)	*AIDS in Asia*, the first Regional AIDS support unit, is established in the East Asia and Pacific Region. (21) Janet de Merode becomes Director of the PHN Division. (12)	*Disease Control Priorities in Developing Countries* provides information on disease control interventions for the most common diseases and injuries in developing countries to help them define essential health service packages. The publication eventually leads to increased Bank lending for disease control. (October) (28*)
1994	A policy paper, *Water Resources Management*, proposes a new approach to managing water resources. The approach advocates a comprehensive policy framework and treatment of water as an economic good, along with decentralized management and delivery structures, greater reliance on pricing, and fuller participation by stakeholder. (29*)	David de Ferranti becomes Director of PHN Division. (12)	*Better Health in Africa*, directed to both Bank and external audiences, argues that because households and communities have the capacity to use knowledge and resources to respond to health problems, policy makers should make efforts to create an enabling environments that stimulate "good" decision making. It also points out that health reforms are necessary, that cost-effective packages of services can meet needs, and that changes in domestic and international financing for health are necessary. The publication was never approved as an official strategy, but the World Bank supported an independent 'Better Health in Africa' Expert Panel that worked to disseminate key messages to African policy makers. (30*) Bank participates in International Conference on Population and Development (ICPD) in Cairo and commits to its plan of action. (31)

(Table continues next page)

Appendix A: World Bank Group HNP Timeline *(continued)*

Year	World Bank group events	HNP sector events	HNP publications and strategies	HNP partnerships and commitments
1995	James Wolfensohn is appointed as the ninth World Bank president. (June) (1) *The Broad Sector Approach to Investment Lending: Sector Investment Programs* defines sector investment programs (SIP), analyzes experience with the new lending instrument and advocates for more learning and support of SIPs, particularly in Africa. (32)	The Human Development Department is established and David de Ferranti serves as Department Director. Richard Feachem (Health), Jorge Barrientos (Implementation), Alan Berg (Nutrition) and Thomas Merrick (Population) are appointed as managers/advisers. (July) (4, 12)		The Bank hosts a conference to launch the African Program for Onchocersiasis Control, a follow-up to a successful project launched in the 1970s. Sponsored by governments, NGOs, bilateral donors and international institutions, it implements community-based drug-treatment programs in 16 African countries. (December) (1)
1995		Learning and Leadership Center-Human Development Network training week initiated to provide staff with intensive training focused on topical issues in the HNP sector. (15)		The Bank participates in the Fourth World Conference on Women in Beijing (FWCW) and agrees to: reduce the gender gap in education and ensure that women have equitable access and control over economic resources. (31)
1996	*World Bank Participation Sourcebook* launched. Wolfensohn announces that the Bank will involve NGOs, the private sector, community groups, cooperatives, women's organizations, and the poor and disadvantaged in decision-making processes. (February) (33) In his Annual Meetings address, Wolfensohn defines the key elements of the Strategic Compact to renew the Bank Group and improve development effectiveness: improving resource mobilization; taking more integrated approaches; building partnerships and sharing knowledge; and restructuring the Bank to be closer to clients through responsive and high-quality products. (October) (33) The Bank announces that three new networks will be created: Environmentally and Socially Sustainable Development (ESSD), Finance, Private Sector and Infrastructure (FPSI), and Poverty	World Bank sponsors tobacco-related and non-communicable disease conference in Washington, DC. (June) (1) The Flagship Program on Health Sector Reform and Sustainable Financing is initiated by the Economic Development Institute (EDI, now World Bank Institute) to provide knowledge and training on options for health sector development, including lessons learned and best practices from country experience. Course is offered at regional and country levels. (1)	IFC launches a global study on "Private Hospital Investment Opportunities" to identify key success factors for investment in hospitals and more generally in health. (2a)	Special UN Initiative for Africa launched; Bank partners with UN to promote an expanded program of assistance to Sub-Saharan Africa and improve cooperation between the Bank and the UN. Bank commits to take special responsibility for mobilizing resources for basic health and education reforms. (March) (1) Wolfensohn announces Bank's support for the G-7's declaration and objective of providing an exit strategy for heavily indebted countries. Bank pledges $500 million to a trust fund for debt relief as its initial contribution. (June) (33) World Bank cosponsors the Joint UN Program on HIV/AIDS (UNAIDS) with UNDP, UNESCO, UNFPA, UNICEF, and WHO. (21)

World Bank becomes a donor to the newly formed International AIDS Vaccine Initiative (IAVI). It is established to ensure the development of an HIV vaccine for use around the world. (35)

Reduction and Economic Management (PREM). (December) (1)

Poverty Reduction and the World Bank: Progress and Challenges in the 1990s is released and vows to redouble Bank's efforts to ensure success in its mandate to help countries reduce poverty. The Bank says that it will judge itself and staff by their contributions to achieving this goal. (June) (1)

The Bank and International Monetary Fund launch the Highly Indebted Poor Country (HIPC) Initiative, creating a framework for creditors to provide debt relief to the world's most poor and indebted countries. The HIPC Trust Fund and HIPC Implementation Unit are established. (November) (1)

Quality Assurance Group (QAG) established with the expressed purpose of improving the quality of the Bank's operational work within the broad context of reducing poverty and achieving development impacts. (34)

1997

World Development Indicators 1997, the first edition, is published. Wolfensohn points to the publication as an example of the World Bank's role in disseminating knowledge to facilitate decision making in development. (April) (33)

The Strategic Compact period, a three-year organization renewal process, is launched. (April) (1)

Bank reorganization leads to the creation of Bank-wide "anchor" units to provide quality support to the Regions. The reorganization was designed to promote balance between "country focus" and "sectoral excellence." (21)

The Human Development Network (HDN) is formed, along with the HNP Sector Board, when Bank reorganization groups sector staff into regional sector units or departments. Sector staff work with county departments in a matrix relationship. This allows Regional managers working in the HNP sector to come together. (21)

David de Ferranti serves as Vice President and Head of HDN. Richard G.A. Feachem is named HNP Director and serves as Chair of the Sector Board. (12)

World Bank organizes and hosts an International Conference on Innovations in Health Financing. (36)

IFC sponsors a global conference on "Investing in Private Hospitals and Other

The 1997 *Health, Nutrition, and Population Sector Strategy Paper* emphasizes the importance of institutional and systemic changes to improve health outcomes for the poor, improve health system performance, and achieve sustainable financing in the health sector. (September) (15*)

Confronting AIDS: Public Priorities in a Global Epidemic makes the case for government intervention to control AIDS in developing countries from epidemiological, public health, and public economics perspectives. The report advocates that donors base their support on evidence of country-specific effectiveness for interventions, and finance key international public goods. (November) (37*)

World Bank collaborates with UN Economic Commission for Africa and UNICEF to organize the Forum on Cost Sharing in the Social Sectors of Sub-Saharan Africa. Fifteen principles for cost sharing in health and education are agreed upon at the Forum. (38)

The World Bank and The Danish Ministry of Foreign Affairs cohost a meeting for donor agencies in Copenhagen to discuss sectorwide approaches. At the meeting the term SWAp is coined, a SWAp guide is commissioned, and an Inter-Agency Group on SWAp is formed. (32)

(Table continues next page)

Appendix A: World Bank Group HNP Timeline *(continued)*

Year	World Bank group events	HNP sector events	HNP publications and strategies	HNP partnerships and commitments
		Health Delivery Systems in Developing Countries: Opportunities and Risks," bringing together IFC and World Bank staff and other major private health care players from developing and developed countries.		
1998	President Wolfensohn's address at the Annual Meetings warns that financial reforms are not sufficient, that human needs and social justice must also be sought. (1)	The World Bank launches AIDS Vaccine Task Force to speed up deployment of effective and affordable AIDS vaccine. It supports high-level dialogue with policy makers and industry, both "push" and "pull" strategies to generate investments in research and development, and sponsors studies of potential demand for a vaccine in developing countries. (April) (1)		The World Bank partners with WHO and Smith Kline Beecham to initiate a Program to Eliminate Elephantiasis by distributing drugs free of charge to governments and collaborating organizations. (January) (1)
	Assessing Aid: What Works, What Doesn't and Why concludes that there is a role for foreign aid and that properly managed aid can contribute to improving people's lives. It argues that institutional development and policy reforms along with strong three-way partnership among recipient countries, aid agencies, and donor countries can improve the impact of foreign assistance. (39*)	The World Bank Institute develops a course and learning program titled "Adapting to Change" as a response to the ICPD. (40)		The World Bank, WHO, UNDP, and UNICEF launch Roll Back Malaria to provide a coordinated global approach to halve malaria by 2010. (41)
	IFC introduces its frontier country strategy to steer resources toward "pioneering" or underserved sectors in high-risk and/or low-income countries. (3a)	Christopher Lovelace is appointed Director of the HNP Sector. (12)		
		The Health Care Best Practice Group is formed in IFC to analyze potential investments in health and to share and leverage knowledge about the health care industry that was developing across IFC departments. Nevertheless, the group has no decision-making role. (4a)		
1999	Wolfensohn calls for development partners to adopt a Comprehensive Development Framework, which aims to improve the effectiveness of development activities and move beyond individual projects, promoting national leadership and consensus, and requiring a commitment to	The AIDS Campaign Team for Africa (ACT *africa*) unit is created to help mainstream HIV/AIDS activities in all sectors. (21)	*Population and the World Bank: Adapting to Change* is shaped largely by its commitment to the 1994 ICPD and by an emphasis on health sector reform in the 1990s. Its objective is to address population issues with a people-centered and multisectoral approach that improves reproductive health through access to information and	The World Bank partners to establish The Global Alliance for Vaccines and Immunization (GAVI), a public-private partnership, to ensure financing to save children's lives and people's health through widespread vaccinations. (46)
		Eduardo A. Doryan is appointed HDN Vice President. (12)		

expanded partnership, transparency, and accountability. (January) (33)

Bolivia becomes the pilot country for the CDF with two loans for health and institutional reform. (June) (1)

In preparation for WDR 2000/2001, the Bank launches the *Voices of the Poor* study. The study focused on perceptions of a quality of life; pressing problems and priorities; the quality of interactions with key public, market and civil society institutions in their lives; and changes in gender and social relations. (September) (42*)

Wolfensohn appointed for second term as World Bank president. (September) (33)

Wolfensohn links corruption and poverty at International Anti-Corruption Conference in Durban. He states that the Bank will position corruption as a central issue to development, apply external pressures for change at the country level while encouraging internal pressures for change, and create partnerships to address corruption issues. (October) (33)

The World Bank and International Monetary Fund announce that concessionary lending to 81 eligible poor countries will be based on poverty reduction strategies, initiating the Poverty Reduction Support Paper process. (43)

Enhanced HIPC launched. HIPC initiative is modified to provide deeper and broader relief, faster relief, and to create a more direct link between debt relief and poverty reduction through Poverty Reduction Strategy Papers. (1)

IEG releases an evaluation of the HNP sector that suggests that the Bank improve knowledge management, develop more flexible instruments, and support increased economic and sector work to help countries identify challenges and improve the efficiency, effectiveness, and equity of health reforms. It argues

The Health and Education Unit is established in IFC.

services, and recognizes the importance of contextual factors such as gender equity and human rights. (January) (31*)

The Bank's new strategy to fight HIV/AIDS in Africa in partnership with African government and Joint UN Program on HIV/AIDS (UNAIDS) approved by Regional Leadership Team. (May) (21)

A Health Sector Strategy for the Europe and Central Asia Region responds to changes in the health care systems, particularly in transition countries, by providing a guide to support regionally appropriate, intersectoral health system reforms. Key priorities are identified as: (i) promoting wellness and reducing the prevalence of avoidable illness; (ii) creating affordable and sustainable delivery systems; and (iii) maintaining functioning health systems during the reform process. (September) (45*)

The document "Investing in Private Health Care: A Note on Strategic Direction for IFC" is prepared by IFC's Health Care Best Practice Group. (5a)

(Table continues next page)

Appendix A: World Bank Group HNP Timeline (continued)

Year	World Bank group events	HNP sector events	HNP publications and strategies	HNP partnerships and commitments
	that projects had been too complex, had neglected institutional analysis and that monitoring and evaluation was almost nonexistent. It urged that the sector "do better, not more," that is, be more selective to do a few things better rather than too much with poor results. (44)			
2000	World Bank announces a plan to work with church groups in Africa to fight poverty and AIDS. (March) (1)

Thousands of demonstrators protest at the Development Committee's Spring meetings in Washington. The Development Committee renews its pledge to speed up debt relief and to support the fight against AIDS. (March) (1) | Wolfensohn addresses the UN Security Council and calls for increased resource allocation to fight a "War on AIDS," noting the epidemic's devastating effects on the developing world, especially Africa. (January) (33)

The first Multicountry AIDS Program (MAP) is approved by the Board and provides a $500 million envelope for financing HIV/AIDS projects in Africa. (September) (21) | The overall objective of the *World Bank Strategy for Health, Nutrition, and Population in East Asia and the Pacific Region* is to improve the Bank's effectiveness in health, nutrition, and population in the region. The strategy urges selectivity and flexibility to develop new approaches, as necessary, based on lessons learned and experience in the region. It prioritizes: improving outcomes for the poor, enhancing the performance of health care systems, and securing sustainable financing. (June) (47*)

World Bank and WHO issue a publication, *Tobacco Control in Developing Countries*. It argues that a reduction in tobacco use is essential to improve global health. (August) (48*)

Intensifying Action Against AIDS in Africa emphasizes the importance of increased advocacy to strengthen political commitment to fighting HIV/AIDS, mobilization of resources, and strengthening the knowledge base. It advocates allocation of increased resources and technical support to assist African partners and the World Bank to mainstream HIV/AIDS into all sectors. (August) (49*)

World Bank releases 44 country reports on Socio-Economic Differences in Health, Nutrition and Population. The reports stress that the poorest sectors of the population must receive adequate healthcare. (November) (50*) | At the World Economic Forum, Wolfensohn urges world leaders to support GAVI and its campaign for children. (January) (33)

At the Second World Water Forum, Wolfensohn pledges the Bank's support to ensure that everyone has water services for health, food, energy, and the environment. The approach he outlines emphasizes participatory institutions as well as technological and financial innovation. (March) (1)

At the XIIIth International AIDS Conference, the World Bank pledges $500 million. The Multicountry AIDS Program, developed with UNAIDS, helps countries to implement national HIV/AIDS programs. (July) (1)

The Bank-Netherlands Water Partnership Program (BNWPP) is established to improve water security by promoting innovative approaches to Integrated Water Resources Management (IWRM), and thereby contribute to poverty reduction. (51) |

2001

WDR 2000/2001: Attacking Poverty emphasizes that insecurity, in income or health services, is one of many deprivations suffered by the poor. (52*)

The World Bank announces that it will join the UN as a full partner to implement the Millennium Development Goals and to put these goals at the center of the development agenda. (September) (1)

World Bank makes a Declaration of Commitment at Special Session of the UN General Assembly, reaffirming pledges made by world leaders to halt and reverse the spread of HIV/AIDS by 2015. (June) (33)

The Water Supply and Sanitation Program (WSP) Council is created to oversee program activities and guide strategic development in water and sanitation. (53)

Board of Executive Directors approves a gender and development mainstreaming strategy. (54)

First poverty reduction support credit (PRSC) approved. (1)

Bank announces it will build upon current programs and follow the Caribbean Regional Strategic Plan of Action for HIV/AIDS, devoting up to $150 million to the fight against HIV/AIDS in the Caribbean. (April) (21)

Joseph Ritzen appointed HDN Vice President. (June) (1)

Leadership Program on AIDS launched by the World Bank Institute (WBI) to build capacity for accelerated implementation of HIV/AIDS programs. (21)

IFC Against AIDS is launched with the idea of accelerating the involvement of the private sector in the fight against HIV/AIDS through risk management and implementation of workplace programs. (6a)

The Health and Education Unit becomes a Department within IFC. (7a)

Sub-regional HIV/AIDS strategy for Caribbean. *HIV/AIDS in the Caribbean: Issues and Options* released. (January) (55*)

The Bank and partners gather in Washington, to further commit to operationalize the Amsterdam Declaration. The Global Plan to Stop TB calls for expansion of access to DOTS and increased financial backing for the program from governments throughout the world. (October) (56)

The Bank's Water and Sanitation Program forms the Private-Public Partnership for Handwashing with the London School of Hygiene and Tropical Medicine, the Academy for Educational Development, USAID, UNICEF, the Bank-Netherlands Water Partnership, and the private sector. (57)

The Bank becomes a trustee of the Global Fund to Fight HIV/AIDS, TB, and Malaria (GFATM), a financing mechanism established to foster partnerships between governments, civil society, the private sector, and affected communities to increase resources and direct financing toward efforts to fight HIV/AIDS, TB, and malaria. (58)

In cooperation with the Gates Foundation and Dutch and Swedish governments, the World Bank Health and Poverty Thematic Group initiates the Reaching the Poor Program (RPP). RPP is an effort to find better ways to ensure that the benefits of HNP programs flow to disadvantaged population groups through research, policy guidance, and advocacy. (1)

The Bank joins the Rockefeller Foundation, Sida/SAREC, and Wellcome Trust to launch the INDEPTH Network, an international platform of sentinel demographic sites that provides health and demographic data and research to enable developing countries to set evidence-based health priorities and policies. (59)

The Bank and USAID cohost the Annual Meetings of the Global Partnership to Eliminate Riverblindness in Washington. The partners pledged to eliminate riverblindness in Africa by 2010. (1)

(Table continues next page)

Appendix A: World Bank Group HNP Timeline *(continued)*

Year	World Bank group events	HNP sector events	HNP publications and strategies	HNP partnerships and commitments
2002	Wolfensohn presents a seven-point Post-Monterrey Action Plan to the Development Committee on how to boost development aid and effectiveness, and translate Monterrey commitments into results. (April) (33) From this point, Country Assistance Strategies (CASs), the main vehicle for making strategic choices about program design and resource allocations for individual countries, were based on Poverty Reduction Support Papers in low-income countries. (July) (60) IDA announces that 18–21 percent of IDA would be in grants and available for specific activities and for the debt-vulnerable poorest countries. (July) (1)	$500 million is approved for the second stage of its Multicountry HIV/AIDS Program for Africa (MAP). (February) (1) WBI's course "Adapting to Change" becomes "Achieving the MDGs: Reproductive Health, Poverty Reduction, and Health Sector Reform." (40)	The HNP Sector Board presents an HNP strategy update to the Board. The presentation reviews trends in project lending and objectives, analytic and advisory services, OAG ratings, IFC lending for HNP, and staffing. The update reconfirms the sector's commitment to the objectives in the 1997 strategy. It also emphasizes that greater country selectivity and diversity in lending instruments will be pursued along with efforts to sharpen the focus on quality and effectiveness, work more closely with clients and communities, and improve training for staff and their allocation to ensure the appropriate skills mix. (March) (61) The 2002 IFC Health Strategy is presented to the Board of Directors.	The Global/HIV AIDS program is created along with the Global Monitoring and Evaluation Team (GAMET). GAMET is housed at the World Bank and supports efforts with UNAIDS to build country-level monitoring and evaluation capacities as well as coordinate technical support. (June) (21) First phase of Bank-Netherlands Water Partnership-Water Supply and Sanitation initiated. (51) Global Alliance for Improved Nutrition (GAIN) created at a special UN session for children. The World Bank is a key partner, mainly managing trust funds and program implementation. (62)
2003	*World Bank Annual Report* describes the Bank's commitment to meeting the MDGs and emphasizes its commitment to four priority sectors including HIV/AIDS, water and sanitation, health, and education for all. (September) (1)	Jean-Louis Sarbib assumes HDN Vice Presidency. (July) (12) Board approves first pilots of buy-down mechanism in several polio eradication projects in Pakistan and Nigeria. Projects were financed by Gates Foundation, UNF, Rotary International, and the Centers for Disease Control and Prevention. (63) Romania Dialysis is the first public-private partnership (PPP) project in health approved by IFC.	Regional AIDS strategy for ECA published: *Averting AIDS Crises in Eastern Europe and Central Asia* (September) (64*)	The Bank and the Pan-American Health Organization (PAHO) inaugurate the "Health Partnership for Knowledge Sharing and Learning in the Americas." The initiative promotes the use of technology to share expertise in order to meet the MDGs across the region. (October) (1)

2004		
Water Resources Sector Strategy: Strategic Directions for World Bank Engagement is published. The strategy highlights the centrality of water resource management and development to sustainable growth and poverty reduction. It argues that the World Bank is perceived to have a comparative advantage in the area. It emphasizes the need to tailor Country Water Assistance Strategies to be consistent with country context, CASs, and Poverty Reduction Support Papers. (January) (65)	Regional HIV/AIDS strategy for East Asia and Pacific published *Addressing HIV/AIDS in East Asia and the Pacific.* (January) (69*)	WHO and the Bank cosponsor the First High-Level Forum on the Health MDGs. Heads of development agencies, bilateral agencies, global health initiatives, and health and finance ministers agree on four action areas: resources for health and poverty reduction papers; aid effectiveness and harmonization; human resources; monitoring performance. (January) (1)
Reaching the Poor Program sponsors global conference for researchers to disseminate evidence of how well health and other social programs reach the poor and to produce policy guidelines based upon the evidence. (February) (66)	*Improving Health, Nutrition, and Population Outcomes in Sub-Saharan Africa—The Role of the World Bank* notes that positive trends in health indicators have slowed or reversed in Sub-Saharan Africa. It argues that the Bank must use its comparative advantage to work with governments and partners to strengthen the capacity of countries to improve health outcomes. Nutrition and population must remain central issues in development in Sub-Saharan Africa and accordingly, the report presents a regional guide to shape strategy formulation at the country or subregional level. (December) (70*)	
The Bank sponsors an event for 35 African ambassadors, Harmonizing Approaches to Health in Africa, to intensify efforts to improve women's health in Africa and plan follow-up activities. (April) (1)	IFC clarifies five strategic priorities, of which health and education are one. (8a)	
IEG releases an evaluation of the Bank's approach to global programs, *Addressing the Challenges of Globalization.* The evaluation recommends that the Bank separate oversight of global programs from management, improve standards of governance and management of individual programs, reevaluate selection and exit criteria, strengthen links between global programs and country strategies, and strengthen evaluations and review of global programs within the Bank. (67*)		
WDR 2004: *Making Services Work for Poor People* identifies good governance and accountability mechanisms as key determinants of health system performance. (68*)		

(Table continues next page)

Appendix A: World Bank Group HNP Timeline *(continued)*

Year	World Bank group events	HNP sector events	HNP publications and strategies	HNP partnerships and commitments
2005	Paul Wolfowitz is approved by the Board of Executive Directors as the World Bank's 10th President. (March) (1) In his speech at the Annual Meetings, Wolfowitz emphasizes the importance of leadership and accountability, civil society and women, and the rule of law as well as focusing on results. When speaking on the importance of health on the development agenda, he emphasizes the World Bank's commitment to fight malaria with the same intensity as HIV/AIDS. (September) (71) An IEG evaluation of the Bank's HIV/AIDS Assistance, *Committing to Results: Improving the Effectiveness of HIV/AIDS Assistance,* is released. It finds that the Bank's support has raised commitment and access to services, but the effect on the spread of HIV and survival is unclear. It recommends that the Bank: help governments to be strategic and selective, and prioritize high-impact activities and the highest-risk behaviors; strengthen national institutions to manage and implement long-run responses; and improve monitoring and evaluation to strengthen the local evidence base for decision making. (21*)	When the Adviser for Population and Reproductive, Maternal and Child Health (Elizabeth Lule) is appointed as manager of ACTAfrica, the Adviser position is eliminated. (January) (72) The Life Sciences Group is established within IFC's Global Manufacturing Department.	*Rolling Back Malaria: The World Bank Global Strategy and Booster Program* provides the basis and rationale for initiating the five-year Booster Program for Malaria Control. Its objectives are to increase coverage, improve outcomes, and build capacity. Described as a "new business model," it prioritizes flexible, country-driven, and results-focused approaches. (January) (41*)	World Bank partners launch the Health Metrics Network, a global partnership to improve the quality, availability, and dissemination of data for decision making in health. (June) (73)

| 2006 | Task Force on Avian Flu for Africa established to manage the information, communication, and coordination aspects of the response to avian influenza. It supports country teams to prepare individual country operations; helps coordinate the region's response with the global and Bank-wide funding programs, with donors, and mobilize additional funding as necessary. (74) | Cristian Baeza appointed as Acting HNP Director (February) (75) | *Repositioning Nutrition as Central to Development: A Strategy for Large-Scale Action* aims to position nutrition as a priority on the development agenda at both the country and international levels to bolster increased commitments and investment to fight malnutrition. It prioritizes: approaches that reach the poor and most vulnerable at strategic stages in their development; scaling-up proven and cost-effective programs; reorienting ineffective programs; improving nutrition through deliberate activities in other sectors; supporting action research and learning by doing; and mainstreaming nutrition into development strategies. (January) (76*)

 Health Financing Revisited: A Practitioner's Guide reviews the policy options and tools available for health finance in low- and middle-income countries. Key priorities include: (i) mobilizing increased and sustainable government health spending; (ii) improving governance and regulation to strengthen the capacity of health systems and ensure that investments are equitable and efficient; and (iii) coordinating donors to make more flexible and longer-term commitments that are aligned with the development goals of a country. (May) (77*) | World Bank cosponsors the International Pledging Conference on Avian and Human Influenza in Beijing to assess financing needs at country, regional and global levels. (January) (74)

 World Bank joins the International Monetary Fund and the African Development Bank in implementing the Multilateral Debt Relief Initiative (MDRI), forgiving 100 percent of eligible outstanding debt owed to these three institutions by all countries reaching the completion point of the HIPC Initiative. The MDRI will effectively double the volume of debt relief already expected from the enhanced HIPC Initiative. (78) |
| 2007 | Paul Wolfowitz resigns as World Bank President. (June) (79)

 Robert Zoellick becomes 11th World Bank President. (July) (80) | Joy Phumaphi becomes Vice President of the Human Development Network. (February) (81)

 Julian Schweitzer becomes HNP Sector Director. (October) (82)

 IFC Against AIDS is integrated into the Small and Medium Enterprises Department. | The objective of the 2007 World Bank Strategy for Health, Nutrition, and Population Results is to use a selective and disciplined framework to redouble efforts to support client countries to: improve HNP outcomes, especially for the poor; protect households from illness; ensure sustainable financing; and improve sector governance and reduce corruption. (April) (63*) | World Bank signs agreement to join the International Health Partnership. The Partnership aims to improve the work of donor and developing countries and international agencies to create and implement plans and services that improve health outcomes for the poor. (September) (84) |

(Table continues next page)

Appendix A: World Bank Group HNP Timeline (continued)

Year	World Bank group events	HNP sector events	HNP publications and strategies	HNP partnerships and commitments
			Population Issues in the 21st Century: The Role of the World Bank focuses on levels and trends in births, deaths, migration and population growth, and related challenges. After analyzing global and regional trends, as well as those for lending for population, the report outlines the Bank's areas of comparative advantage. It concludes that the Bank must focus analytical work on population issues, and collaborate with the private sector and global partners to develop and mainstream multisectoral population policies appropriate for low-, middle-, and high-fertility countries. (April) (83*)	
			The IFC Africa Health Strategy is presented to the Board of Directors. (9a)	

Sources: The World Bank part of this timeline was compiled by Mollie Fair, and is extracted from appendix C of "From Population Lending to HNP Results: The Evolution of the World Bank's Strategies in Health, Nutrition, and Population," IEG Working Paper, no. 2008/3, February 2008.

1. World Bank Group Archives 2005.
2. World Bank Web site. "Water Supply and Sanitation Projects the Bank's Experience: 1967–1989." (http://go.worldbank.org/8LRMSA1520)
3. King 2007.
4. World Bank Group Archives, "Sector Department Chart."
5. World Bank 1972a.
6. World Bank 1972b.
7. Golladay and Liese 1980.
8. World Bank 1973.
9. World Bank 1974.
10. World Bank 1975.
11. United Nations System Web site. "Standing Committee on Nutrition." (http://www.unsystem.org/SCN/Publications/html/mandate.html).
12. World Bank Group Archives, World Bank Group Staff Directories.
13. World Bank 1980b.
14. World Bank 1980a.
15. World Bank 1997b.
16. World Bank 1984.
17. Grosh and Muñoz 1996.
18. Harvard School of Public Health Web site. (http://www.hsph.harvard.edu/review/fellow.shtml).
19. Kapur and others 1997.
20. World Bank 1986b.
21. IEG 2005a.
22. World Bank 1986a.
23. World Bank 1988.
24. Nassim 1991.
25. World Bank 1989.
26. People and Planet. Net Web site. (http://www.peopleandplanet.net/doc.php?id=1740).
27. World Bank 1993c.
28. Jamison and others 1993.
29. World Bank 1993b.
30. World Bank 1994a.
31. World Bank 1999c.
32. Vaillancourt forthcoming.
33. World Bank Group Archives. "James D. Wolfensohn Timeline of Major Developments."
34. World Bank Web site. "Quality Assurance Group." (http://web.worldbank.org/WBSITE/EXTERNAL/PROJECTS/QAG/0,,contentMDK:20067126~menuPK:114865~pagePK:109617~piPK:109636~theSitePK:109609,00.html).
35. IAVI Web Site (http://www.iavi.org/viewpage.cfm?aid=24).
36. Schieber 1997.
37. World Bank 1997a.
38. UNECA, UNICEF, and World Bank. 1998.
39. World Bank 1998a.
40. White, Merrick, and Yazbeck 2006.
41. World Bank 2005b.
42. Narayan and Petesch 2002.
43. Wagstaff and Claeson 2004.
44. IEG 1999.
45. World Bank 1999a.
46. Walt and Buse 2006.
47. World Bank 2000b.
48. Jha and Chaloupka 2000.
49. World Bank 2000a.
50. Gwatkin and others 2000.
51. Bank-Netherlands Water Partnership Program Web site (http://www-esd.worldbank.org/bnwpp/).
52. World Bank 2001c.
53. WSP Web site (http://www.wsp.org).
54. World Bank Web site. "Gender and Development." (http://web.worldbank.org/WBSITE/EXTERNAL/TOPICS/EXTGENDER/0,,menuPK:336874~pagePK:149018~piPK:149093~theSitePK:336868,00.html).
55. World Bank 2001a.
56. Stop TB Partnership Web site (http://www.stoptb.org/stop_tb_initiative/).
57. Global Public-Private Partnership for Handwashing with Soap Web site (http://www.globalhandwashing.org/).
58. Kaiser Family Foundation Web site (www.kff.org/hivaids/timeline).
59. INDEPTH Web site (http://www.indepth-network.org/core_documents/vision.htm).
60. World Bank Web site. "Strategies." (http://intranet.worldbank.org/WBSITE/INTRANET/SECTORS/HEALTHNUTRITIONANDPOPULATION/INTHIVAIDS/0,,contentMDK:20120702~menuPK:375837~pagePK:210082~piPK:210098~theSitePK:375799,00.html).
61. HNP Sector Board. (draft, February 7, 2002). "Health, Nutrition and Population Sector Strategy Briefing."
62. GAIN Web site (http://www.gainhealth.org/gain/ch/en-en/index.cfm?page-/gain/home/about_gain/history).

63. World Bank 2007a.
64. World Bank 2003b.
65. World Bank 2004d.
66. World Bank Web site. (http://web.worldbank.org/WBSITE/EXTERNAL/TOPICS/EXTHEALTHNUTRITIONANDPOPULATION/EXTPAH/0,,contentMDK:20744334~pagePK:210058~piPK:210062~theSitePK:400476,00.html).
67. IEG 2004a.
68. World Bank 2003b.
69. World Bank 2004a.
70. World Bank 2004c.
71. World Bank Web site. News and Broadcast. "Annual Meetings 2005 Opening Press Conference with Paul Wolfowitz." (http://web.worldbank.org/WBSITE/EXTERNAL/NEWS/0,,contentMDK:20656903~pagePK:64257043~piPK:437376~theSitePK:4607,00.html).
72. World Bank Web site. "News and Broadcasts>" http://web.worldbank.org/WBSITE/EXTERNAL/NEWS/0,,contentMDK:20138122~pagePK:64257043~piPK:437376~theSitePK:4607,00.html
73. WHO Web site. "What is HMN?" (http://www.who.int/healthmetrics/about/whatishmn/en/index.html).
74. World Bank Web site. "Avian and Pandemic Influenza." (http://web.worldbank.org/WBSITE/EXTERNAL/TOPICS/EXTHEALTHNUTRITIONAND

POPULATION/EXTTOPAVFLU/0,,menuPK:1793605~pagePK:64168427~piPK:64168435~theSitePK:1793593,00.html).
75. World Bank Web site. "Acting Assignments in HNP." (http://intranet.worldbank.org/WBSITE/INTRANET/SECTORS/HEALTHNUTRITIONANDPOPULATION/0,,contentMDK:20131131~pagePK:210082~piPK:210098~theSitePK:281628,00.html)
76. World Bank 2006c.
77. Gottret and Schieber 2006.
78. World Bank Web site. "Debt issues." (http://web.worldbank.org/WBSITE/EXTERNAL/TOPICS/EXTDEBTDEPT/0,,menuPK:64166739~pagePK:64166681~piPK:64166725~theSitePK:469043,00.html).
79. World Bank Web site. "Statements of Executive Director and President Wolfowitz." (http://intranet.worldbank.org/WBSITE/INTRANET/UNITS/INTPRESIDENT2007/INTPASTPRESIDENTS/INTPRESIDENTSTAFCONN/0,,contentMDK:21339650~menuPK:64324835~pagePK:64259040~piPK:64258864~theSitePK:1014519,00.html).
80. World Bank Web site. "President's Staff Connection." http://intranet.worldbank.org/WBSITE/INTRANET/UNITS/INTPRESIDENT2007/0,,contentMDK:21477815~menuPK:64821535~pagePK:64821348~piPK:64821341~theSitePK:3915045,00.html
81. World Bank Web site. January 30, 2007. "Interview with Joy Phumaphi, New HD Vice President." (http://intranet.worldbank.org/WBSITE/INTRANET/

UNITS/INTHDNETWORK/0,,contentMDK:21199087~menuPK:514396~pagePK:64156298~piPK:64152276~theSitePK:514373,00.html).
82. World Bank Web site. "Julian Schweitzer, Sector Director, HNP, Human Development Network." http://intranet.worldbank.org/WBSITE/INTRANET/K I O S K /0,,contentMDK:21473063~menuPK:34897~pagePK:37626~piPK:37631~theSitePK:3664,00.html
83. World Bank 2007g.
84. Department for International Development Web Site. "International Health Partnership launched today." (http://www.dfid.gov.uk/news/files/ihp/default.asp).

1a IFC 1982.
2a IFC 2002, p. 24.
3a IFC 1998.
4a IFC 2002, p. 24.
5a IFC 1999.
6a Lutalo 2006.
7a IFC 2002, p. 24.
8a IFC 2004.
9a IFC 2007a.

Note: * indicates the publication itself, otherwise, facts are reported in the cited reference.

A show of hands among Nepalese children who wash their hands after using their new latrine. Photo courtesy of George T. Keith Pitman.

APPENDIX B: DEFINITION OF THE SAMPLES USED FOR PORTFOLIO REVIEWS AND WORLD BANK HNP STAFF ANALYSIS

World Bank HNP Project Portfolio

Projects

The review of the portfolio managed by the HNP sector that is presented in chapters 2–4 included all 220 active and closed projects approved from fiscal 1997 to 2006 (table B.1). The 220 projects are listed in appendix C. Approvals of supplemental allocations for active projects are attributed to the original project; they are not considered separate operations. The count of projects in other sectors with HNP components included any project with HNP commitments, as defined below.

HNP Commitments

Up to five sector codes are assigned to every World Bank lending operation, and the percentage of the loan to be dedicated to each sector code was noted in the project design documents. HNP commitments include the amounts committed under sector codes JA (health), BK (compulsory health finance), FB (noncompulsory health finance) and other historic codes used for the health sector (HB, HC, HE, HH, HP, HR, HT, HY).

Total commitments to HNP were calculated by taking the total amount of each project allocated to these codes.[1] Because there is often more than one sector code, even for HNP-managed projects, it means that less than 100 percent of the cost of a loan or credit is actually being counted. Note, too, that for multisectoral Development Policy Loans that are essentially direct budget support to the government, the allocation across sector codes is entirely notional and does not reflect earmarked funds for any sector.

World Bank Water Supply and Sanitation Project Portfolio

The water supply and sanitation projects reviewed in chapter 4 include all 117 active and closed projects approved from fiscal 1997 to 2006 (table B.2) with financial commitments to sector codes WA (sanitation), WC (water supply), WS (sewerage), and WZ (general water, sanitation, and flood protection), and managed by the Water Supply and Sanitation Sector Board. Projects that are solely aimed at flood protection (WD) and solid waste management (WB) are not included. Supplemental credits and projects approved under emergency

Table B.1: Projects Managed by the HNP Sector by Fiscal Year of Approval and Project Status

Project status	Fiscal years					
	1997–2001		2002–06		1997–2006	
	Projects	Percent	Projects	Percent	Projects	Percent
Active	9	9	101	83	110	50
Closed	90	91	20	17	110[a]	50
Total	99	100	121	100	220	100

a. Of these, 99 had been reviewed and rated by IEG as of September 30, 2008. In addition, 2 projects were cancelled before they were implemented and thus did not receive an outcome rating.

Table B.2: Water Supply and Sanitation Projects Included in the Portfolio Review

| Project status | Fiscal years | | | | | |
| | 1997–2001 | | 2002–06 | | 1997–2006 | |
	Projects	Percent	Projects	Percent	Projects	Percent
Active	33	53	55	100	88	75
Closed[a]	29	47	0	0	29	25
Total	62	100	55	100	117	100

a. As of October 31, 2007. Implementation Completion Reports had not been received by IEG for 3 of the 29 projects at the time of the review, reducing to 26 the number of completed projects reviewed.

Table B.3: Transport Projects Included in the Portfolio Review

| Project status | Fiscal years | | | | | |
| | 1997–2001 | | 2002–06 | | 1997–2006 | |
	Projects	Percent	Projects	Percent	Projects	Percent
Active	28	22	96	93	124	54
Closed[a]	98	78	7	7	105	46
Total	126	100	103	100	229	100

a. As of June 25, 2007.

procedures were also excluded. Greater detail and the list of projects can be found in Overbey (2008).

World Bank Transport Project Portfolio

The transport projects reviewed in chapter 4 include all 229 active and closed projects approved from fiscal 1997 to 2006 (table B.3). Only projects managed by the Transport Sector Board and that had financial commitments under the sector codes TA (roads and highways), TP (ports, waterways, and shipping), TV (aviation), TW (railways), and TZ (general transportation, which includes urban transport) were included. Supplemental credits and projects approved under emergency procedures are excluded. Transport projects managed by other sector boards were excluded because the resources needed to track down the relatively small number of such projects were not warranted.[2] Thus, transport projects related to improvements of air quality that fell either under the Environment Sector Board or were funded through the Global Environment Facility (GEF) have not been reviewed.

World Bank HNP Staffing

The analysis of HNP staffing in chapter 2 uses four sets of data on World Bank staff in the HNP sector provided by the Bank's Human Resources Department:

1. **Master dataset of HNP staff.** This is a master dataset of all Bank staff at levels GF and higher as of the end of every fiscal year (June 30), from fiscal 1997 to 2007, who were mapped to the HNP sector. Staff members below level GF are not systematically mapped to a sector, so are excluded from the analysis. The datasets included the following data for each individual: fiscal year; UPI (staff identification) number; primary managing unit (PMU); unit of assignment; entry on duty (EOD); appointment type; level; job title; age; gender; whether Part I or II; years in the Bank; years in the PMU; whether posted at headquarters or in the field; duty country; whether a coterminous appointment;[3] program name; whether a manager; and whether a former Young Professional. The information

was provided separately for each fiscal year and merged by IEG. This provided the basis for a master panel dataset from which it is possible to track the movement of staff into and out of the sector, using the UPI number as the identifier.

2. **Hub dataset.** This is a dataset of all Bank staff and consultants level GE and higher assigned to the "hub" or "anchor," for the period fiscal 1997–2007. The "hub" was defined as including the units HDDHE and its successor HDNHE (the HNP hub), and HDNGA (the central unit for the AIDS program, established in 2004). The data and variables assembled for hub staff levels GF and higher are identical to those for the master HNP staff dataset. However, this dataset also includes staff at level GE and in other categories, such as junior professional associates, junior professional officers, coterminous staff, and special assignments, who were working in those units.

3. **New hires.** A dataset of all new hires of individuals directly into the World Bank HNP sector. The variables available included all of the variables in the master HNP staff dataset, plus the effective date of the hire.

4. **Exits.** A dataset of all terminations of individuals from the World Bank who were mapped to the HNP sector at the time that they left. This includes, for example, resignations, retirements, and deaths of HNP staff. The variables available for analysis included all of the variables in the master HNP staff dataset, plus the effective date that of the hire and the reason for termination.

Only a few corrections were made to the original data for the analysis. First, the original data included several individuals mapped to units in IFC who were dropped. No other individuals were dropped, though in a number of instances the unit codes did not seem to pertain to health (for example, the Board, Staff Association, External Affairs, Commodity Risk Group). Second, in the new hire and exit datasets there were often duplicates associated with conversions from one type of assignment to another—for example, the person appears as a new hire, then an exit, then a new hire shortly thereafter in another assign-

ment type. In those instances, the first time that the individual appears was used for the purposes of counting the number of new hires and their age, and in the exit dataset instances were excluded of those who had been converted to a new assignment type. The last observation was used if there was more than one appearance and the person was no longer at the Bank (or at least no longer in the HNP sector at the Bank).

Country Assistance Strategies

The desk review of CASs included a sample of the 211 CASs approved from fiscal 1997 to 2006. In light of the large number of countries in three Regions, the study reviewed: (a) all CASs for East Asia, the Middle East and North Africa, and South Asia; and (b) a random sample consisting of roughly half of all CASs for Europe and Central Asia, Latin America and the Caribbean, and Africa (table B.4). The results reported in chapters 2 and 4 have been weighted to take the stratification of the sample into account. A list of the CASs actually reviewed can be found in Sinha and Gaubatz 2009.

IFC Portfolio of Investment Projects and Advisory Services

The portfolio of 52 IFC health projects reviewed in chapter 5 includes 35 active and 17 closed projects approved from fiscal 1997 to 2007 (appendix D). Active projects are those for which IFC has financial exposure; closed projects are those with which IFC no longer has a financial relationship. Health sector projects included those with the health and pharmaceuticals sector code and additional projects with business objectives related to health (for example, a medical training project with an education sector code). Dropped projects, cancellations, rights issues, reschedulings, restructurings, supplementary investments made in the context of previously approved projects, investments through the Africa Enterprise Fund and Small Enterprise Fund, and individual investments under agency lines were excluded.[4]

Chapter 5 assesses the performance of IFC projects that reached "early operating maturity."[5] The performance of mature projects was assessed through either detailed Expanded Project Supervision Reports (XPSRs) prepared by the investment

Table B.4: Country Assistance Strategies Issued in Fiscal Years 1997–2006, by Region and Year, and the IEG Sample for Review

Region	1997–2001	2002–06	Total	Reviewed sample
Sub-Saharan Africa	29	26	55	31
Europe and Central Asia	31	29	60	29
Latin America and the Caribbean	20	20	40	21
East Asia & Pacific	12	11	23	23
Middle East and North Africa	9	10	19	19
South Asia	7	7	14	14
Total	108	103	211	137

departments and validated by IEG, or by IEG's desk review of project information for those not covered by an Expanded Project Supervision Report. For projects that had not yet reached early operating maturity, IEG gathered information about each project's characteristics and design, as well as information on implementation status in the supervision reports. Field visits supplemented the information gathered by the desk review. The objective of the field visits was to conduct in-depth validation and interviews linked to ongoing and completed investments and Advisory Services. The five countries visited were selected to achieve Regional balance, to have more than one current or past IFC health investment, to include investments in different time periods, and to include different types of investments (for example, hospitals

and pharmaceuticals). During field visits, IFC clients, government agency officials, health-related professional and business associations, relevant multilateral and/or bilateral development organizations with private sector portfolios, and other stakeholders were interviewed.

For Advisory Service projects, the monitoring and evaluation system was still in a pilot phase. IEG reviewed all health projects covered by the previous rounds of project completion report (PCR) pilots, as well as desk review of approval and supervision documents for projects not covered by the PCR. Interviews were conducted with IFC and World Bank managers, sector specialists, investment officers, and project task managers.

Appendix C: World Bank HNP Sector Projects Approved in Fiscal Years 1997–2007							
				HNP commitment ($US millions)			
Fiscal year approved	Project ID	Project name	Country	IBRD	IDA	Total HNP	Total commitment
1997	P006059	Maternal and Child Health and Nutrition II	Argentina	95.0	0.0	95.0	100.0
1997	P043418	AIDS and STD Control	Argentina	11.9	0.0	11.9	15.0
1997	P044522	Essential Hospital Services	Bosnia-Herzegovina	0.0	14.4	14.4	15.0
1997	P004034	Disease Control and Health Development	Cambodia	0.0	27.7	27.7	30.4
1997	P010473	Tuberculosis Control	India	0.0	129.6	129.6	142.4
1997	P010511	Malaria Control	India	0.0	159.9	159.9	164.8
1997	P010531	Reproductive Health	India	0.0	223.5	223.5	248.3
1997	P042540	Iodine Deficiency Control	Indonesia	19.1	0.0	19.1	28.5
1997	P001999	Health Sector Development Program	Niger	0.0	37.6	37.6	40.0
1997	P007927	Maternal Health/Child Development	Paraguay	19.2	0.0	19.2	21.8
1997	P008814	Health Reform Pilot	Russian Federation	66.0	0.0	66.0	66.0
1997	P041567	Endemic Disease	Senegal	0.0	13.9	13.9	14.9
1997	P010526	Health Services	Sri Lanka	0.0	17.5	17.5	18.8
1997	P009095	Primary Health Care Services	Turkey	13.3	0.0	13.3	14.5
1998	P045312	Health Recovery	Albania	0.0	13.9	13.9	17.0
1998	P050140	Health	Armenia	0.0	8.4	8.4	10.0
1998	P037857	Health and Population Program	Bangladesh	0.0	242.5	242.5	250.0
1998	P003566	Basic Health (Health VIII)	China	0.0	78.2	78.2	85.0
1998	P052887	Health	Comoros	0.0	6.7	6.7	8.4
1998	P007015	Provincial Health Services	Dominican Republic	28.2	0.0	28.2	30.0
1998	P039084	Health Services Modernization	Ecuador	40.5	0.0	40.5	45.0
1998	P045175	Health Sector	Egypt, Arab Rep. of	0.0	90.0	90.0	90.0
1998	P043124	Health	Eritrea	0.0	17.2	17.2	18.3
1998	P000825	Participatory HNP	Gambia	0.0	17.8	17.8	18.0
1998	P000949	Health Sector Support	Ghana	0.0	33.6	33.6	35.0
1998	P035688	National Health Development Program	Guinea-Bissau	0.0	10.8	10.8	11.7
1998	P010496	Orissa Health Systems	India	0.0	69.5	69.5	76.4
1998	P049385	Economic Restructuring	India	72.3	58.1	130.4	543.2
1998	P035827	Women and Child Development	India	0.0	273.0	273.0	300.0
1998	P036956	Safe Motherhood	Indonesia	41.2	0.0	41.2	42.5

(Table continues next page)

Appendix C: World Bank HNP Sector Projects Approved in Fiscal Years 1997–2007 *(continued)*

Fiscal year approved	Project ID	Project name	Country	HNP commitment ($US millions) IBRD	IDA	Total HNP	Total commitment
1998	P001568	Community Nutrition II	Madagascar	0.0	19.3	19.3	27.6
1998	P035689	Health Sector Investment Program	Mauritania	0.0	23.8	23.8	24.0
1998	P007720	Health System Reform - SAL	Mexico	700.0	0.0	700.0	700.0
1998	P055061	Health System Reform TA	Mexico	21.5	0.0	21.5	25.0
1998	P035753	Health Sector II	Nicaragua	0.0	18.2	18.2	24.0
1998	P004566	Early Childhood Development	Philippines	17.1	0.0	17.1	19.0
1998	P002369	Integrated Health Sector Development	Senegal	0.0	42.0	42.0	50.0
1998	P005746	Health Sector	Tunisia	48.5	0.0	48.5	50.0
1998	P040551	Nutrition and Early Childhood Development SIL	Uganda	0.0	22.1	22.1	34.0
1999	P060392	Health Reform-APL I	Bolivia	0.0	20.5	20.5	25.0
1999	P044523	Basic Health	Bosnia-Herzegovina	0.0	8.2	8.2	10.0
1999	P043874	Disease Surveillance - VIGISUS	Brazil	94.0	0.0	94.0	100.0
1999	P054120	AIDS and STD Control II	Brazil	165.0	0.0	165.0	165.0
1999	P036953	Health IX	China	9.4	47.0	56.4	60.0
1999	P000756	Health Sector Development	Ethiopia	0.0	99.0	99.0	100.0
1999	P052154	Structural Reform Support	Georgia	0.0	8.3	8.3	16.5
1999	P041568	Population and Reproductive Health	Guinea	0.0	9.9	9.9	11.3
1999	P045051	HIV/AIDS II	India	0.0	183.4	183.4	191.0
1999	P050651	Maharashtra Health System	India	0.0	123.3	123.3	134.0
1999	P003967	Health V	Indonesia	38.0	0.0	38.0	44.7
1999	P039749	Health Sector Reform	Jordan	34.0	0.0	34.0	35.0
1999	P046499	Health Restructuring	Kazakhstan	39.5	0.0	39.5	42.5
1999	P058520	Health	Latvia	10.8	0.0	10.8	12.0
1999	P036038	Population/Family Planning	Malawi	0.0	5.0	5.0	5.0
1999	P040652	Health Sector Development Program (PRODESS)	Mali	0.0	40.0	40.0	40.0
1999	P055003	Nutrition, Food Security and Social Mobilization LIL	Mauritania	0.0	1.9	1.9	4.9
1999	P005525	Health Management	Morocco	64.0	0.0	64.0	66.0
1999	P040179	Health Pilot	Panama	2.2	0.0	2.2	4.3
1999	P009125	Health	Uzbekistan	26.7	0.0	26.7	30.0
2000	P055482	Public Health Surveillance and Disease Control	Argentina	50.4	0.0	50.4	52.5
2000	P063388	Health Insurance for the Uninsured	Argentina	3.3	0.0	3.3	4.9
2000	P050751	National Nutrition Program	Bangladesh	0.0	82.8	82.8	92.0
2000	P055157	Health Sector Reform	Bulgaria	51.3	0.0	51.3	63.3
2000	P055122	Health Sector Support	Chad	0.0	33.6	33.6	41.5
2000	P051273	Health System	Croatia	27.3	0.0	27.3	29.0
2000	P067330	Immunization Strengthening	India	0.0	129.8	129.8	142.6
2000	P050657	Health Systems Development	India	0.0	95.7	95.7	110.0

Appendix C: World Bank HNP Sector Projects Approved in Fiscal Years 1997–2007 *(continued)*

Fiscal year approved	Project ID	Project name	Country	HNP commitment ($US millions)			Total commitment
				IBRD	IDA	Total HNP	
2000	P049545	Provincial Health I	Indonesia	0.0	33.8	33.8	38.0
2000	P059477	Water and Sanitation for Low Income Communities II	Indonesia	0.0	24.0	24.0	77.4
2000	P069943	Primary Health Care and Nutrition II	Iran	82.7	0.0	82.7	87.0
2000	P053200	Health Sector Reform	Lesotho	0.0	4.5	4.5	6.5
2000	P035780	Health	Lithuania	18.7	0.0	18.7	21.2
2000	P051741	Health Sector Support II	Madagascar	0.0	38.4	38.4	40.0
2000	P062932	Health Reform Program	Peru	77.6	0.0	77.6	80.0
2000	P008797	Health Sector Reform	Romania	37.6	0.0	37.6	40.0
2000	P051418	Health Sector Management	Slovenia	5.9	0.0	5.9	9.5
2000	P058358	Health Sector Development Project	Solomon Islands	0.0	3.5	3.5	4.0
2000	P049894	Primary Health Care	Tajikistan	0.0	4.8	4.8	5.4
2000	P058627	Health Sector Development Program	Tanzania	0.0	20.5	20.5	22.0
2001	P069293	Health Reform LIL	Azerbaijan	0.0	4.0	4.0	5.0
2001	P069933	HIV/AIDS Prevention	Bangladesh	0.0	39.2	39.2	40.0
2001	P075220	HIV/AIDS I	Barbados	14.4	0.0	14.4	15.2
2001	P074212	Health Sector Reform APL II	Bolivia	0.0	32.2	32.2	35.0
2001	P073065	Multisectoral HIV/AIDS	Cameroon	0.0	20.0	20.0	50.0
2001	P071505	HIV/AIDS Prevention & Control Project	Dominican Republic	21.8	0.0	21.8	25.0
2001	P065713	HIV/AIDS, Malaria, STD, and TB Control	Eritrea	0.0	33.2	33.2	40.0
2001	P069886	MAP	Ethiopia	0.0	47.8	47.8	59.7
2001	P060329	HIV/AIDS Rapid Response	Gambia	0.0	11.0	11.0	15.0
2001	P071617	AIDS Response Project (GARFUND)	Ghana	0.0	21.3	21.3	25.0
2001	P067543	Leprosy II	India	0.0	27.3	27.3	30.0
2001	P049539	Provincial Health II	Indonesia	58.8	37.2	96.0	103.2
2001	P070920	HIV/AIDS Disaster Response	Kenya	0.0	31.5	31.5	50.0
2001	P066486	Decentralized Reproductive Health and HIV/AIDS	Kenya	0.0	46.0	46.0	50.0
2001	P051372	Health II	Kyrgyz Republic	0.0	12.5	12.5	15.0
2001	P066321	Basic Health Care III	Mexico	343.0	0.0	343.0	350.0
2001	P051174	Health Investment Fund	Moldova	0.0	9.5	9.5	10.0
2001	P064926	Health Sector Management	Samoa	0.0	3.9	3.9	5.0
2001	P072482	HIV/AIDS Control	Uganda	0.0	36.6	36.6	47.5
2001	P050495	Caracas Metropolitan Health	Venezuela, R. B. de	28.8	0.0	28.8	30.3
2002	P073118	Multisectoral HIV/AIDS	Benin	0.0	13.6	13.6	23.0
2002	P057665	Family Health Extension Project I	Brazil	64.6	0.0	64.6	68.0
2002	P071433	HIV/AIDS Disaster Response	Burkina Faso	0.0	16.3	16.3	22.0
2002	P071371	Multisectoral HIV/AIDS Control and Orphans	Burundi	0.0	10.8	10.8	36.0
2002	P073525	HIV/AIDS	Central African Rep.	0.0	8.0	8.0	17.0
2002	P074249	HIV/AIDS	Cape Verde	0.0	6.5	6.5	9.0

(Table continues next page)

Appendix C: World Bank HNP Sector Projects Approved in Fiscal Years 1997–2007 *(continued)*

Fiscal year approved	Project ID	Project name	Country	HNP commitment ($US millions) IBRD	IDA	Total HNP	Total commitment
2002	P072226	Population and AIDS II	Chad	0.0	16.5	16.5	24.6
2002	P071147	Tuberculosis Control	China	96.7	0.0	96.7	104.0
2002	P073892	Health Sector Strengthening and Modernization	Costa Rica	16.2	0.0	16.2	17.0
2002	P071062	Health Sector Development	Djibouti	0.0	15.0	15.0	15.0
2002	P067986	Earthquake Emergency Reconstruction and Health Services Extension	El Salvador	135.5	0.0	135.5	142.6
2002	P053575	Health System Reform	Honduras	0.0	26.6	26.6	27.1
2002	P074641	HIV/AIDS Prevention and Control II	Jamaica	13.5	0.0	13.5	15.0
2002	P072987	Multisectoral STI/HIV/AIDS Prevention I	Madagascar	0.0	15.4	15.4	20.0
2002	P070290	Health System Development II	Nigeria	0.0	111.8	111.8	127.0
2002	P070291	HIV/AIDS Program Development	Nigeria	0.0	82.2	82.2	90.3
2002	P069916	Social Expenditure Management II	Philippines	20.0	0.0	20.0	100.0
2002	P074059	HIV/AIDS Prevention and Control	Senegal	0.0	25.8	25.8	30.0
2002	P070541	Nutrition Enhancement Program	Senegal	0.0	11.3	11.3	14.7
2002	P073883	HIV/AIDS Response	Sierra Leone	0.0	13.1	13.1	15.0
2002	P073305	Regional Blood Transfusion Centers	Vietnam	0.0	38.2	38.2	38.2
2002	P043254	Health Reform Support	Yemen	0.0	25.1	25.1	27.5
2003	P078324	Health Sector Emergency Rehabilitation	Afghanistan	0.0	53.0	53.0	59.6
2003	P071004	Social Insurance TA	Bosnia-Herzegovina	0.0	4.6	4.6	7.0
2003	P080400	AIDS and STD Control III	Brazil	100.0	0.0	100.0	100.0
2003	P054119	Bahia Development (Health)	Brazil	9.0	0.0	9.0	30.0
2003	P070542	Health Sector Support	Cambodia	0.0	24.3	24.3	27.0
2003	P073603	HIV/AIDS, Malaria and TB Control	Djibouti	0.0	3.6	3.6	12.0
2003	P076802	Health Reform Support	Dominican Republic	30.0	0.0	30.0	30.0
2003	P082395	First Programmatic Human Dev. Reform	Ecuador	14.0	0.0	14.0	50.0
2003	P040555	Primary Health Care Development	Georgia	0.0	17.3	17.3	20.3
2003	P073649	Health Sector Program Support II	Ghana	0.0	89.6	89.6	89.6
2003	P076715	HIV/AIDS Prevention and Control II	Grenada	1.5	1.5	3.0	6.0
2003	P073378	Multi-Sectoral AIDS	Guinea	0.0	7.1	7.1	20.3
2003	P075056	Food and Drugs Capacity Building	India	0.0	54.0	54.0	54.0
2003	P073772	Health Workforce and Services (PHP III)	Indonesia	21.8	52.2	73.9	105.6
2003	P074122	AIDS Control	Moldova	0.0	5.5	5.5	5.5
2003	P078053	HIV/AIDS Response	Mozambique	0.0	22.0	22.0	55.0
2003	P071612	Multisectoral STI/HIV/AIDS II	Niger	0.0	10.0	10.0	25.0
2003	P080295	Polio Eradication	Nigeria	0.0	28.7	28.7	28.7
2003	P074856	HIV/AIDS Prevention Project	Pakistan	0.0	37.1	37.1	37.1
2003	P081909	Partnership For Polio Eradication	Pakistan	0.0	20.0	20.0	20.0
2003	P064237	TB/AIDS Control	Russia	150.0	0.0	150.0	150.0
2003	P046497	Health Reform Implementation	Russia	24.0	0.0	24.0	30.0
2003	P071374	Multisectoral HIV/AIDS	Rwanda	0.0	10.7	10.7	30.5

Appendix C: World Bank HNP Sector Projects Approved in Fiscal Years 1997–2007 *(continued)*

Fiscal year approved	Project ID	Project name	Country	HNP commitment ($US millions)			Total commitment
				IBRD	IDA	Total HNP	
2003	P077675	Health	Serbia	0.0	20.0	20.0	20.0
2003	P074128	Health Sector Reconstruction and Development	Sierra Leone	0.0	14.0	14.0	20.0
2003	P074730	National HIV/AIDS Prevention	Sri Lanka	0.0	6.3	6.3	12.6
2003	P076798	HIV/AIDS Prevention and Control Project	St . Kitts & Nevis	2.9	0.0	2.9	4.1
2003	P075528	HIV/AIDS Prevention and Control	Trinidad & Tobago	20.0	0.0	20.0	20.0
2003	P069857	TB/AIDS Control	Ukraine	45.0	0.0	45.0	60.0
2003	P003248	Zanara HIV/AIDS APL	Zambia	0.0	16.8	16.8	42.0
2004	P082613	Regional HIVAIDS Treatment Acceleration	Africa	0.0	38.9	38.9	59.8
2004	P074850	HIV/AIDS Project for Abidjan Lagos Transport Corridor	Africa	0.0	6.8	6.8	16.6
2004	P071025	Provincial Maternal-Child Health	Argentina	115.4	0.0	115.4	135.8
2004	P072637	Provincial Maternal-Child Health Sector Adjustment	Argentina	675.0	0.0	675.0	750.0
2004	P073974	Health Systems Modernization	Armenia	0.0	17.9	17.9	19.0
2004	P083169	HIV/AIDS and STI Prevention and Control	Bhutan	0.0	2.6	2.6	5.8
2004	P087841	Social Sector Programmatic Credit	Bolivia	0.0	6.3	6.3	25.0
2004	P083013	Disease Surveillance and Control II	Brazil	57.0	0.0	57.0	100.0
2004	P080721	HIV/AIDS Prevention and Control	Caribbean Region	0.0	2.3	2.3	9.0
2004	P077513	HIV/AIDS & Health	Congo, Rep. of	0.0	4.6	4.6	19.0
2004	P073442	HIV/AIDS Global Mitigation Support	Guinea-Bissau	0.0	1.4	1.4	7.0
2004	P076722	HIV/AIDS Prevention and Control	Guyana	0.0	4.7	4.7	10.0
2004	P050655	Rajasthan Health Systems Development	India	0.0	71.2	71.2	89.0
2004	P086670	Health Sector Management	Macedonia, FYR	9.0	0.0	9.0	10.0
2004	P073821	Multi-Sectoral AIDS	Malawi	0.0	3.5	3.5	35.0
2004	P078368	Multisectoral HIV/AIDS Control	Mauritania	0.0	4.2	4.2	21.0
2004	P082223	Health System (Montenegro)	Montenegro	0.0	4.9	4.9	7.0
2004	P075979	Social Sector Support	São Tomé & Principe	0.0	1.7	1.7	6.5
2004	P082879	Health TA	Slovak Republic	4.3	0.0	4.3	12.4
2004	P065954	Health Reform - SECAL	Slovak Republic	50.3	0.0	50.3	62.9
2004	P050740	Health Sector Development	Sri Lanka	0.0	26.4	26.4	60.0
2004	P082335	Health Sector Development II	Tanzania	0.0	58.5	58.5	65.0
2004	P071014	HIV/AIDS	Tanzania	0.0	10.5	10.5	70.0
2004	P075230	Health Sector Support	Tonga	0.0	10.6	10.6	10.9
2004	P074053	Health Transition	Turkey	24.2	0.0	24.2	60.6
2005	P080406	African Regional Capacity Building Network for HIV/AIDS Prevention, Treatment, & Care	Africa	0.0	8.5	8.5	10.0
2005	P080413	HIV/AIDS Great Lakes Initiative APL	Africa	0.0	11.0	11.0	20.0
2005	P083180	HAMSET SIL	Angola	0.0	1.9	1.9	21.0
2005	P074841	HNP Sector Program	Bangladesh	0.0	120.0	120.0	300.0
2005	P091365	Social Sector Programmatic Credit II	Bolivia	0.0	3.8	3.8	15.0

(Table continues next page)

Appendix C: World Bank HNP Sector Projects Approved in Fiscal Years 1997–2007 *(continued)*

Fiscal year approved	Project ID	Project name	Country	HNP commitment ($US millions) IBRD	IDA	Total HNP	Total commitment
2005	P088663	Health Sector Enhancement	Bosnia-Herzegovina	0.0	9.4	9.4	17.0
2005	P082243	HIV/AIDS	Central America	0.0	6.0	6.0	8.0
2005	P087003	AIDS Control	Central Asia	0.0	16.3	16.3	25.0
2005	P094694	HIV/AIDS/STI/TB/Malaria/Reproductive Health	Eritrea	0.0	12.0	12.0	24.0
2005	P065126	Health Sector Support	Guinea	0.0	17.5	17.5	25.0
2005	P073651	Disease Surveillance	India	0.0	37.4	37.4	68.0
2005	P075058	Health Systems	India	0.0	88.7	88.7	110.8
2005	P087843	HIV/AIDS Capacity Building TAL	Lesotho	0.0	3.0	3.0	5.0
2005	P083401	Health Sector Support	Malawi	0.0	12.0	12.0	15.0
2005	P040613	Health Sector Program Project	Nepal	0.0	43.5	43.5	50.0
2005	P078991	Health Sector II (APL 2)	Nicaragua	0.0	10.2	10.2	11.0
2005	P079628	Women's Health and Safe Motherhood II	Philippines	12.5	0.0	12.5	16.0
2005	P078971	Health Sector Reform II	Romania	76.8	0.0	76.8	80.0
2005	P076795	HIV/AIDS Prevention and Control	St Lucia	0.8	0.8	1.7	6.4
2005	P076799	HIV/AIDS Prevention and Control	St. Vincent & the Grenadines	1.0	1.0	2.0	7.0
2005	P051370	Health II	Uzbekistan	0.0	40.0	40.0	40.0
2005	P082604	HIV/AIDS Prevention	Vietnam	0.0	24.5	24.5	35.0
2006	P082814	Health System Modernization	Albania	0.0	13.1	13.1	15.4
2006	P094220	Health Sector Reform	Azerbaijan	0.0	43.0	43.0	50.0
2006	P096482	Malaria Control Booster Program	Benin	0.0	18.6	18.6	31.0
2006	P093987	Health Sector Support and AIDS	Burkina Faso	0.0	35.3	35.3	47.7
2006	P088751	Health Sector Rehabilitation Support	Congo, Dem. Rep. (Zaire)	0.0	135.0	135.0	150.0
2006	P088575	Health Insurance Strategy	Ecuador	90.0	0.0	90.0	90.0
2006	P088797	Multisectoral HIV/AIDS	Ghana	0.0	6.2	6.2	20.0
2006	P077756	Maternal and Infant Health and Nutrition	Guatemala	31.9	0.0	31.9	49.0
2006	P085375	Water Supply and Sanitation for Low-Income Communities III	Indonesia	0.0	6.9	6.9	137.5
2006	P084977	Health and Social Protection	Kyrgyz Republic	0.0	10.8	10.8	15.0
2006	P100081	Avian and Human Influenza Control	Lao, PDR	0.0	1.2	1.2	4.0
2006	P074027	Health Services Improvement Project	Lao, PDR	0.0	14.3	14.3	15.0
2006	P076658	Health Sector Reform Phase II	Lesotho	0.0	4.6	4.6	6.5
2006	P090615	Multisectoral STI/HIV/AIDS Prevention II	Madagascar	0.0	10.5	10.5	30.0
2006	P094278	Health and Nutrition Support	Mauritania	0.0	7.3	7.3	10.0
2006	P083350	Institutional Strengthening & Health Sector Support Program	Niger	0.0	22.8	22.8	35.0
2006	P097402	Second Partnership For Polio Eradication	Pakistan	0.0	46.7	46.7	46.7
2006	P082056	Mother and Child Basic Health Insurance	Paraguay	12.1	0.0	12.1	22.0
2006	P075464	National Sector Support For Health Reform	Philippines	99.0	0.0	99.0	110.0
2006	P078978	Community and Basic Health	Tajikistan	0.0	8.0	8.0	10.0
2006	P079663	Mekong Regional Health Support	Vietnam	0.0	69.3	69.3	70.0
2006	P096131	Malaria Health Booster	Zambia	0.0	5.8	5.8	20.0

APPENDIX D: IFC HEALTH INVESTMENTS, FISCAL YEARS 1997–2007

Appendix D: IFC Health Investments Approved in Fiscal Years 1997–2007

Country	Project name	Approval date	Commitment date	Project size (US$ 000)	Primary sector	Secondary sector	IFC loans ($ 000)	IFC equity ($ 000)	Total IFC commitment (net, US$ 000)
Uzbekistan	Core Pharm	30-Jun-97	01-Oct-97	12,200	Chemicals	Pharmaceuticals	3,350	500	3,850
India	Duncan Hospital	30-Jun-97	31-Oct-97	29,300	Health Care	Hospitals, Clinics, Laboratories & Other	7,000	87	7,087
Latin America Region	MSF Holding	20-Nov-97	27-Apr-98	90,000	Finance & Insurance	Rental & Leasing Services	15,000	2,000	17,000
Argentina	Hospital Privado	30-Apr-98	31-Aug-98	21,200	Health Care	Hospitals, Clinics, Laboratories & Other	9,600	0	9,600
Sri Lanka	Apollo Lanka	06-May-98	20-Jun-01	32,000	Health Care	Hospitals, Clinics, Laboratories & Other	5,350	1,096	6,447
Mexico	CIMA Mexico	30-Jun-98	04-Nov-98	11,200	Health Care	Hospitals, Clinics, Laboratories & Other	0	4,800	4,800
Mexico	CIMA Puebla	30-Jun-98	06-Jan-99	32,500	Health Care	Hospitals, Clinics, Laboratories & Other	3,500	0	3,500
Costa Rica	CIMA Costa Rica	30-Jun-98	04-Nov-98	2,800	Health Care	Hospitals, Clinics, Laboratories & Other	0	1,200	1,200
Brazil	Itaberaba	04-Mar-99	24-Feb-00	25,000	Health Care	Hospitals, Clinics, Laboratories & Other	0	5,340	5,340
Central Europe Region	Medicover	15-Apr-99	14-May-99	22,000	Health Care	Hospitals, Clinics, Laboratories & Other	7,000	0	7,000
Macedonia, FYR	Alkaloid	30-Jun-99	20-Jul-99	38,200	Chemicals	Pharmaceuticals	4,473	0	4,473
Dominican Republic	Hospital	16-Jul-99	07-Apr-00	45,900	Health Care	Hospitals, Clinics, Laboratories & Other	2,000	0	2,000
Brazil	Fleury	17-Aug-99	08-May-00	58,000	Health Care	Hospitals, Clinics, Laboratories & Other	15,000	0	15,000
Philippines	Asian Hospital	14-Feb-00	19-Dec-00	88,475	Health Care	Hospitals, Clinics, Laboratories & Other	5,000	0	5,000
Mexico	Hospital ABC	02-May-00	07-Feb-01	81,800	Health Care	Hospitals, Clinics, Laboratories & Other	10,294	0	10,294
China	Wan Jie Hospital	26-Jun-00	28-Nov-01	57,300	Health Care	Hospitals, Clinics, Laboratories & Other	15,000	0	15,000
Croatia	Pliva	09-Nov-00	17-Nov-00	113,000	Chemicals	Pharmaceuticals	35,000	0	35,000
Russian Federation	NMC	27-Dec-00	11-Apr-01	9,000	Health Care	Hospitals, Clinics, Laboratories & Other	2,100	0	2,100
India	Orchid	01-Mar-01	19-May-01	116,000	Chemicals	Pharmaceuticals	20,000	0	20,000
Philippines	AEI	07-Jun-01	20-May-03	4,200	Health Care	Hospitals, Clinics, Laboratories & Other	1,000	0	1,000
Latin America Region	Salutia	12-Jul-01	04-Jan-02	10,000	Health Care	Hospitals, Clinics, Laboratories & Other	0	2,500	2,500
Eastern Europe Region	Euromedic	09-Oct-01	14-Nov-01	33,000	Health Care	Hospitals, Clinics, Laboratories & Other	12,976	0	12,976
Vietnam	F-V Hospital	11-Oct-01	30-Nov-01	40,000	Health Care	Hospitals, Clinics, Laboratories & Other	8,000	0	8,000
Egypt, Arab Rep. of	SEKEM	28-Mar-02	16-Jan-03	13,300	Chemicals	Pharmaceuticals	5,000	0	5,000
Costa Rica	Gutis	24-Jun-02	10-Jan-03	15,800	Health Care	Hospitals, Clinics, Laboratories & Other	6,000	0	6,000
India	Max Healthcare	04-Apr-03	03-Sep-03	84,000	Health Care	Hospitals, Clinics, Laboratories & Other	128	0	128

Country/Region	Company	Date 1	Date 2	Amount	Sector	Subsector			
Latin America Region	Hospital II	09-Apr-03	26-May-03	42,200	Health Care	Hospitals, Clinics, Laboratories & Other	12,000	0	12,000
Jordan	Hikma	19-Jun-03	27-Jun-03	32,000	Chemicals	Pharmaceuticals	14,866	0	14,866
Turkey	MESA Hospital	23-Jun-03	22-Jul-03	45,000	Health Care	Hospitals, Clinics, Laboratories & Other	11,000	0	11,000
Southern Europe Region	Euromedic II	04-Mar-04	12-Mar-04	25,800	Health Care	Hospitals, Clinics, Laboratories & Other	12,644	0	12,644
Turkey	Acibadem	29-Oct-04	11-Nov-04	40,900	Health Care	Hospitals, Clinics, Laboratories & Other	20,000	0	20,000
India	Bharat Biotech	16-Feb-05	26-May-05	4,500	Chemicals	Pharmaceuticals	0	4,500	4,500
China	BioChina	11-Apr-05	10-May-05	25,000	Collective Investment Vehicles	Private Equity Funds	0	4,650	4,650
Mexico	CentroMedico PDH	27-Apr-05	10-Jun-05	69,000	Health Care	Hospitals, Clinics, Laboratories & Other	14,500	0	14,500
Bosnia and Herzegovina	Bosnalijek expan	16-May-05	13-Jun-05	24,273	Chemicals	Pharmaceuticals	9,403	0	9,403
India	Dabur Pharma	03-Jun-05	07-Jun-05	69,000	Chemicals	Pharmaceuticals	0	15,064	15,064
Mexico	Centro Espanol	07-Jun-05	27-Apr-06	15,000	Health Care	Hospitals, Clinics, Laboratories & Other	5,000	0	5,000
India	Apollo equity	08-Aug-05	10-Aug-05	NA	Health Care	Hospitals, Clinics, Laboratories & Other	0	5,085	5,085
China	United Family	16-Sep-05	13-Oct-05	16,000	Health Care	Hospitals, Clinics, Laboratories & Other	8,018	0	8,018
China	SAC	04-Nov-05	22-Nov-05	13,000	Education Services	Education	3,000	1,600	4,600
Ukraine	Biocon Group	31-Jan-06	15-May-06	7,223	Chemicals	Pharmaceuticals	3,500	0	3,500
Turkey	Acibadem II	24-Feb-06	14-Mar-06	112,894	Health Care	Hospitals, Clinics, Laboratories & Other	40,000	0	40,000
Kenya	Adv Bio-Extracts	23-Jun-06	18-Jan-07	29,300	Chemicals	Pharmaceuticals	9,000	0	9,000
Egypt, Arab Rep. of	Dar Al Fouad	01-Aug-06	29-Apr-07	31,000	Health Care	Hospitals, Clinics, Laboratories & Other	4,000	0	4,000
Romania	MedLife	13-Oct-06	16-Oct-06	30,000	Health Care	Hospitals, Clinics, Laboratories & Other	6,348	5,000	11,348
China	Aier Eye	25-Oct-06	06-Nov-06	29,825	Health Care	Hospitals, Clinics, Laboratories & Other	8,112	0	8,112
India	Ocimum Bio	01-Nov-06	03-Nov-06	19,760	Health Care	Hospitals, Clinics, Laboratories & Other	2,600	3,900	6,500
China	Fosun Pharma	08-Nov-06	08-Nov-06	104,000	Chemicals	Pharmaceuticals	40,560	0	40,560
Nigeria	Hygeia Expansion	25-Jan-07	30-Jan-07	6,230	Health Care	Hospitals, Clinics, Laboratories & Other	3,033	0	3,033
China	Weigao	23-Feb-07	02-Mar-07	20,000	Chemicals	Pharmaceuticals	20,000	0	20,000
India	Max Phase II	24-May-07	29-Jun-07	146,861	Health Care	Hospitals, Clinics, Laboratories & Other	0	67,144	67,144
India	Granules	07-Jun-07	08-Jun-07	31,900	Chemicals	Pharmaceuticals	9,000	6,000	15,000

Indian woman with her children, who help her run her business. Photo by Curt Carnemark, courtesy of the World Bank Photo Library.

The World Bank's population strategies and lending over the past decade took place in the context of a shifting international consensus on approaches to population control and reproductive health and a number of competing agendas.[1] The Bank's initial involvement in the HNP sector in the 1970s arose primarily over concern for the adverse impacts of rapid population growth and high fertility.

However, the 1994 International Conference on Population and Development (ICPD) in Cairo shifted the focus of population programs away from fertility reduction and family planning and toward women's health, economic and social factors affecting the demand for children, and the right to reproductive health care (Robinson and Ross 2007). Shortly thereafter, the international community's attention was drawn to addressing the rising threat of HIV/AIDS; sectorwide approaches in health; and, following the recommendations of the *World Development Report 1993,* delivery of a package of basic or essential health services for the poor.

The Bank's 1999 population strategy (World Bank 1999c) committed to assist countries to link population to poverty reduction and human development; advocate for cost-effective policies that reflect country context; build on analysis and dialogue; provide sustained support; and strengthen skills and partnerships. A year later, the MDGs were adopted with no explicit family planning or reproductive health goal, even though both are key to achieving many of the other MDGs.

The focus of the Bank's support for reducing fertility and population growth declined over the decade, and family planning became one of many components of an essential package of health or reproductive health services. Over the period fiscal 1997 to 2006, the Bank approved only 14 population projects, defined for the purposes of the review as those with population in the title and/or including an objective to reduce fertility, or with a population or family planning component or subcomponent.[2] Population projects thus defined represented about 6 percent of the HNP lending portfolio, declining from 11 to 2 percent of the portfolio over the decade. The population projects approved in three-quarters of the countries were preceded by population projects. Those in Bangladesh, India, Indonesia, and Kenya represented the last in a long series stretching back to the 1970s. However, the series ended during the period under review, replaced by operations focusing on reproductive health or sectorwide activities.

The Bank's population support was directed to only about a quarter of the 35 countries with high fertility. Among the 13 countries that received Bank support, 8 had a total fertility rate of 5.0 or greater. Only one freestanding population project was approved—the Population and Family Planning Learning and Innovation Loan in Malawi, which implemented community-based distribution of family planning in rural areas on a pilot basis. Two of the projects packaged population and AIDS activities, three were linked to maternal and child health or reproductive health, and eight were part of a health or HNP sector project. The main activities financed by these projects included: training health workers; information, education, and communication on family planning and the benefits of smaller families; contraceptives, including social marketing; civil works; community funds; policy reform; and economic activities for women and youth. Almost all of the support was to low-income countries.

None of the projects with explicit fertility or population objectives achieved them. The three projects with population or family planning components but no explicit fertility objective[3] at least partially achieved their objectives. Eleven of the population projects approved from fiscal 1997 to 2006 have closed; only 3 had satisfactory outcomes. In Guinea, India, Kenya, and Mali, modern contraceptive use and fertility were scarcely affected.[4] In Russia, the abortion rate declined in project areas at the same rate as in nonproject areas, while modern contraceptive use was stagnant. In Bangladesh, Gambia, and Senegal, fertility declined somewhat, but there is significant doubt about links to the support of the Bank, other donors, or public policy more generally.[5] Bangladesh had experienced a spectacular decline in fertility—from 7 children per woman in the 1970s to 3.3 by 1999—in large part because of a highly successful family planning program supported by the Bank and other donors (IEG 2005b). From 1999 to 2004, fertility continued to decline to 3.0 and the contraceptive prevalence rate rose from about 50 to 60 percent, but it is unlikely that this is primarily attributable to the family planning program supported by the Health and Population Sector Program, given the disruption in service delivery caused by the controversy in attempting (without success) to absorb the vertical family planning program into other health services.

Shortcomings in project preparation contributed to poor outcomes.[6] According to completion reports and IEG fieldwork, project designs were often excessively complex, driven by participatory or sectorwide approaches. This often resulted in a failure to prioritize activities, which reduced the project's feasibility and ultimate impact in the face of low implementation capacity. Also frequently noted was a lack of up-front risk analysis, risk mitigation actions, and institutional analysis. An IEG field evaluation of the Vietnam Population and Family Health Project (1996–2003) (IEG 2006d), for example, found very little increase in oral contraceptive use, partly because the

existing incentives for two-child families within the family planning delivery structure were not taken into account. This is something that institutional analysis in advance of the project should have been able to anticipate.

The absorption of population and family planning into sectorwide programs—be they SWAps or health reform projects—may have contributed to the lack of results. There were significant improvements in the modern contraceptive prevalence rate and a reduction in the total fertility rate during Ghana's Second Population and Family Health Project (1991–97). However, under the subsequent Health Sector Support Project (1998–2002), which supported a sectorwide approach, there was no progress on either of these outcomes (IEG 2005b, 2007d). A similar situation occurred in Bangladesh, between the Fourth Population and Health Project (1991–98) and the subsequent Health and Family Planning Program (1998–2005) (IEG 2006b). In both cases, the transition to a SWAp increased the emphasis on process, but did not ensure the achievement of health-service performance and output targets, including those for population (IEG 2007d). Field visits in Egypt underscored the findings of a recent study that family planning and reproductive health services are diluted within the basic package of services delivered through new family health facilities supported by the Health Reform Project (1998–present) (IEG 2008b). Clients report that there are no longer special rooms in facilities for family planning clients; female physicians or specialists to discuss the topic are not available; and family physicians have less specialized training and less time to devote to the clients (Zaky and others 2007 as reported in IEG 2008b).

Nevertheless, there were some important successes in raising contraceptive use and support for fertility decline in high-fertility environments, particularly with respect to use of family planning. The Egypt Population Project (1996–2005) contributed to raising contraceptive use and lowering fertility in rural Upper Egypt, while the Malawi Population and Family Planning Project was able to raise modern contraceptive use in rural areas through community-based distributors. Both of these projects included important demand-generation activities. The Madagascar Second Health Program Support Project financed training and contraceptives, with a particular focus on a new, long-duration implantable contraceptive that is easily inserted and especially convenient in rural and remote areas. The number of locations offering family planning services increased by 45 percent from 2003 to 2007, and the contraceptive prevalence rate rose from 9.7 to 24 percent (World Bank 2008e). Unfortunately, the successful investment in pilot family planning activities in Malawi was not replicated nationally, and contraceptive use remains low, with little change (figure E.1). There has been virtually no improvement in Ghana despite support by the Bank and other donors for a health SWAp over the past decade, and there has been modest improvement in Bangladesh, despite the disruption in family planning services by the unpopular and ultimately failed attempt to unify the delivery of health and family planning services.

The problems of high fertility and rapid population growth have regained prominence internationally and in the Bank's population strategy. There is greater recognition that lowering fertility and population growth through demand-side activities alone will take a very long time, while simply providing family planning as part of a package of basic services is unlikely to raise contraceptive prevalence dramatically in high-fertility countries or to lower fertility among the very poor. Both demand- and supply-side activities are important. Universal

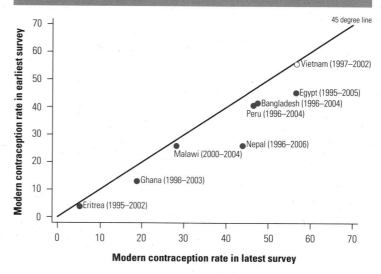

Figure E.1: Trends in Modern Contraceptive Use Rates, Case Study Countries

Source: Nankhuni forthcoming, based on demographic and health survey reports (www.measuredhs.com)
Note: Solid circle indicates that the change is statistically significant at 5 or 10 percent level, hollow circle indicates that the change is not statistically significant, and solid triangle indicates that it was not possible to determine statistical significance. Countries below the 45-degree line experienced improvements in uptake of modern contraception rates.

access to reproductive health was added as an MDG in 2007.[7] The Bank's 2007 population strategy (World Bank 2007g) differentiates between reproductive, maternal, and sexual health and the services that address them and factors that affect demographic outcomes. It links population, economic growth, and poverty reduction and advocates targeting assistance to the 35 countries with total fertility rates exceeding 5.0, many of which are also among the poorest countries in the world.

Woman in Burkina Faso cooking a typical meal over a wood fire. Photo by Ray Witlin, courtesy of the World Bank Photo Library.

The 2006 World Bank publication, *Repositioning Nutrition as Central to Development: A Strategy for Large Scale Action* (World Bank 2006c), argues that malnutrition is one of the world's most serious health problems and the largest contributor to child mortality. About a third of children in developing countries are underweight (low weight for age) or stunted (low height for age), and about 30 percent of the population of those countries suffers from deficiencies in micronutrients such as vitamin A, iodine, or iron.[1] Women and children are particularly affected, and nutritional deficiencies in children while they are still in the womb and up to age 2 can have lifelong consequences. Malnutrition among children is highest in South Asia and is high and increasing in Sub-Saharan Africa. It affects both the poor and the non-poor, but is greater among the poor: in 39 out of 46 countries with recent household surveys, more than half of children are stunted, and stunting is as much as eight times higher among the poorest wealth quintile than among the richest.[2] **Tackling malnutrition not only contributes to the MDG of halving the share of people who suffer from hunger, but also to other MDGs that deal with reducing child mortality, improving maternal health, raising school achievement, and reducing income poverty.**

The causes of malnutrition are diverse and include inadequate breastfeeding, poor child feeding practices, diarrheal disease and other illness, intestinal parasites, frequent and closely spaced childbearing, inadequate diet, low access to health care, unsafe water, poor sanitation, low purchasing power, and in some cases inadequate food production. However, the fact that the non-poor also have significant levels of malnutrition indicates that knowledge and behavior are often key.

World Bank support is in countries with high malnutrition, but coverage of the worst-affected countries is low. IEG undertook an in-depth desk review of the 21 projects approved from fiscal 1997 to 2006 with nutrition objectives (10 percent of the HNP lending portfolio),[3] plus 6 additional projects with nutrition in the title or nutrition components or subcomponents, for a total of 27 projects, henceforth called "nutrition projects."[4] About half of them are general health or HNP projects, five are freestanding nutrition projects, four are mother and/or child health projects, and the remaining five are emergency or multisectoral programmatic lending.[5] While about two-thirds of the nutrition projects were in countries with average child stunting of 30 percent or more, only about a quarter of countries with such high levels of malnutrition were receiving World Bank nutrition support.[6] Two-thirds of nutrition projects were in low-income countries. While Africa had the largest number of nutrition projects (9), South Asia had the highest share of nutrition projects relative to the rest of the Regional portfolio (29 percent).[7] The share of projects with nutrition objectives declined from 12 to 7 percent between the first and second half of the decade.

The types of interventions supported by these operations included growth monitoring and nutritional surveillance (100 percent), micronutrient supplements (52 percent), behavior change (nutrition education, promotion of growth monitoring, breastfeeding, specific dietary changes, and hygiene, 48 percent), and feeding supplements or rehabilitation of malnourished children (41 percent). The projects also supported ca-

Figure F.1: Trends in Stunting in the Rural Areas of Case Study Countries, 1995–2006

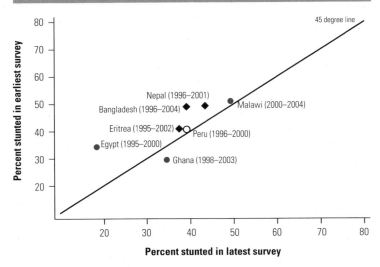

Source: Nankhuni forthcoming, based on demographic and health survey reports.
Note: Solid circle indicates statistically significant change at p<.05 or p<.10; empty circle indicates that the change is not statistically significant; solid diamond indicates that it was not possible to determine statistical significance. Countries above the 45-degree line experienced reductions in stunting levels, those below the line experienced increases, and those along the line experienced no change.

Several of the case study countries suffered from high levels of child malnutrition, overall and among the poor, and in most cases there was little improvement (figure F.1). A 2005 IEG impact evaluation found that, although nutritional status in Bangladesh has improved over time, the link between the interventions and outcomes was weak (box F.1). Although the interventions produced some modest improvements, most nutrition improvements over the period were brought about by better food availability and lower prices linked to the increase in rice yields since the late 1990s. The case study teams pointed to malnutrition as particularly neglected in the Bank's support over the past decade in Nepal, Peru, and (at least until recently) Malawi. The observed improvements in rural Nepal could also have been affected through interventions in other sectors, such as water supply and sanitation.[9] Ghana has had no specific nutrition support from the Bank, but experienced an *increase* in rural stunting over the course of sectorwide Bank support.

The overall performance of the nutrition projects was weak. Fifteen of the nutrition projects had closed and been reviewed by IEG; 64 percent had satisfactory outcomes—about the same as the rest of the portfolio. But this statistic is deceptive, since nutrition is often only one of several objectives, and in some cases only a small component of a larger project.[10] Only two projects—Indonesia Iodine Deficiency Control and Senegal Nutrition—demonstrated substantial efficacy in meeting their objectives, with resulting changes in nutritional outcomes. In Indonesia, increased consumption of iodized salt and targeted distribution of iodine capsules helped reduce the total goiter rate by 35 percent in highly endemic provinces and by more than 50 percent in a few others.[11] The Senegal project surpassed almost all of its targets in terms of outputs (training, children and mothers reached, health posts equipped) and demonstrated improvements in some nutrition indicators (exclusive breastfeeding), though for a few indicators, only by slightly more than in control areas (World Bank 2007c). Among the remaining 12 projects, the completion reports for 4 suggested little or no impact,[12] and for 8 projects

pacity building in the form of nutrition policy development, training, and data collection. However, 4 of the 27 projects had an explicit objective to improve nutrition, with no nutrition components or subcomponents in the appraisal document.[8]

The diverse causes of malnutrition made nutrition projects organizationally complex—about half were multisectoral in implementation and in half of the multisectoral projects, the executing agency was outside of the Ministry of Health. The projects were managed by the Ministry of Health or by the Ministry of Finance/ Economy/ Plan (four projects each); jointly executed by multiple ministries, one of which was the Ministry of Health (three projects); by a nonhealth ministry (two projects); or by the Office of the President or Prime Minister (one project). The number of implementing agencies was often greater, with six projects relying on three implementing ministries and two projects on four implementing agencies.

Box F.1: Reductions in Malnutrition in Bangladesh: Lessons from the Integrated Nutrition Project

The Bank has supported improved nutrition in Bangladesh through two freestanding nutrition projects—the Bangladesh Integrated Nutrition Project (BINP, 1995–2002) and the National Nutrition Project (2000–07)—and as part of two projects supporting sectorwide approaches in HNP. In 2005, IEG evaluated the impact of the BINP, which was based on a community-based approach that provided nutrition counseling to bring about behavior change and supplementary feeding for pregnant women and young children.

The evaluation found that coverage of the intervention was high in project areas in general, but that the causal link between the interventions and nutrition outcomes was weakened by targeting deficiencies; large shares of mothers and children receiving supplemental feeding but no counseling; and the focus of behavior change almost exclusively on mothers, who are often not the main decision makers on nutrition-related practices (both husbands and mothers-in-law have an important influence). Supplementary feeding had some impact among the most malnourished, but was a costly part of the program and not sustainable in the long run.

The follow-on National Nutrition Program revised the targeting criteria and attempted to reach out to men with behavior-change messages. The program was delayed and scaled back, but was able to maintain the achievements of micronutrient coverage and to promote adoption of new behaviors. It was unable to demonstrate sustainable improvements in birth weights and nutrition status of vulnerable groups; however, the baseline was collected only two years before the end of the project and monitoring data were not collected.

Source: IEG 2005c, World Bank 2007d.

---

the impact was unclear, often due to the failure to collect data or report on nutrition outcomes.

Complexity was cited as contributing to the shortcomings in more than half of the weak-performing projects. Projects in Bangladesh, Indonesia, Nicaragua, and Sri Lanka had to be scaled back and the efforts prioritized to include fewer activities or a smaller geographic area. The Food Security and Social Mobilization Project in Mauritania suffered from the inexperience and institutional weaknesses of the Executive State Secretariat for Promotion of Women, in addition to high project complexity. The Uganda Nutrition and Child Development Project was designed as a pilot intended for only a few districts; expansion of its geographical coverage without additional resources greatly increased its complexity.

M&E were particularly weak for both projects with nutrition components and the freestanding nutrition projects. Nutrition outcomes are affected by many factors beyond the interventions in these projects; it is thus very important to attempt to monitor other important factors that could be affecting outcomes, a lesson of the project in Senegal. However, these projects failed even to collect basic data on nutrition outcomes, such as micronutrient consumption (Gambia, Mauritania, Sri Lanka) or the projects' main outputs (Sri Lanka). The Bangladesh project did not collect baseline data until two years before the end of the project; the Indonesia project produced baseline and final data from different groups of people; the India Women and Child Development Project collected data on children aged 0–3 when the target group was aged 0–6. The completion report for the Nicaragua project reported no outcomes at all.

This experience nevertheless presents some important lessons for future nutrition projects. Several projects reported success in the use of community volunteers to mobilize communities or deliver services (Gambia, Senegal, Nicaragua), while one of the reasons for poor performance in Mauritania was the limited capacity of communities to undertake growth-promotion activities. The experience also highlighted the importance of demand generation for nutrition services and behavior change communication for success in Senegal: lack of demand was a factor in weak results in India and Mauritania. Multisectoral coordination and the engagement of sectors outside of health was lacking in India and Mauritania. Two early child development projects pointed to the need for better targeting of children in a more appropriate age range (Uganda) or with more education and counseling (India). Finally, a number of projects cited the need to develop simpler indicators for use by grassroots groups, to adopt more realistic and measurable targets (Bangladesh), and to identify monitoring indicators for improved supervision (Sri Lanka).

To summarize, the need to address malnutrition in client countries is great, and the coverage of Bank support for the hardest-hit countries is low. However, the multidimensional determinants of nutrition tend to lead to complex projects that involve multiple sectors. While there have been demonstrable results in a few cases, the overall results for the HNP-managed nutrition portfolio were thin.

APPENDIX G: WORLD BANK SUPPORT FOR ANALYTIC WORK ON HNP

The Bank's analytic work in HNP includes both the products of the lending part of the institution and research products and other publications of Bank staff. Official economic and sector work (ESW) financed directly from the Bank budget for country, Regional, or global-level HNP analysis is tracked in an internal database.[1]

Between fiscal 2000 and 2008 the Bank spent $43 million of its own budget and trust funds on a total of 218 ESW tasks that generated reports, policy notes, conferences, workshops, consultations, and country dialogue on HNP.[2] This amounts to about 4 percent of ESW Bank-wide for those years, whether measured in costs or number of activities.

However, the true amount of HNP analytic work undertaken by the Bank far exceeds what is in the official database. The tracking system excludes the work of the Bank's Research Department and major undertakings, such as the *World Development Report 2004: Making Services Work for the Poor* and the multiyear research on *Reaching the Poor with Health, Nutrition, and Population Services* (World Bank 2005a).[3] An exhaustive search for all individual articles, working papers, studies, toolkits, reports, and research published by the Bank or Bank staff on HNP topics counted a total of 1,457 pieces issued over fiscal 1997–2006—six times more than implied by the official ESW database.[4]

ESW on HNP tripled over fiscal 2001–05, then dropped to half its previous levels in fiscal 2006–08 (figure G.1). About two-thirds of these activities were conducted at the country level, about a quarter at the Regional level, and 7 percent at the global level.[5] The largest shares of these ESW activities were country-level HNP sector studies (42 percent), studies of health finance (33 percent), HIV/AIDS studies (31 percent), or health strategies or policies (29 percent). The increase in ESW in fiscal 2002 and 2004–05 is mostly attributable to an increase in country-level sector studies or reviews in those years; there followed a large drop in fiscal 2007–08.

Prominent among the country-level studies was a series of more than a dozen HNP *Country Status Reports* launched by the Africa Region in 2003, with the purpose of informing the HNP discussion in Poverty Reduction Strategies. Most used the analytic framework proposed in the HNP chapter of the *Sourcebook for Poverty Reduction Strategies* (Claeson and others 2002), linking health outcomes, household and community characteristics and behaviors, health care delivery and financing, and other sectors affecting health. All focused on the relationship between health and poverty to differing degrees and included a chapter on public expenditures in health and health financing.

Nearly two-thirds of all ESW tasks since 2002 that stated an objective were intended to inform government policy, while only half aimed to inform lending.[6] Other main objectives of the HNP ESW portfolio were to inform public debate (42 percent), inform the development community (32 percent), and build capacity (25 percent). Not surprisingly, country and Regional ESW were more likely intended to inform government policy, and country-level ESW was the most likely to have an objective to inform lending (55 percent), while all—or nearly all—global HNP ESW intended to inform public debate or the

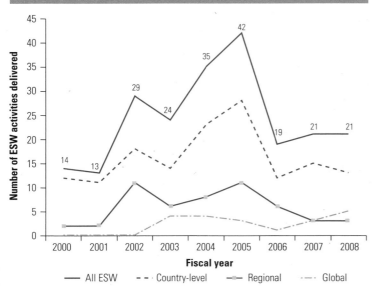

Figure G.1: Trend in Official HNP ESW Tasks, Fiscal Years 2000–08

Source: World Bank data.

Table G.1: Coverage of Topics in an Inventory of HNP Analytic Work, Fiscal 1997–2006 (n =1,457)

Topic	Number	Percent
Health system performance	597	41.0
HIV/AIDS and STIs	321	22.0
Child health	152	10.4
Communicable diseases other than AIDS	109	7.5
Injuries and noncommunicable diseases	109	7.5
Nutrition and food security	99	6.8
Population and reproductive health[a]	74	5.1
Other HNP and human development	367	25.2

Source: IEG inventory of HNP analytic work.
Note: Categories are not mutually exclusive; percentages add to more than 100 percent.
a. Of which only 11 deal exclusively with population/family planning.

development community. IEG's recent evaluation of Bank-wide ESW found that it led to higher project quality at entry (IEG 2008h).

The broader inventory of analytic work conducted for this evaluation found that health system performance was the most common topic, treated in 41 percent of all analytic work (table G.1). HIV/AIDS was the second-most common topic, while only 1 in 10 publications addressed child health.

Health is also frequently analyzed in public expenditure reviews (PERs), a category of formal ESW usually conducted by staff in other sectors, and thus not included in the statistics for the HNP sector.[7] PERs are often the basis for discussion with the Ministry of Finance about sectoral budget allocations, and about allocations within sectors. Thus, they are an important input into discussions of efficiency and sustainability of finance. *However, about a third of PERs delivered from fiscal 2000 to 2007 had no chapter or subchapter on health.* The health focus of PERs has declined over time: between fiscal 2000–03 and 2004–07, the share with health chapters or subchapters declined from 71 to 59 percent. Only 3 percent of PERs had a chapter or subchapter on nutrition or on population, fertility, or family planning. Of the five PERs with a population chapter or subchapter, only one (Ethiopia) was in a high-fertility country. Given the close relationship between rapid population growth, the dependency ratio, and sustainability of public expenditure, it is particularly surprising that population is not more widely discussed.

APPENDIX H: ADDITIONAL FIGURES ON WORLD BANK HNP LENDING, ANALYTIC WORK, AND STAFFING

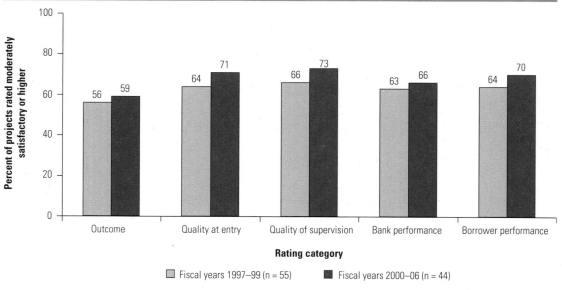

Figure H.1: IEG Ratings for Closed HNP Projects Approved in Fiscal 1997–2006, by Year of Approval

Source: World Bank data.

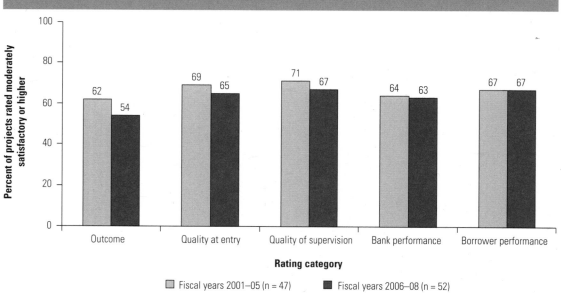

Figure H.2: IEG Ratings for Closed HNP Projects Approved in Fiscal 1997–2006, by Year of Exit

Source: World Bank data.

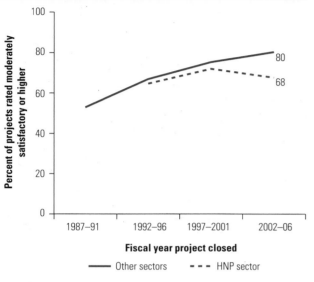

Figure H.3: IEG Bank Performance Ratings, by Sector Board and Fiscal Year of Exit

Source: World Bank data.

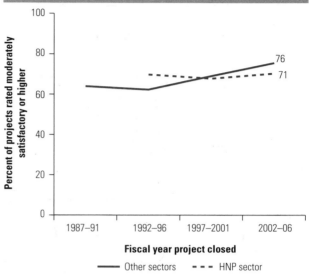

Figure H.4: IEG Borrower Performance Ratings, by Sector Board and Fiscal Year of Exit

Source: World Bank data.

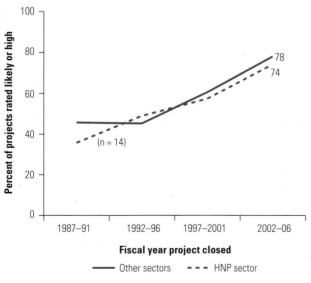

Figure H.5: IEG Sustainability Ratings, HNP and Other Sectors, by Fiscal Year of Exit

Source: World Bank data.

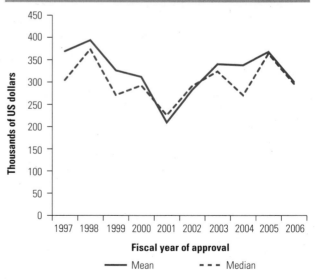

Figure H.6: Mean and Median HNP Project Preparation Costs, by Fiscal Year of Approval (nominal dollars)

Note: N = 220 projects.

Figure H.7: Duration of HNP Project Preparation, by Fiscal Year of Approval

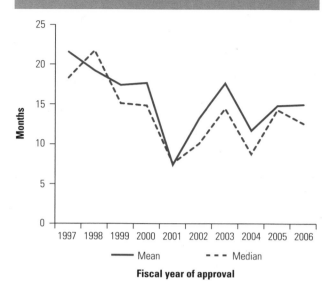

Fiscal year of approval

Note: N = 220 projects.

Figure H.8: Average Annual Supervision Costs for Investment Projects Managed by HNP and Other Sectors

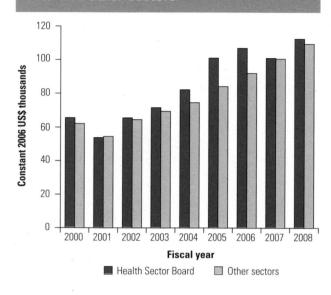

Fiscal year

Source: World Bank data.

Figure H.9: Trends in HNP and Hub-Mapped Staff of Level GF+ (excluding coterms), Fiscal 1997–2007

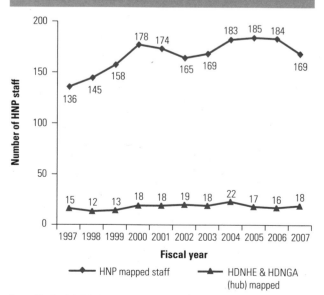

Fiscal year

Source: Nankhuni and Modi 2008.

Figure H.10: HNP Operational Staff, by Region and Fiscal Year

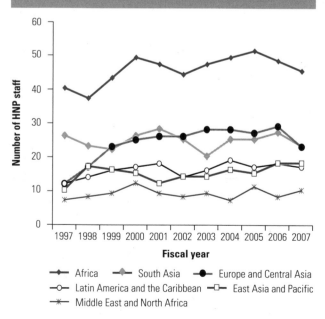

Fiscal year

Source: Nankhuni and Modi 2008.

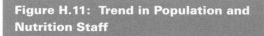

Figure H.11: Trend in Population and Nutrition Staff

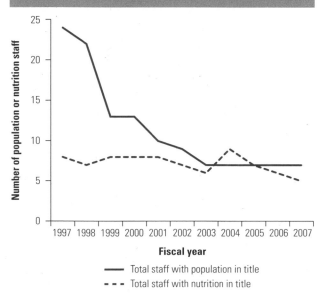

Source: Nankhuni and Modi 2008.

Note: If staff have both population and nutrition in their title, they are counted in both categories.

Table H.1: Frequency of Bank Performance Issues in Closed HNP Projects Approved in Fiscal 1997–2006, by Project Outcome

Bank performance issue	Projects with unsatisfactory outcome		Projects with satisfactory outcome		Ratio of percent unsatisfactory to percent satisfactory outcome
	Number	Percent	Number	Percent	
Inadequate risk assessment	17	(40)	2	(4)	10:1
Inadequate technical design	17	(40)	3	(5)	8:1
Inadequate supervision	18	(43)	5	(9)	5:1
Inadequate political or institutional analysis	17	(40)	8	(14)	3:1
Inadequate baseline data or unrealistic targets	17	(40)	8	(14)	3:1
Inadequate M&E framework, poor data quality	36	(86)	26	(46)	2:1
Overly complex design	12	(29)	8	(14)	2:1
Inadequate partner financing or coordination	5	(12)	4	(7)	2:1
Implementation disrupted by a crisis	7	(17)	8	(14)	1:1
Inadequate prior analytic work	5	(12)	0	(0)	—
Number of projects	42		57		

Source: IEG review of ICRs.

Table H.2: Probit Regressions on the Determinants of Project Outcome Ratings
(n = 94 investment projects approved from fiscal 1997–2006)

Variable	(1) dP/dx	(1) T	(2) dP/dx	(2) T	(3) dP/dx	(3) T	(4) dP/dx	(4) T	(5) dP/dx	(5) T	(6) dP/dx	(6) T	(7) dP/dx	(7) T	(8) dP/dx	(8) T
Satisfactory Bank quality at entry	0.309	1.43	0.325	1.36	0.308	1.44	**0.537**	3.02	**0.580**	3.61	**0.549**	3.12				
Satisfactory Bank supervision	0.187	0.97	0.225	0.98	0.209	1.02	0.341	1.89	0.339	2.02	*0.337*	1.89				
Satisfactory borrower performance	**0.800**	4.04	**0.822**	4.06	**0.799**	4.10										
IDA	−0.097	−0.05	0.055	0.23	−0.054	−0.28	0.224	0.86	0.056	0.29	0.219	0.84	0.089	0.63	*0.369*	1.90
Multisectoral	0.050	0.29	0.040	0.23	0.112	0.68	0.227	0.68			0.234	0.71	0.323	1.45	0.424	1.46
IDA* multisectoral	**−0.554**	−2.69	**−0.627**	−2.96	*−0.456*	−1.90	−0.531	−1.46			−0.505	−1.34	**−0.689**	−3.14	**−0.700**	−2.47
Europe and Central Asia							**0.518**	2.93	**0.495**	2.88	**0.510**	2.75			**0.442**	2.63
Middle East and North Africa							**0.479**	2.58	**0.486**	2.52	**0.481**	2.54			0.442	2.07
East Asia and Pacific							0.288	1.32	0.306	1.44	0.266	1.16			*0.345*	1.74
Latin America and Caribbean							*0.417*	1.84	0.355	1.52	*0.402*	1.68			**0.500**	2.82
South Asia							**0.580**	3.65	**0.578**	3.08	**0.572**	3.38			**0.468**	3.01
$10–50 million	−0.027	−0.17	−0.004	−0.02	0.052	0.33	0.258	1.05	0.197	0.83	0.276	1.11	0.082	0.42	0.099	0.42
$50–100 million	0.034	0.22	0.070	0.38	0.101	0.66	0.193	0.74	0.120	0.45	0.203	0.78	0.089	0.44	0.030	0.12
>$100 million	0.379	1.33	0.399	1.29	0.365	0.22	−0.118	−0.24	−0.194	−0.42	−0.093	−0.19	0.113	0.31	−0.220	−0.50
Approved fiscal 2000–06	0.018	0.12	0.009	0.06	0.142	0.91	0.171	1.16	0.139	0.95	0.192	1.23	0.133	1.10	*0.204*	1.64
Support for SWAp	−0.450	−2.30	−0.450	−2.30	−0.45	−2.10							−0.339	−1.98	−0.096	−0.47
Africa MAP (HIV) project									−0.303	−1.20	−0.150	0.52				
Pseudo R²	0.6433		0.6736		0.6615		0.4551		0.4372		0.4568		0.1443		0.2515	
Joint tests (p value)																
Quality at entry, Bank supervision, borrower performance	**0.0010**		**0.0008**		**0.0007**		**0.0000**		**0.0000**		**0.0000**					
Regions							**0.0008**		**0.0069**		**0.0028**				0.0157	
Loan size	0.6180		0.6304		0.6103		0.6073		0.6408		0.5800		0.9746		0.7956	
IDA, multisectoral, interaction	**0.0032**		**0.0006**		0.1505		0.2701				0.4436		**0.0017**			
IDA, multisectoral, Africa MAP					**0.0028**						0.3892				0.0333	

a. Figures in **bold** are significant at p < .01; figures underlined are significant at p < .05; figures in *italics* are significant at p < .10.

b. The comparison groups are: Africa Region; projects of less than $10 million; approved in fiscal years 1997–99.

The **Medicines for Malaria Venture** (MMV) funds and manages the discovery, development, and registration of new medicines for the treatment of malaria in disease-endemic countries in response to the increasing incidence of and mortality from malaria, the declining efficiency of first- and second-line treatments, and the limited response of the pharmaceutical industry to discover and develop new antimalarial drugs. The MMV has been highly successful at achieving its initial objectives—to establish and manage a portfolio of antimalarial drug candidates—and the public sector target price of a full course of treatment of a dollar or less appears within reach.

The MMV's mandate has been expanded to include improving access and delivery of antimalarial drugs. It is less clear whether MMV has the organizational arrangement and institutional relationships (notably with countries) to deliver on the highly demanding downstream access and delivery activities and whether it will be able to reconcile its private sector entrepreneurial style with the public sector requirements for resolution of policy and institutional issues in access and delivery (IEG 2007e).

The **Population and Reproductive Health Capacity Building Program** (PRHCBP), established in 1999, is a merger of three programs: Population and Reproductive Health, Safe Motherhood, and the Program to Reduce the Practice of Female Genital Mutilation and Improve Adolescent Health. Its objective is to build the capacity of civil society organizations to develop and implement culturally appropriate interventions in population and reproductive health. It does this by providing grants to international intermediaries, which then make grants to grassroots groups, and supporting operations research and technology and information transfer. It is financed entirely by the Bank's Development Grant Facility, managed within the Bank structure, and with no steering committee or other structure that would enable actors external to the Bank to participate in decision making and oversight. To date, the Bank has allocated $18.3 million of Development Grant Facility funding to the PRHCBP. The evaluation found that the objectives of the program were highly relevant, but that both efficacy and efficiency were difficult to assess because there was no systematic measurement of the achievement of the program's stated objectives. Grant decision making by the Review Committee was a very informal process. It was only in 2006 that public solicitation of proposals became practice, and in 2007 that criteria for evaluating proposals were established. For almost a quarter of all grants awarded through fiscal 2007, there was no written record of review decisions. Under the operations research component, PRHCBP has supported the International Partnership for Microbicides to develop new technologies to prevent HIV/AIDS and unwanted pregnancy. The consolidation of the three programs did not lead to clear objectives and the links to country-level Bank operations were weak (IEG 2008e).

This mobile health education van covers rural areas in Sri Lanka. Photo by Dominic Sansoni, courtesy of the World Bank Photo Library.

Management highly values IEG's evaluation of World Bank Group support in the health, nutrition and population sector, an important assessment after 10 years of implementation of the 1997 health, nutrition and population (HNP) strategy.[1] The evaluation is helpful in articulating some of the contextual difficulties the Bank Group faces as a key partner in the international health environment. Management has some general comments on the changing context for its support, followed by comments on the evaluation's main findings and recommendations. Lastly, the Response cites the International Finance Corporation's (IFC) evolving role in the sector. The Management Action Record (attached to the Management Response Summary at the front of this volume) provides a Bank Group response to IEG's recommendations. As noted below, the 2007 Health Strategy (World Bank 2007a) found issues similar to those raised by IEG, not surprising because there was regular interaction between HNP staff and the IEG team in the process of preparing the new strategy. The recent health Strategy Progress Report (World Bank 2009) lays out the Bank's actions to strengthen its support, including taking into account all of the major IEG analysis and recommendations. Annex 2 of the Progress Report, the Management Action Plan, summarizes how the actions being taken correspond to IEG's recommendations, including assigning responsibilities and setting benchmarks for measuring progress. For reference it is appended to this response.

Changing Context for WBG Support

The context in which the Bank Group provides support in this sector has changed dramatically during the last decade. That context affects how the World Bank Group works.

A Changing Global Environment Requires More from the Bank. The last 10 years have seen the creation of new international health institutions and foundations, as well as the emergence of many different innovative health funding mechanisms.[2] The welcome result has been sharply increased global funding for HNP. The Bank's role has undergone a similar paradigm shift. Although lending investment remains significant, we now play a much more nuanced role, working with and through partners and new international institutions.[3] This changing role, anchored in the Paris and Accra Declarations, is desirable from a development perspective, but it also imposes significant additional challenges in attributing development outcomes to Bank finance or technical contributions. The sector is constantly adapting to this rapidly evolving environment, using the full spectrum of the Bank's comparative advantages beyond traditional lending and economic and sector work (ESW). The benefits are clear, as are the risks of working in a complex development area, investing in complex health systems while respecting the multiplicity of synergies necessary for a continuum of care and service delivery, essential for public health and disease control, and in some instances relying on partners to deliver results.

A Mandate to Achieve Health Outcomes through Health in All Policies. The international health community and the World Bank Group have recognized that, in addition to stand-alone interventions and sector-specific policies, we must focus on more comprehensive "health in all policies." Given how the Bank Group is organized, this is our comparative advantage—and the HNP sector has been moving in this direction over the past years. The 2007 HNP strategy (World Bank

2007a) included a critical self-assessment of the sector's performance since 1997. The IEG evaluation reconfirms much of this self-assessment, and many of IEG's recommendations are helpful in achieving greater effectiveness and impact.

Main Findings and Recommendations

Management agrees with many of the findings, and appreciates the recommendations. Management has taken them into account in the Progress Report and the Plan of Action (see the attached Action Plan). While not detracting from the importance that it gives to the evaluation and its usefulness for the Strategy Progress Report, management has a set of observations on some of the findings.

Health Status Has More than One Development Dimension. Management considers better health a development outcome in and of itself, irrespective of its contributions to other goals. In addition to improving health status, the HNP sector aims to cushion the financial shocks of health costs, which can be substantial in many client countries, where out-of-pocket payments dominate. Thus, while we agree that investments should focus on health outcomes for the poor, it is also vital to protect those above the poverty line from financial shocks from poor health that push families into poverty.

The World Bank Group's Global HNP Engagements Go Beyond Projects and ESW. The evaluation emphasizes lending, with some attention to policy dialogue and analytic work. But the HNP sector has expanded the paradigm over the past decade. The World Bank Group uses a range of engagement instruments, such as analytic and advisory activities (including IFC Advisory Services),[4] just-in-time policy advice, policy-based lending led by other sectors, subnational lending without a sovereign guarantee (through IFC), and working through international networks and partnerships, such as the Global Alliance for Vaccines Initiative (GAVI), the Global Fund to Fight AIDS, Tuberculosis and Malaria (GFATM), and the European Union (EU) Observatory. Working with partners through pooled funding, country systems and joint strategies and supervision (as opposed

to ring-fenced Bank operations) is also anchored in international commitments and agreements such as the Paris and Accra Declarations. The success of the Joint United Nations Program on HIV/AIDS (UNAIDS), GFATM, GAVI, Roll Back Malaria, EU Observatory and other major international partnerships is also the shared success of the Bank Group's HNP work, as we exercise substantial technical and financial influence in these networks and partnerships. Over the past decade, we have also enhanced internal collaborations to improve the Bank Group's impact on global health: Examples include work across units (notably with Concessional Finance and Global Partnerships, Operations Policy and Country Services, and Treasury for innovative financing mechanisms—the International Finance Facility for Immunization, Advance Market Commitment, and Treasury services) and partnerships with GFATM, GAVI, UNAIDS, and others. Harnessing the Bank's broader development expertise has significantly impacted the structure of the global health architecture, in addition to saving millions of lives.

The Evaluation Framework Does Not Assess the World Bank Group's Non-Traditional Contributions to Global Health and Client Support. The evaluation's review of four approaches misses much of the work carried out in support of global public health, including key analytical pieces, the global work on core public health functions, water and sanitation, surveillance and vital statistics, indoor air pollution, avian and human influenza, and so forth. The evaluation does not evaluate performance-based approaches, which we believe have delivered impressive results. Regarding SWAPs, we note that before reaching any conclusions on their effectiveness we need to take into account elements beyond the evaluation that reflect the Bank's support for greater donor coordination and the use of country systems as enshrined in the Paris and Accra Declarations.

Coverage of Analytic Work. Much of the nontraditional analytical work has a potentially large or larger impact than the Bank's lending, especially since Bank financing is usually a small share of overall health spending in middle-income countries.[5] Knowledge-product tasks are often preferred to ESW to get findings out more quickly or provide just-in-time advice to clients and partners. The evaluation does not sufficiently account for the role of analytic and advisory activities in engaging clients and advancing policy dialogue, either as a stand-alone tool to support the client (in particular in middle-income countries) or as a parallel track dialogue to investment and policy-based lending. The evaluation could also have taken greater account of other knowledge products, such as a large portfolio of Japan Policy and Human Resources Development Fund (PHRD) grant-financed analytic and advisory activities in support of project preparation, as well as non-formal ESW and technical assistance.

Improving Poverty Targeting. Management agrees with the need to ensure that project design responds to the priorities and needs of the poor, and to measure the full impact of improved health services for the poor. Indeed, the 2007 HNP strategy explicitly recognizes the need to focus not only on levels of HNP outcomes but also on their distribution, especially among the poor. This focus in the strategy drew heavily on HNP's path-breaking Reaching the Poor Program, active since 2001. Reaching the Poor has delivered global leadership in the measurement of disparities in HNP health-service coverage and outcome indicators among the poor versus the non-poor, as well as of the financial burden on households from seeking care. In 2005, Reaching the Poor published a review of interventions and programs that had been successful in reaching the poor (Gwatkin, Wagstaff, and Yazbeck 2005). A new report (Yazbeck 2009) has been produced in the period since the adoption of the 2007 HNP strategy and was launched in January 2009. This volume lays out a policy menu emphasizing pro-poor policy reform along six dimensions, and a list of the analytical tools to better understand the constraints to pro-poor targeting of public health investments.[6] Management will use these findings to ensure a better pro-poor focus in future lending operations.

Disease Control Programs and Targeting. As opposed to specific income groups, disease control programs must focus on the prevailing epi-demiology. For example, an AIDS program must focus on high-risk groups—irrespective of income. A malaria program focused solely on the poor would fail to eliminate malaria. Polio could only be eradicated from the Western Hemisphere by focusing on large, inclusive campaigns targeting all income groups. Such investments in public health and control of communicable diseases are global public goods, generating positive externalities for society, irrespective of income status.

Investments in Health Systems. The 2007 HNP strategy underscores the need to focus on health systems for delivering improved HNP results, particularly for the poorest and the most vulnerable, and the Bank has emerged as a strategic leader in advancing health systems strengthening for improved HNP results. Over the past two years, projects with a primary focus on health systems have increased twofold. In line with the strategy, 67 percent of Bank programs approved since fiscal year 2007 that focus on priority disease areas also include strong components on health systems strengthening. A new Health Systems for the Health MDGs initiative was launched in 2008 to bring together the resources and efforts to fund and implement coherent, country-led health sector programs in Africa and selected countries in Asia.[7] This program will improve the Bank's ability to rapidly assist and advise HNP operations on the ground, particularly in the areas of health finance and risk pooling mechanisms, human resources for health, governance, supply chain management, as well as infrastructure planning.

HNP in Poverty Assessments and CASs. Management notes the substantive improvements over the past years in quantity and quality of HNP involvement in the Poverty Reduction and Economic Management Network–led analytical work, and agrees that HNP must be fully included in all Poverty Assessments and fully examined in the preparation of CASs.

Cross-Sector Work. Management welcomes the suggestion to expand cooperation and cross-sector work with the Transport, Water and Sanitation sectors. More will be done to harness cross-sectoral results along the notion of "health in all policies." The 2007 HNP strategy is a good conduit to foster improved collaboration across sectors in support of health outcomes. We note the recommendation that "when the benefits are potentially great in relation to the marginal costs," health objectives should be incorporated into non-health projects, but also note that clients undertake such operations largely for non-health objectives and it would be unrealistic within current resources to burden all such projects with potentially small (albeit cost effective) health impact objectives, or to demonstrate and document empirically such impact and outcomes in each case.

The Quality of the Bank HNP Portfolio. Management appreciates the concern for the quality of the Bank HNP portfolio—in particular in Africa. The current data on riskiness of the HNP portfolio confirms the fact that the problems are most acute in the Africa Region, and that HNP's performance across most other Regions is approaching other sectors' performance. An additional area of concern is the underperformance of projects that have a significant HIV/AIDS component, a high percentage of which have received unsatisfactory ratings from IEG[8,9] (with a relatively high disconnect—as management rated the outcomes of several of these operations as satisfactory) and which also constitute a disproportionate number of projects at risk in the current portfolio.

The HNP Action Plan for the Portfolio. As outlined in the Strategy Progress Report, the HNP sector is making major efforts to improve the quality of the existing portfolio and ensure the quality of new operations entering the portfolio. These efforts include increasing candor in reporting to close the realism gap and improving other portfolio indicators. The Africa Region has implemented several changes aimed at improving HNP's portfolio in the Region. In March 2008, the Quality Assurance Group (QAG) was asked to review the performance of HNP projects that were categorized as being at risk. The QAG panel indicated important areas for urgent attention: strengthening sector management oversight; reviewing current resources for preparation/supervision; and addressing two key weaknesses: monitoring

and evaluation (M&E) and institutional analysis. A detailed Portfolio Improvement Action Plan that includes all at-risk projects, as well as projects needing additional management oversight to avoid falling into at-risk status, has been developed and is being monitored on a quarterly basis by the HNP Sector Board.[10] The Portfolio Improvement Action Plan addresses some of the key concerns raised by the various reviews, namely, intensifying management oversight, targeting of resources to projects most in need, strengthening project implementation to focus on monitoring and evaluation, and matching project interventions to the country's institutional capacity. A comprehensive approach has also been adopted to improve the quality of HIV/AIDS projects, and this included an umbrella restructuring package of 11 Multi-Country HIV/AIDS Programs (MAP) for Africa projects in fiscal year 2007. Additional technical support is being provided to improve implementation, develop impact evaluation capacity, and strengthen governance and accountability within national AIDS programs.

Doing More in Population and Reproductive Health. The Strategy Progress Report highlights plans for strengthening support for population and reproductive health in a health systems approach. That strengthening is critical to improving maternal and child survival rates.

Investing in Nutrition Support. We also agree with the evaluation's findings that nutrition has played a less prominent role within HNP over the past 10 years. The need for action is even more important today in the context of the aftermath of the crises in fuel, food, and fertilizers, as well as the escalating effects of the financial crisis. Management is therefore investing significant resources in the next few years to ramp up the Bank's analytical and investment work and leverage resources from other donors. The agenda for scaling-up nutrition is being catalyzed with additional budget resources starting in 2009, and continuing for three years. The increased allocations are being utilized principally in Africa and South Asia, two Regions where the malnutrition burden is highest. These funds will be complemented by additional trust fund resources from

Japan, and possibly from other donors that are currently engaged in discussions on this issue.

Needed Improvement in Monitoring and Evaluation. Management agrees that M&E needs to be improved, and it is an important part of Strategy implementation, as noted in the Strategy Progress Report (including the work on retrofitting projects and improving the design of new projects). The evaluation proposes a focus on strengthening health information systems. However, in some cases, routine health monitoring systems (including surveillance, facility reporting, vital registration, census data, resource tracking, and household surveys) first need to be strengthened to provide the data and indicators that are needed. The Bank has deepened its collaboration with the Health Metrics Network, a global partnership aimed at building statistical capacity in countries to improve the collection and use of health information. The Bank has produced a toolkit on measuring health system governance to better monitor accountability in the sector, and this is being piloted in five countries with support of the Governance and Anti-Corruption Trust Fund. One of the largest impact evaluation trust funds at the Bank, the Spanish Trust Fund for Impact Evaluation, is housed in the human development sector. The trust fund, which was initiated in 2007 and will continue until 2010, finances rigorous impact evaluations of interventions aimed at enhancing human development as well as learning and dissemination activities to help promote knowledge and awareness of "what works" in the human development Sector. The Bank is also working with partners, such as WHO, to develop better ways to monitor the health MDGs, including the estimation of trends in child and maternal mortality for which updates have recently been issued.

The Problem of Attribution. The evaluation argues for a better attribution of health outcomes to inputs financed by the World Bank Group. Health outcomes are hard to evaluate within the timeframe of a project and are influenced by multiple determinants. Also, the Paris and Accra Declarations emphasize the greater development impact of pooled funding, use of country systems, and country-based M&E. The Bank's policy on M&E (OP 13.60) likewise emphasizes the use of country-level M&E systems. Strictly speaking, attribution is only possible in a tightly designed randomized trial, which will rarely be feasible in Bank-supported investment projects or sector support. The standard should be that sufficient evidence on outputs, intermediate outcomes, and outcomes should be collected to establish a credible results chain regarding the link between Bank-financed investments and sector progress.

Cost of M&E. Borrowing countries have many development and poverty-reduction priorities and worry about the opportunity cost of complex M&E systems, especially those that are separate from country systems. They see that large-scale evaluations have an important global public good aspect, justifying external (grant) financing in most cases. This may delay the establishment of appropriate baseline data and results frameworks prior to project approval, notably with regard to impact evaluations.

Operational Complexity. Management agrees that we need to strive to reduce complexity in Bank-financed HNP operations. However, HNP operations can rarely be institutionally or technically simple, since the desired outcome usually depends on a complex and interacting set of social, cultural, and institutional factors. Investing in simple programs would not necessarily provide for lasting impact. Management acknowledges, however, that complexity can be at least partially addressed by some of the recommendations of the evaluation, such as thorough technical preparation, including solid analytical underpinning, political mapping, high quality at entry including a good results framework, and finally in-depth supervision and parallel policy dialogue with client and partners.

The 2007 Health Sector Strategy and IEG Recommendations. The 2007 strategy actually cited findings that were similar to the IEG findings, as would be expected since IEG staff worked with the strategy team to share preliminary results of their work. Annex 2 of the Progress Report summarizes how the overall actions being taken to strengthen the Bank's HNP support correspond to IEG's recommendations (see attached).

IFC's HNP Footprint

IFC has considerably increased its footprint in HNP over the past decade and is prepared to intensify collaboration within the World Bank Group. During the period under review, much has occurred, both in IFC's health activities and in the private health sector in developing countries. There is a growing acknowledgement of the role of the private sector in health care in developing countries. Indeed, in many low-income countries, the private sector pays for a far larger part of health care than the public one, and in many more, it is at least of equal size. Furthermore, joint research by the World Bank, IFC, and the U.S. Agency for International Development (USAID) conducted in Africa showed that very poor people often obtain health care in the private sector and that the public sector often subsidizes health care for the rich. These findings have led to the Bank and its partners designing innovative consumer-focused approaches to addressing major health financing challenges; such as the AMFm (Affordable Medicines Facility for Malaria), which will reduce the price of Artemisinin-based Combination Therapy (ACT), and therefore out-of-pocket payments.

In a world of growing, aging populations in developing countries that are likely to "get old before they get rich," both public and private sector resources are needed to tackle the health needs of the population, as neither has the resources by itself. Indeed, all countries' health systems are financed by both sectors; it is only the proportions that vary.

IFC therefore has taken up the challenge to grow its work to support the private health sector in developing countries to complement the larger, more established work done with the public sector by the World Bank. The period under review has seen a marked increase in IFC's activity in health, the creation of a dedicated Health and Education Department, and a specific focus on pharmaceutical and life sciences activities within IFC's Global Manufacturing and Services Department. During this time, many lessons have been learned, specialist knowledge has deepened, and performance has improved by any measure applied. As in other sectors, IFC continues to strive for greater development impact, and we therefore welcome all input that could help us to do better.

World Bank Management Action Plan

IEG Recommendation	Actions to Be Taken	How Much & by When	By Whom
I. Intensify efforts to improve the performance of the World Bank's health, nutrition, and population support.			
(a) Match project design to country context and capacity and reduce the complexity of projects in low-capacity settings through greater selectivity, prioritization, and sequencing of activities, particularly in Sub-Saharan Africa.	– Carry out Quality Enhancement Reviews focusing on technical preparation, M&E, and institutional and risk assessments and mitigation measures. – Reviews of HNP portfolio.	– 75% of all new HNP projects have an intensive Quality Enhancement Review focusing on technical preparation, M&E, and institutional and risk assessments and mitigation measures, starting fiscal year 2010. – Quarterly reviews of HNP portfolio by HNP Sector Board ongoing.	HNP Sector Board, HNP Hub, and Regional quality teams.
(b) Thoroughly and carefully assess the risks of proposed HNP support and strategies to mitigate them, particularly the political risks and the interests of different stakeholders, and how they will be addressed.	– Concentrate on risk management and mitigation during Quality Enhancement Reviews. – Expand learning on HNP sector risk assessments and mitigation strategies.	– Of the Quality Enhancement Reviews conducted, 100% include focus on risk, starting fiscal year 2010. – Develop and roll out course on project risk analysis for HNP teams, and disseminate best practices and lessons learned, starting fiscal 2010.	HNP Sector Board, HNP Hub, World Bank Institute.
(c) Phase reforms to maximize the probability of success.	– Increase analytical work focusing on reform for those HNP projects focusing on health system reform.	– 100% of new HNP projects focusing on health system strengthening or broadly on health reform to be based on analytical work, including political risks and the interests of different stakeholders, starting fiscal 2010.	HNP Sector Board, with technical support from HNP Hub, as needed.
(d) Undertake thorough institutional analysis, including an assessment of alternatives, as an input into more realistic project design.	– Increase analytic and advisory activities for institutional analysis, with increased attention through better policy dialogue and analytical work, adapted to country context. – Learning program focusing on HNP sector institutional and stakeholder analysis.	– 80% of new HNP projects to be based on institutional analysis, starting fiscal 2010. – Training program designed and delivered, starting fiscal 2010.	HNP Sector Board, HNP Hub.
(e) Support intensified supervision in the field by the Bank and the borrower to ensure that civil works, equipment, and other outputs have been delivered as specified, are functioning, and are being maintained.	– Project design to specify borrower responsibilities for civil works and equipment maintenance. – Project design to ensure adequate recurrent cost budgeting for civil works and equipment maintenance.	– All new HNP projects starting preparation in fiscal 2010. – All new HNP projects starting preparation in fiscal 2010.	HNP Sector Board, HNP Hub.

(Table continues on next page)

World Bank Management Action Plan *(continued)*

IEG Recommendation	Actions to Be Taken	How Much & by When	By Whom
	– Develop guidelines and standard specifications for civil works and equipment and other health inputs, and their maintenance.	– By fiscal 2010.	

II. Renew the commitment to health, nutrition, and population outcomes among the poor.

IEG Recommendation	Actions to Be Taken	How Much & by When	By Whom
(a) Boost *population* and *family planning* support in the form of analytic work, policy dialogue, and financing to high-fertility countries and countries with pockets of high fertility.	– Analytic and advisory activity policy note on reproductive health, including family planning. – Incorporate family planning into health-system strengthening projects. – In high-fertility countries, incorporate population and family planning issue into CAS.	– By fiscal 2010. – 2 health system strengthening projects in high-fertility countries include strengthening of family planning delivery, by fiscal 2010. – 50% of CASs for high-fertility countries, starting fiscal 2010.	HNP Sector Board, HNP Hub.
(b) Incorporate the poverty dimension into project objectives to increase accountability for health, nutrition, and population outcomes among the poor.	– Ensure adequate attention is given to poverty dimensions in project design and supervision, particularly project development objectives and key performance indicators.	– 80% of all new HNP projects incorporate the poverty dimension, where appropriate, starting fiscal 2010.	HNP Sector Board, with technical support from HNP Hub, as needed.
(c) Increase support to reduce *malnutrition* among the poor, whether originating in the HNP sector or other sectors.	– Scale-up the Bank's analytical and investment work and leverage resources from other donors.	– President's Regional Reprioritization Fund to hire 6 additional Bank staff (US$4 million committed for fiscal years 2009–11); Japan TF (US$2 million with potential for additional US$20 million); possibly funds from other donors that are currently engaged in discussions on this issue. – Global Action Plan designed and agreed with key partners, by fiscal 2010. – Six to 8 analytic and advisory activitiess or new investment in nutrition by fiscal 2011.	HNP Sector Board, HNP Hub.
(d) Monitoring health, nutrition, and population outcomes among the poor, however defined.	– Track health outcomes and intervention coverage among the poor. – Publish report on health indicators of poor people.	– Annual review of health indicators among the poor, starting fiscal 2010. – Annual report, starting fiscal 2010.	HNP Hub

World Bank Management Action Plan *(continued)*

IEG Recommendation	Actions to Be Taken	How Much & by When	By Whom
(e) Bring the health and nutrition of the poor and the links between high fertility, poor health, and poverty back into poverty assessments in countries where this has been neglected.	– Increase inclusion of HNP in poverty assessments.	– 90% of all poverty assessments and at least 40% of all CASs should assess the health status of the poor, starting fiscal 2010.	HNP Sector Board, with technical support from HNP Hub and PREM, as needed.

III. Strengthen the World Bank Group's ability to help countries to improve the efficiency of their health systems.

IEG Recommendation	Actions to Be Taken	How Much & by When	By Whom
(a) Better define the efficiency objectives of its support and how efficiency improvements will be improved and monitored.	– Expanded PAD definition and discussion of efficiency objectives, measures and monitoring framework to be expanded and more explicit. – Analytic and advisory activities to analyze and review experience in improving health system efficiency.	– 70% of HNP projects to include definition and analysis of improving HNP sector efficiency, including discussion of efficiency-equity trade-off, starting fiscal 2010. – Start fiscal 2010.	HNP Sector Board, HNP Hub.
(b) Carefully assess decisions to finance additional earmarked communicable disease activities in countries where other donors are contributing large amounts of earmarked disease funding and additional funds could result in distortion in allocations and inefficiencies in the rest of the health system.	– Closely coordinate proposals for Bank support for new disease-specific programs with other partners.	– 100% of HNP projects with significant priority-disease components to map contributions from other donors and ensure strengthening of health systems, starting fiscal 2010.	HNP Sector Board, with technical support from HNP Hub, as needed.
(c) Support improved health information systems and more frequent and vigorous evaluation of specific reforms or program innovations to provide timely information for improving efficiency and efficacy.	– Build statistical capacity for client countries on priority HNP outcome indicators directly through Bank operations and/or supporting global partner's country support (e.g., MDGs). – Continue support of the International Health Partnership's (IHP+) efforts to strengthen monitoring and evaluation and health information systems in countries. – Conduct country assessments of health information systems.	– 50% of new HNP projects include strengthening of country M&E systems, by fiscal 2010. – Strategy for global monitoring arrangement designed (in collaboration with global partners), by fiscal 2009. – Country assessments in 10 countries in fiscal 2010.	HNP Sector Board, HNP Hub.

(Table continues on next page)

World Bank Management Action Plan (continued)

IEG Recommendation	Actions to Be Taken	How Much & by When	By Whom
IV. Enhance the contribution of support from other sectors to health, nutrition, and population outcomes.			
(a) When the benefits are potentially great in relation to the marginal costs, incorporate health objectives into non-health projects, for which they are accountable.	– Provide incentives to non-HNP task team leaders to incorporate health objectives into non-health projects.	– Intersectoral coordination thematic group for HNP results established to identify constraints and incentives, by fiscal 2010.	HNP Sector Board, HNP Hub, Country Directors.
(b) Improve the complementarity of investment operations in health and other sectors to achieve health, nutrition, and population outcomes, particularly between health and water supply and sanitation.	– Develop, implement, and manage an intersectoral coordination thematic group for HNP results.	– Group Functioning by fiscal 2010.	HNP Sector Board, HNP Hub.
(c) Prioritize sectoral participation in multisectoral HNP projects according to the comparative advantages and institutional mandates, to reduce complexity.	– Invite other sectors' participation to HNP project design reviews (e.g., Quality Enhancement Reviews) where appropriate.	– 100% of all HNP projects, starting fiscal 2010.	HNP Sector Board.
(d) Identify new incentives for Bank staff to work cross-sectorally for improving HNP outcomes.	– See response to IV (a) above.	– See response to IV (a) above.	– See response to IV (a) above.
(e) Develop mechanisms to ensure that the implementation and results for small health components retrofitted into projects are properly documented and evaluated.	– Strengthen HNP portfolio monitoring, including non-HNP projects, to document health results achieved through non-HNP sectors.	– 50% of all HNP and non-HNP Sector Board operations tracked, starting fiscal 2010.	HNP Sector Board, HNP Hub.
V. Implement the results agenda and improve governance by boosting investment in and incentives for evaluation.			
(a) Create new incentives for monitoring and evaluation for both the Bank and the borrower linked to the project approval process and the mid-term review. This would include requirements for baseline data, explicit evaluation designs for pilot activities in Project Appraisal Documents, and periodic evaluation of main project activities as a management tool.	– Implement US$2.8 million Spanish Trust Fund (SIEF), supporting impact evaluations. – Pilot and evaluate impact of output- and performance-based financing for HNP-related projects/programs. – Introduce Results Frameworks targeting HNP outcomes, output, and system performance, including baseline data and output targets and programs.	– 15 HNP projects, fiscal 2011. – 16 active projects with most loan proceeds allocated to output-based financing, fiscal 2010. – At least 70% of new projects/ programs approved by the Board, starting fiscal 2009.	HNP Sector Board, HNP Hub.

Chapter 1

1. Michaud 2003. The share of IDA averaged 11.1 percent of the total for 1997–99.

2. IEG calculation based on an annual average of $1 billion of World Bank HNP assistance, of a total calculated by C. Michaud of $16.665 billion in 2006 (World Bank 2008a).

3. http://www.unicef.org/publications/index_23557.html

4. World Bank 2008a. About 536,000 women die annually worldwide from complications of pregnancy and childbirth; the mortality rate in Africa is about 900 maternal deaths per 100,000 live births.

5. The World Bank's commitments include loans from the IBRD and the credits and grants from IDA.

6. This excludes 17 IFC health projects funded through the Africa Enterprise Fund (AEF) and Small Enterprise Fund (SEF), totaling $14 million, which are not evaluated here.

7. In many countries, access to basic health care is considered a basic human right.

8. World Bank 1993b, p. 5. An example of a *public good* is information—one person's consumption does not reduce the information available to others. *Externalities* occur when consumption of a good or service by one individual affects others—for example, children immunized against a disease are not only less likely to get the disease themselves, but so are others they come into contact with (a positive externality). At the same time, industries and automobiles generate air pollution, which conveys a *negative health externality* for the surrounding population. Insurance companies seek to avoid *adverse selection*—in which people who are the most likely to be sick enroll—by targeting people with the lowest health risks, making it difficult for people with pre-existing conditions to obtain insurance. *Moral hazard* occurs when people who are insured have less of an incentive to avoid health risks or demand more expensive or unnecessary care because they are insured.

9. Before 2006, IEG-World Bank was known as the Operations Evaluation Department (OED).

10. A forthcoming IEG evaluation will evaluate support for HNP outcomes through multisectoral development policy lending in the form of Poverty Reduction Support Credits (PRSC). That support is not assessed here.

11. Improving the selectivity and strategic engagement of the Bank in global programs is one of the five strategic directions in the 2007 HNP strategy.

12. This was also maintained in the preceding strategy, from 1997.

Chapter 2

1. The trends in formal ESW are described in appendix G, as well as the results of an inventory of HNP analytic work undertaken by IEG.

2. Investment operations provide funding in the form of IBRD loans or IDA credits and grants to governments to cover specific expenditures related to economic and social development projects. Development Policy Loans provide untied, direct budget support to governments for policy and institutional reforms aimed at achieving a set of specific development results. They may be freestanding operations or, more often, part of a programmatic series of operations. Of the 220 HNP-managed projects approved over fiscal years 1997–2006, only 6 were Development Policy Loans.

3. The number of IDA projects increased by 46 percent, while the number of IBRD projects declined by 20 percent.

4. The results, findings, and lessons from lending for communicable diseases and SWAps are discussed in chapter 3; results for multisectoral HNP projects are taken up in chapter 4.

5. The absolute number of projects with these types of formal objectives declined from 44 in fiscal 1997–2001 to 29 in 2002–06. There may be other projects in the portfolio that include financing, health insurance, and activities with the private sector for which these are not expressed as objectives. They are not included in the table.

6. Staff at level GF+ or higher mapped to the HNP sector (Nankhuni and Modi 2008).

7. As explained in appendix B, the analysis of staff specialties is based on job titles only; there was no known reliable data source that would have allowed tracking by actual staff expertise over the period. The extent to which the job titles accurately reflect staff expertise is unclear.

8. IEG evaluates projects by assessing their results in relation to their stated objectives. The *outcome* rating is based on: (a) the *relevance* of the project's objectives and design in relation to country needs and institutional priorities; (b) *efficacy*, which is the extent to which the project's objectives have been (or are expected to be) achieved; and (c) *efficiency*, which is the extent to which the objectives have been (or are expected to be) achieved without using more resources than necessary. Outcome is rated on a six-point scale: highly satisfactory, satisfactory, moderately satisfactory, moderately unsatisfactory, unsatisfactory, and highly unsatisfactory. For ease of comparison, this report uses the percentage of ratings that are moderately satisfactory or higher in making comparisons across project groupings.

9. The share of project exits in other sectors that were Development Policy Loans remained a constant 15–16 percent between the two periods.

10. The share of Africa Region projects with satisfactory outcomes rose from 60 to 67 percent among projects exiting in fiscal 1998–2001 and fiscal 2003–07, compared with an increase from 73 to 78 percent Bankwide. Outcome ratings for African HNP projects are thus considerably lower than the Regional average across all sectors.

11. However, it is important to note that there was a large increase in HNP project approvals in the Africa Region in fiscal 2002–06 and they will constitute a much larger share of exits in the HNP portfolio over the next five years.

12. While Africa Region projects performed less well on average in other sectors than did the other Regions combined (64 percent satisfactory in Africa, 79 percent in other Regions over the 10-year period), the outcome ratings of Africa Region projects increased at a faster rate (from 58 to 72 percent satisfactory over the two periods). When Africa Region projects are excluded, the ratings for other Regions and sectors combined are higher, but the amount of increase is lower (rising only from 78 to 81 percent satisfactory, as opposed to 72 to 79 percent satisfactory if Africa is included).

13. Ratings on institutional development impact of HNP-managed projects (a rating that was discontinued in fiscal 2006) are as low as those for other sectors.

14. Of the 220 projects approved from fiscal 1997 to 2006 that were subjected to in-depth review, 110 had closed and 99 had been rated by IEG as of September 30, 2008. Fifty-eight percent of the HNP projects approved from 1997 to 2006 that had closed had satisfactory outcomes, while about two-thirds had satisfactory Bank and borrower performance. The outcome ratings for the sample in the portfolio review (58 percent satisfactory) are different from those in figure 2.4 (68 percent satisfactory) because they apply to a different group of projects. Figure 2.4 shows the outcomes for all projects that closed in a given fiscal year, irrespective of when they were approved, while the IEG sample is of 220 projects approved from fiscal 1997 to 2006, only half of which have closed to date. Most of the projects that have closed were approved in fiscal 1997–2001, but a few approved in fiscal 2002–06 (for example, Development Policy Loans) are also included. The performance of most of the projects approved more recently is unknown.

15. While there are several possible explanations for the overall increase in supervision costs across all sectors, examination of the supervision cost data by Region reveals no pattern that would explain why average HNP supervision costs for three years were so much greater than for the rest of the Bank.

16. The ratio of the percent of unsatisfactory projects with this characteristic relative to the percent of satisfactory projects with the characteristic.

17. Projects in Africa are also largely responsible for lower outcomes for IDA projects. Half of IDA-financed HNP projects had satisfactory outcomes, compared to about three-quarters of IBRD projects. However, this rises to 77 percent if IDA projects in Africa are excluded.

18. For a fuller definition and discussion of sector-wide approaches (SWAps), see chapter 3.

19. See appendix F for more on the performance of these projects.

20. World Bank Group 2007. The Detailed Implementation Review (DIR) was conducted by the Department of Institutional Integrity.

21. World Bank Group 2007, p. 11. The DIR team visited all 15 food and drug laboratories and 2 offices that received equipment from the project (p. 67).

22. World Bank Group 2007, p. 12. The DIR team visited 55 hospitals in 23 districts, representing 35 per-

cent of project sites. They were selected based on diversity in size and geographic areas, including remote areas and sites visited and not visited previously by Bank supervision missions (p. 191).

23. World Bank Group 2007, p. 22. For example, in the case of the Orissa project, it noted that it was not until after 6 years of implementation and two project extensions that the Bank began to "extensively" visit and report on project sites (p. 186). In response, the South Asia Region developed an action plan that included stronger supervision structured around the project supply chain and vulnerable points, use of multiple information sources, more use of community and third-party mechanisms, and dedicated consultants to conduct random visits.

24. The average length of the M&E section of the PAD has also increased between the two years, from 445 to 1,272 words.

25. This reflects results for HNP projects reviewed through October 31, 2008. These 45 projects were approved roughly between 1998 and 2000. There have been substantial additional efforts to improve the monitoring of results since then, partly by incorporating logframes or results frameworks that try to measure all of the different links in the results chain. However, these improvements cannot yet be evaluated.

26. The HNP impact evaluations addressed the following types of interventions: nutrition (20 percent), HIV/AIDS (17 percent), malaria (13 percent), health insurance (9 percent), other health financing and performance-based contracting (9 percent), de-worming (6 percent), PROGRESA conditional cash transfers (5 percent), health reform (2 percent), and other (21 percent).

27. This is probably an understatement of the true number of intended evaluations of pilot activities or impact evaluations, as some may not be mentioned in the PAD but rather in the detailed project implementation plans. Impact evaluations that were retrofitted into projects after they were approved are also not included.

28. In a similar vein, Loevinsohn and Pande (2006) found that a typical HNP project in South Asia averages about two innovations, neither of which are typically evaluated.

29. One additional project—the Bangladesh National Nutrition Program (fiscal 2000)—had an impact evaluation conducted by an external entity, as reported in the completion report.

30. TB, malaria, schistosomiasis, leprosy, and polio.

31. For the purpose of this analysis, projects were flagged if they had any mention of "the poor" or "poor regions" in their objectives. To the extent that the projects selected poor regions of the country for implementation and this is not reflected in the objectives, the poverty focus of the portfolio is understated by the objectives. IEG reviewed the design documents for the 47 projects with objectives to improve general health status, to identify projects that targeted poor areas, even if this was not explicit in the objectives. If one were to include projects that had poverty targeting in their design but not in the objectives, the overall share of projects targeting health outcomes among the poor would double, from 8 to 16 percent.

32. A third or more of projects expressed a non-specific objective to improve equity in health services or in the health system, without specifying whether the intent was access to or use of services, distribution of resources, or health status of the population.

33. Two of the 14 projects were cancelled before they were implemented, so it is not possible to assess whether they achieved their objectives. Both of the cancelled operations involved extending health insurance to the poor.

34. Six major studies, all in the first five years covered by the inventory, generated a large number of country reports linked to a single program and account for a total of 184 pieces of analytic work. They were all related to poverty and equity.

Chapter 3

1. The Zaire National AIDS Control Project and the Brazil Amazon Basin Malaria Control Project were both approved in fiscal 1989.

2. For freestanding projects, the full project cost is included, for projects with components, only the cost of the communicable disease component is included (Martin 2009). This is likely an understatement, since many HNP projects finance childhood immunization as an activity, even when it does not appear as a formal component. A search of "immunization" and "vaccine" in project appraisal documents identified 13 additional projects with either immunization subcomponents or mention of immunization as an activity. However, there is often insufficient information available in project completion documents to assess the efficacy of subcomponents in a desk study.

3. Seven regional AIDS projects were approved, covering parts of Africa, the Caribbean, Central America, and

Central Asia. The two main rationales for regional projects, according to design documents, are: (a) to address externalities that individual country programs may not be able to address and (b) to achieve economies of scale and where investments by individual countries will likely result in duplication. The first rationale would cover the projects that dealt with truckers, migrants, and other mobile populations that cross international borders, like the Abidjan-Lagos Transport Corridor Project. The second rationale would cover projects like the Central Asia AIDS Control Project, which aims to strengthen regional laboratory services and disease surveillance. However, several are operating in countries where there is also a freestanding AIDS project. IEG has yet to conduct an in-depth field evaluation of these projects; only one has closed to date.

4. The Bank approved the first of two umbrella commitments for the Africa Multicountry AIDS Program in 2001, together totaling $1 billion.

5. "G8 Summit Communiqué," Okinawa, Japan, July 23, 2000.

6. The Africa Multicountry HIV/AIDS Program, or MAP.

7. GFATM Web site. Commitments are as of November 2007.

8. The World Bank serves on the governing boards for Stop TB and Roll Back Malaria. It also serves on the board of GAVI, leads the Financing Task Force, and is the treasury manager for the International Finance Facility for Immunization.

9. Bangladesh Fourth Population and Health; Cambodia Disease Control and Health Development; Egypt Schistosomiasis Control; Eritrea HIV/AIDS, Malaria, STDs and TB (HAMSET) Control; Eritrea Health; Ghana AIDS Response (GARFUND); Kyrgyz Health Reform I.

10. Communicable disease projects here are defined as projects with a communicable disease objective, title, or component.

11. Only half of projects with communicable disease components had satisfactory outcomes, although the ratings apply to the overall objectives of the projects, which may include more than communicable disease control.

12. Neither of the two completed Africa MAP projects that received satisfactory outcome ratings are country-level freestanding AIDS projects. The Eritrea HAMSET Project was a multiple disease project (AIDS, malaria, TB, STDs) that was rated moderately satisfactory based on the strong performance of the malaria

activities, highlighted in box 3.1. The Abidjan-Lagos Transport Corridor Project aimed at high-risk groups and risk areas along border crossings; it was rated satisfactory. There is also a group of Caribbean MAP projects, but none had been rated by IEG as of September 30, 2008.

13. Martin 2009. The M&E rating is a rating launched on an informal and experimental basis by IEG in 2006. The rating measures M&E design, implementation of M&E, and use of the data.

14. Problems were noted in the India AIDS II Project by the Detailed Implementation Report of health projects in India prepared by the Bank's Integrity Department. Among the African MAP projects, issues concerning corruption were noted in project completion reports for Kenya and Cameroon. In Sierra Leone, the National AIDS Commission forwarded irregularities to a local investigative body that then published the names of illicit nongovernmental organizations and barred them from participation.

15. Malawi (fiscal 2007) and Mozambique (fiscal 2003).

16. The 2007 strategy refers to synergy 32 times, in the context of synergy between disease-specific interventions and health-systems strengthening, and the need for synergy underpins 1 of 5 strategic directions articulated in the HNP strategy. However, nowhere in the strategy is synergy defined.

17. The countries are Malawi (43.5 percent), Mozambique (33.2 percent), Rwanda (45.0 percent), and Uganda (42.0 percent) (Zaky and others 2008).

18. Of course, the severity of any distortion is related to what is actually being financed.

19. IEG defined health-reform projects based on stated objectives and the project title. However, there were a number of projects with neither characteristic that had components that clearly indicated reform activities—for example, the Bangladesh Health and Population Control Program, the Panama Health Pilot, the Moldova Health Investment Fund, the Ghana Health Sector Program II, and the Nepal Health Sector Program. Many of these projects adopted overall objectives to improve health outcomes or to improve efficiency, without mention of reform.

20. Overall, 28 percent of the projects approved from fiscal 1997 to 2006 had objectives to improve efficiency, and nearly half of health reform projects as defined above (48 percent) had an explicit objective to improve efficiency or cost-effectiveness. Most projects with efficiency objectives that are not in health reform

have titles that indicate that they are health-system projects (15/24 projects with efficiency objectives but not health reform). The share of projects with efficiency objectives has also been in decline—from 37 percent of projects approved in fiscal 1997–2001 to 20 percent of projects approved in fiscal 2002–06.

21. Even when additional projects known to have health reform content but without explicit objectives or a title are included, the share with health reform declines from 48 to 28 percent over the period.

22. In the case of low-income Africa, this decline reflects a large increase in the share of communicable disease projects. See the earlier discussion of communicable disease projects.

23. China Health VIII; Peru Health Reform; Samoa Health Sector Management; Argentina Provincial Maternal and Child Health Sector Adjustment; Kyrgyz Health Reform.

24. Moldova Health Investment Fund.

25. China Health VIII, Kyrgyz Health Reform I and II, Moldova Health Investment Fund; Samoa Health Sector Management; Mali Health Sector Development; Argentina Provincial Maternal and Child Health Sector Adjustment.

26. Kyrgyz Health Reform II (Good Governance Structural Adjustment Credit), Peru Health Reform II (Programmatic Social Reform Loans I-IV).

27. Lithuania Health; Venezuela Caracas Metropolitan Health; Kenya DARE; Chad Health Sector Support.

28. There were probably also efficiency gains in Peru since there was increased utilization of public facilities nationwide and no significant expansion in human resources. However, these efficiencies are not well documented.

29. Although initially the funding for insurance was to be financed from the World Bank and the Inter-American Development Bank, the government of Peru decided to fully finance that component. However, insurance remained part of the PARSALUD project and the Bank provided continuous technical and analytical support.

30. ESSALUD is funded by employers, who pay monthly the equivalent of 9 percent of a worker's salary.

31. The Peru Health Reform Project was launched during the administration of President Fujimori, who later resigned. The new leadership distrusted programs from the previous administration and was not interested in pursuing comprehensive reforms that some stakeholders would object to. Yet the principle of extending insurance endured, based on previous analytic work. The part of the reforms that extended coverage was politically popular; the new leadership consolidated the existing insurance programs into the SIS and expanded it nationwide, ahead of schedule, even while resistance to more ambitious reforms of other public sector insurers persists. The Bank addressed needed expansion of community-managed health facility networks, which the new administration was lukewarm to, through conditions in the four Programmatic Social Reform Loans, particularly the first two.

32. Only 3 of the 37 were given a risk rating of high, and one of these projects was so risky that it never became effective (Argentina Health Insurance for the Poor).

33. In the Kyrgyz Republic and Russia, capacity building in primary care through family medicine reforms was a precondition for hospital rationalization and established a quality alternative to hospital care. Financing and service delivery reforms made possible the later benefits package and copayment schemes; changes in revenue collection and pooling were prerequisites to introduction of new purchasing arrangements. However, in Bangladesh, too many reforms were packed into a single project: unification of health and family planning, decentralization, a new tier of service delivery at the community level, in addition to the launching of a sectorwide approach. Community clinics were launched before staff were available.

34. "[T]his resulted in considerable inertia in the types of service being provided, but did provide a platform to attempt to shift the focus from costly curative care." IEG 2006b, p. 8.

35. The team tried to reduce the complexity by reducing the number of regions from three to two, but each still entailed multiple reforms and links to a national component.

36. *Peru: Poverty Assessment and Social Policies and Programs for the Poor* (1993, before the Basic Health and Nutrition Project); *Peru: Improving Health Care for the Poor* (1999, before PARSALUD); *A New Social Contract in Peru* and *An Opportunity for a Different Peru* (2006, before the current election cycle). The 1999 piece recommended: (i) allocating funds with a sharper focus on the needs of the poor; (ii) reinforce pro-poor focus among Ministry of Health providers by targeting, increase access of the poor to hospitals, more community participation; (iii) create new insurance mecha-

nisms to finance health care for the poor; (iv) improve Ministry of Health's information and management systems; (v) refine human resource skill requirements and incentives to better serve poverty-oriented programs. These were all issues addressed in PARSALUD.

37. Analytic work prior to the first Health Reform Project included analyses of: the sexually transmitted infection (STI) program (1994); the TB situation (1995); maternal and perinatal health (1995); acute respiratory infection and diarrhea control; and health spending (1995). A detailed burden of disease analysis was used to identify areas where health status could be promoted through ambulatory care in the most cost-effective manner. Significant analytic work was undertaken for the second project as well: health expenditures in the Kyrgyz Republic (1999); *Who Is Paying for Health Care in Eastern Europe and Central Asia?* (Lewis 2000); *"Analysis of Kyrgyz Health Expenditures"* (Kutzin 1999); *Informal Health Payments in Eastern Europe and Central Asia* (Lewis 2002); *Review of the Sanitary Epidemiological Services in Kyrgyz Republic* (Kyrgyz Ministry of Health and others 2000); and a social expenditure review (World Bank 2001b).

38. Its technical strength, comprehensiveness, and consistency were not enough to ensure ownership (Gonzalez-Rosetti forthcoming, p. 37).

39. The official World Bank definition of a SWAp is "an approach to support a locally-owned program for a coherent sector in a comprehensive and coordinated manner, moving toward the use of country systems" (World Bank Operations Policy and Country Services).

40. The broad international consensus that country-led management of aid was more likely to promote development was evident by the endorsement of over 100 countries and donor organizations of the *Paris Declaration on Aid Effectiveness* in 2005.

41. Parallel funding is earmarked for project financing that supports implementation of the national health plan.

42. Pooled funding is the pooling of Bank support together with the financial resources of other development partners for the purpose of supporting the implementation of national health plans and programs. These funds, allocated and managed by the government, can be channeled through the budget or in a separate account that is a supplement to the health budget. In all of the examples analyzed for this review, the pooled funds remained separate from the rest of the government budget, as a supplement to the health sector.

43. These 28 projects were defined as having the following characteristics in their design documents: (a) explicitly reference support of a sectorwide approach; (b) appear to support a program or sectorwide approach, even without explicit reference to a SWAp; or (c) provide for the pooling and joint management of donor funding. Among that list of projects, those were retained that had: (d) mechanisms for coordination between the government and donors, and among donors; and (e) a common M&E framework for measuring program performance used by most donors and government and a mechanism for joint reviews of program performance. Support of a sector policy and program is another fundamental characteristic of a SWAp, but is also a common feature of non-SWAp Bank support, so was not used as a defining criterion.

44. The portfolio review understates the extent of World Bank support for health SWAps to the extent that operations outside of the HNP sector that also support health SWAps are excluded. Two examples are the health SWAps in Rwanda and Uganda, which are supported by Poverty Reduction Support Credits (PRSC).

45. The countries in which Bank support was not pooled included: Mauritania (2 projects), Ethiopia, Senegal, Guinea-Bissau, Mali, Sri Lanka, and Lesotho. The Bank's decision not to pool appears to be linked to weak country systems and capacities for the allocation and management of pooled funds and, as a consequence, a decision to undertake a more gradual approach both to build country capacity and to nurture and encourage other partners to move in this direction.

46. Other sectors are discussing adopting internationally accepted procedures for procurement, financial management, and audit. The Ministry of Finance has noted its appreciation for the fiduciary rigor of the SWAp procedures, as it insulates the sector from corruption.

47. This is in contrast to pre-SWAp arrangements, in which donor financing did not appear routinely in the government health budget and thus could not be used for purposes of government planning.

48. Malawi also lacks a sound public expenditure framework.

49. Use of country M&E systems still does not absolve the responsibility of the development partners and government to physically verify that implementation is taking place.

50. For example, the underfunding of malaria control in Ghana; this was also the case with the SWAp in Malawi.

Chapter 4

1. The 2007 HNP strategy proposes a new line of ESW called the Multisectoral Constraints Assessment, to help country teams identify the investments and sector work most likely to result in improved health outcomes, especially among the poor, in the preparation of CASs. Such analysis might result in either multisectoral operations or strategically complementary sectoral lending. The specifics of this new analytic instrument have yet to be elaborated. There has been no systematic review of the extent to which the Bank's CASs over the past decade have already addressed health in a multisectoral way, and the lessons learned.

2. The sample of CASs reviewed included all those approved from fiscal 1997 to 2006 from South Asia, East Asia and the Pacific, and the Middle East and North Africa, and a 50 percent random sample of the CASs from the other three larger Regions (Latin America and Caribbean, Europe and Central Asia, and Africa). This amounted to 65 percent of all CASs issued over the period. In addition, all 30 CAS Completion Report Reviews to date were reviewed to assess the extent to which planned multisectoral action actually occurred. Unless otherwise noted, the results cited in the text are weighted to take into account the stratification of the sample. See Sinha and Gaubatz 2008.

3. Only 18 percent of CASs acknowledged the impact of HNP outcomes on other sectors. The most commonly cited linkage was environmental—the impact of population growth on natural resources (6 percent). All of these were in low-income countries and almost all were in Africa. *Only 5 percent of CASs acknowledged the impact of HNP status on poverty reduction.*

4. This includes 9 percent that had both multisectoral and complementary lending.

5. There was one example in each of three regions where there were some linkages between the HNP sector and sectors proposed for complementary lending—child and maternal health objectives in a water supply and sanitation project in Ghana, indicator for increased number of trips to health clinics for transport project in Laos, and health care centers as an indicator for infrastructure in Sri Lanka. The lack of coordination across sectoral lending programs does not imply that each of the sectoral programs individually has not produced benefits for HNP outcomes indirectly, but rather that the closer coordination and synergies envisioned in the strategy have not really been attempted.

6. In fact, implementing a multisectoral response was itself an objective in many of these projects. A case in point is the Ghana AIDS Response Project (GARFUND), for which the first objective was "to intensify multisectoral activities designed to combat the spread of HIV/AIDS."

7. The main challenge of these projects has to do with the number of actors and the need to generate intersectoral collaboration, not the number of components. Multisectoral projects had a mean of 3.7 components (3.9 for HIV/AIDS projects and 3.3 for other multisectoral HNP projects), compared with 3.6 components for HNP projects that were not multisectoral.

8. The most frequently cited implementing agencies were the ministries of health (91 percent); education (25 percent); labor, social security, or employment (12 percent); social welfare, social affairs, or gender (11 percent); agriculture (7 percent); justice or prisons (6 percent); economy, finance, or planning (5 percent); and information (5 percent).

9. Indonesia Iodine Deficiency Control, Senegal Nutrition Enhancement Program.

10. Outcome ratings can also be compared for multisectoral projects according to the executing agency arrangements: managed by the Ministry of Health (9 projects, 44 percent satisfactory); managed by unit under the office of the president or prime minister (8 projects, none satisfactory); managed by finance or other ministries (8 projects, 75 percent satisfactory); managed by multiple ministries (3 projects, 67 percent satisfactory). However, all of the projects managed by multisectoral commissions had other common design features that could have influenced outcomes independently of the management structure. The borrower's performance for that subset of multisectoral projects was 63 percent satisfactory, but the Bank's performance was only 35 percent satisfactory.

11. IDI and sustainability ratings have been discontinued, so not all closed projects have them. Fourteen multisectoral projects had closed that had IDI ratings, of which 4 were HIV/AIDS projects and 10 were other multisectoral HNP projects; 41 single-sector HNP projects had closed and received IDI ratings. The percent of projects with IDI ratings of substantial or higher was: all multisectoral (43 percent), multisectoral

AIDS (50 percent), other multisectoral HNP (40 percent), and single-sector HNP projects (61 percent). There were no significant differences in the sustainability ratings across these four categories—in all cases, 70 percent or more of the projects got ratings of likely or higher on sustainability.

12. Social funds are multisectoral programs that provide financing (usually grants) for small-scale public investments targeted at meeting the needs of the poor and vulnerable communities, and at contributing to social capital and development at the local level.

13. In fact, although in the Bank's internal financial system certain percentages of Development Policy Loans (including PRSCs) are notionally attributed to the sector, these funds are not earmarked to the health sector, nor can they even be linked to higher spending in the health sector. (See note 2 in chapter 2 for a definition of DPL.)

14. *Social Funds: Assessing Effectiveness* found that social fund projects, many of which have invested in health infrastructure, have been highly effective in delivering small-scale infrastructure, but less so in achieving consistently positive and significant improvements in outcomes and welfare impacts. While they have delivered slightly more than proportional benefits to the poor and the poorest, there have also been a significant number of non-poor beneficiaries. Most social fund beneficiaries are satisfied with the subprojects, but the greatest community problems have not necessarily been addressed and there is no assurance that the selected subprojects ensure the highest net benefits to the community. While social fund facilities are generally operating and equipped, they have not been immune to staffing and equipment shortages. Social fund agencies have developed capacity as effective and innovative organizations; wider impacts on existing institutions have been much more limited.

15. For the full portfolio reviews, see Overbey 2008 for water supply and sanitation and Freeman and Mathur 2008 for transport. The transport review included only projects linked to the Transport Sector Board, with commitments under sector codes TA (roads and highways), TP (ports, waterways, and shipping), TV (aviation), TW (railways), and TZ (general transportation, including urban transport).

16. Aziz and others 1990, Curtis and Cairncross 2003, Daniels and others 1990, Esrey and Habicht 1985, Esrey and others 1991, Fewtrell and others 2005, Hut-

tly and others 1997, Strina and others 2003, VanDerslice and Briscoe 1995, Zwane and Kremer 2007. Water-related diseases include waterborne diseases, water-washed (or water scarce) diseases that are transmitted because of a lack of water for hygiene, water-related vector-borne diseases, transmitted by insects that breed in water or bite near water, like dengue, malaria, and trypanosomiasis; and water-based diseases that transmit via an aquatic intermediate host, such as schistosomiasis and guinea worm.

17. Three of the closed projects had explicit health objectives and planned to collect health outcome data, but only two actually did so—the Morocco and Nepal Rural Water Supply and Sanitation Projects. Among the 23 closed water supply and sanitation projects without a health objective, 3 nevertheless planned to collect health data, but only the Kazakhstan Atryau Pilot Water Supply and Sanitation Project did so, documenting a decline in dysentery, typhoid, intestinal infections, and hepatitis A from 1999 to 2002. A fourth project without health objectives and that did not plan to collect health data nevertheless did—the Madagascar Rural Water Supply and Sanitation Pilot, documenting a decline in water-borne diseases (cholera, bilharzias, and diarrhea) from 2002 to 2004.

18. WHO 2004. Losses were measured in terms of disability-adjusted life years.

19. The review included only projects under the responsibility of the Transport Sector Board; projects with air quality objectives and that fell either under the Environment Sector Board or that were funded through the Global Environment Facility (GEF) are therefore not in the sample.

20. The lack of data on outcomes of HIV/AIDS components of transport projects mirrors the experience of transport components in HIV/AIDS projects. Among five recently completed HIV/AIDS projects managed by the health sector with activities aimed at transport workers or Ministry of Transport civil service, none reported baseline or end-point data on risk behavior or condom use among transport workers. None of the ICRs provided information on the impact of the transport sector interventions.

21. This is not meant to imply that coordination across the complementary sectors is necessary to contribute to HNP outcomes; it is possible that investments in complementary sectors, even if not coordinated, are sufficient. However, the outputs and outcomes of in-

vestments in complementary sectors are integral to the results chain contributing to HNP outcomes and would warrant monitoring.

Chapter 5

1. "[O]ne of our key objectives is to complement the World Bank's work in areas of policy advice and dialogue, lending, and analysis in the health sector. Thus, we believe it is essential that the process feature the closest collaboration possible with the HNP anchor and regional staff in the Bank." IFC 2002, p. 3.

2. IFC Strategic Directions, March 23, 2004, pp. 5–16. IFC produces a Strategic Directions paper every year. This refers 2004 corporate strategy.

3. In September 2006, IFC and the Bill and Melinda Gates Foundation partnered on a research project that investigated the best private health care business models in Africa, conducted by McKinsey and Company and published as *The Business of Health in Africa: Partnering with the Private Sector to Improve People's Lives*" (IFC 2007a). Based on that report, IFC established its Africa Health Initiatives with the objective of mobilizing up to $1 billion over five years to boost health care in the Region. The Gates Foundation also committed to cofinance technical assistance activities related to the implementation of the said initiative.

4. The commitment amount (net of cancellations) represents IFC's legally binding potential financial exposure to the client. It is the standard measurement of IFC's financial exposure in its Annual Report and financial statements, as well as the standard reference of multilateral development bank activities in the "Good Practice Standards for Evaluation of Private Sector Investment Operations" (MDB/ ECG/WGPSE 2006, p. 2).

5. IFC invested in small hospitals and clinics through special promotional facilities such as Africa Enterprise Fund (AEF) and Small Enterprise Fund (SEF). These initiatives are for IFC to make direct investments in small and medium-size enterprises where local intermediaries were not providing sufficient financing to viable projects. IEG evaluated the AEF program as a whole and found mixed results. While most projects had positive features, only about half were successful. The program has been costly and required a $5 million fund injection for operating costs. The hospital investments share this feature. IFC committed 15 projects (average investment amount was $0.9 million) from 1997 until 2001, when the programs were restructured and ef-

fectively limited its operations. More than half of the projects failed to generate sufficient revenue to repay loans or provide any returns on equity. Half of the projects experienced some write-off of IFC investment; IFC investments were fully written off for a third. They are not featured in this study because, in line with the multilateral development banks' best practice on private sector evaluation, they were promotional activities with their own investment criteria outside of conventional IFC operations, and only used selectively.

6. The hospital projects approved after fiscal 2002 are focused on modern urban hospitals, but they have started to incorporate new features to enhance their potential development impact. For example, one project in Sub-Saharan Africa has a link with output-based aid that provides health insurance to the poor, enabling the hospital to provide services to underserved segments of the population. This is consistent with the approach proposed in the 2002 strategy for the Bank Group. Moreover, IFC emphasizes repeat investment with the same clients and investment that moves downmarket, that is, into local markets and out of those dominated by foreigners. Still, it is too soon to evaluate the outreach to local patients. Since 2005, IFC has invested in new areas, such as distance medical education in China. The client company provides distance education for nurses and other medical professions through public-private partnership between local medial universities, local public hospitals, and doctors' associations.

7. Life science projects are also increasing in variety, as they relate not only to generic drug production (five of them) but also to vaccine production, drug distribution, and research and development. All of the projects have focused on research and development. Out of 11 life science projects in the third period, 3 have activities related to antimalaria drugs/vaccines; 1 has focused its research and development on country-specific diseases.

8. The AEF was established in 1988 to make direct investment in small- and medium-size enterprises in Sub-Saharan Africa. It was established because of a shortage of suitable private sector intermediaries in the Region willing and capable of providing long-term finance to such enterprises.

9. IFC's *investment outcome rating* is an assessment of the gross profit contribution quality of an IFC loan and/or equity investment, i.e., without taking into account transaction costs or the cost of IFC equity capi-

tal. Loans are rated satisfactory provided they are expected to be repaid in full with interest and fees as scheduled (or are prepaid or rescheduled without loss). Equities are rated satisfactory if they yield an appropriate premium on the return on a loan to the same company (a nominal U.S. dollar internal rate of return greater than or equal to the fixed loan interest rate plus 5 percent).

10. For real sector projects, like those in health, *project business success* is assessed according to whether they generated a project financial rate of return at least equal to the company's cost of capital (with a 350 basis-point spread to its equity investors over its lenders' nominal yield). *Economic sustainability* is assessed according to whether the project generated an economic rate of return of at least 10 percent (in cases in which it can be assessed). *Environmental and social effects* are measured by whether environmental performance meets IFC's requirements and by the projects' net beneficial impact in terms of pollution loads, conservation of biodiversity and natural resources, social, cultural and community health aspects, as well as labor and working conditions and workers' health and safety. *Private sector development impacts* measure impacts beyond the project company, demonstrating effects in creating a sustainable enterprise capable of attracting finance, increasing competition, and establishing linkages with other firms.

11. A blockbuster drug is a drug generating more than $1 billion of revenue for its owner each year.

12. Advisory Services specifically refers to a service product category in IFC. These services cover a broad range of activities including technical assistance to IFC client companies, fee-based advice to governments on privatization, and feasibility and market studies. Some Advisory Services projects are funded by trust funds and others by IFC's own account.

13. According to the rating methodology for Advisory Services, development effectiveness can be rated for projects even if the impact dimension cannot be determined (because of lack of information, for example). This explains why six projects could be rated overall on development effectiveness, even though only two had a rating on the impact dimension.

14. The 2002 health strategy mentions that an entry strategy was under development to identify the most promising investment opportunities in the biotechnology industry. It envisioned that IFC would initially emphasize opportunities with significant downstream potential (product development and commercialization), rather than upstream basic research. IFC 2002, p. 38.

15. For example, see Roland Berger's research at http://www.rolandberger.com/expertise/industries/healthcare.

16. Full-time/full-year staff refers to staff that worked for more than 2,040 hours in a given year in the Health and Education Department (CHE).

17. The Health Insurance Reform Project (fiscal 1996, opening competition among the social insurance funds), the Provincial Health Sector Development Project (fiscal 1996), the Second Provincial Reform Project (fiscal 1998) and the Second Maternal and Child Health and Nutrition Project (fiscal 1997, basic health services). Based on IEG's field visit, this collaboration between the World Bank and IFC was effective until the Argentina financial crisis in 2001, after which communication and collaboration were reduced as the Bank and IFC took wider actions to avoid actual and perceived conflicts of interest within the World Bank Group. These actions resulted in increased barriers in sharing information.

18. As of end of fiscal 2008, about one-third of active CASs were done jointly by the World Bank and IFC. IFC's engagement in the World Bank Group CAS has been ad hoc and uneven. For much detailed assessment of IFC's involvement in the CAS in general, see IEG's "Biennial Report on Operations Evaluation in IFC 2008" (August 2008).

Appendix B

1. For the two projects managed by the HNP sector that had no HNP sector code—the HIV/AIDS Great Lakes Initiative (fiscal 2005) and the Indonesia WSSLIC III (fiscal 2006)—design documents were reviewed and the projects were manually coded to accurately reflect the projects' true allocation to health.

2. According to the IEG review of the transport sector (IEG 2007a), only 16 percent of all transport projects were managed under sector boards other than transport.

3. A coterminous appointment is a term (maximum of 4 years) or open-ended appointment of indefinite duration funded 100 percent from sources other than the Bank's budget.

4. A rights issue is the additional purchase of a company's equities in the event of a new issue and exercising shareholders' rights to avoid dilution of its position.

Rescheduling of a project often involves a new project ID, but there is no new investment; for evaluation purposes, it is bundled with the original project. These exclusions are consistent with the Expanded Project Supervision Report sampling methodology, as well as the Good Practice Standards.

5. The projects meet early operating maturity and are subject of performance assessment when: (a) the project has been substantially completed; (b) it has generated at least 18 months of operating revenues for the company; and (c) IFC has received at least one set of audited annual financial statements covering at least 12 months of operating revenues generated by the project.

Appendix E

1. This appendix draws on the background paper by Fair (forthcoming).

2. These projects were studied in greater depth because they had a population or family planning focus. They understate the extent of Bank support for family planning, which is often financed as part of maternal and child health, safe motherhood, reproductive health, or general health investments. Eight of the projects had explicit objectives to reduce fertility or population growth, three had objectives to improve the distribution or quality of family planning, two aimed to improve reproductive health outcomes, and one supported better access to an essential health package that included family planning. This discussion is based on the background paper by Fair (forthcoming).

3. Malawi Population and Family Planning, Indonesia Safe Motherhood, and Madagascar Health Sector Support Program II.

4. According to demographic and health survey data, the total fertility rate in Guinea *increased* from 5.5 to 5.7 over 1999–2005 and modern contraceptive use rose only from 4.9 to 6.8.

5. The total fertility rate declined in Gambia from about 6.0 to 5.1, which could be attributable in part to higher female education and delays in marriage of younger cohorts of women or to social marketing and greater availability of family planning services supported under the project. The total fertility rate in Senegal declined from 5.7 to 5.3 over the period 1997–2004. However, the modern contraceptive prevalence rose only from 9 to 10.3 percent, and only half of women who wanted more children had access to contraception.

6. The quality at entry was unsatisfactory for six of the eight projects with unsatisfactory outcome ratings; for all eight projects with unsatisfactory outcome ratings, the quality of Bank supervision was also in the unsatisfactory range.

7. Target 5b is to achieve, by 2015, universal access to reproductive health. The main indicators are the contraceptive prevalence rate, the adolescent birth rate, antenatal care coverage (at least one visit and at least four visits), and unmet need for family planning.

Appendix F

1. Shekar, Heaver, and Lee 2006, pp. 3–4. Overnutrition, or obesity, is an increasing problem contributing to morbidity and mortality in developing countries, and is often found in the same households as undernutrition.

2. Ergo, Shekar, and Gwatkin 2008, pp. 7–8. The greatest inequality in stunting is in Latin America and the Caribbean, while the greatest average levels are found in South Asia (more than 50 percent of children are stunted in all four countries), followed by Sub-Saharan Africa (average of 41 percent stunted across 26 countries with recent household surveys).

3. Three-quarters of these projects had an objective of improving nutritional status, including child growth and reducing nutrient deficiencies, and about one in five aimed to increase the access to or quality of nutrition services. One project aimed to mitigate the impact of malnutrition.

4. This understates the Bank's support for nutrition to the extent that nutrition activities are often included in the basic health care packages, yet not mentioned in the PAD. In addition, it is likely that projects in other sectors make major contributions to nutritional status (such as agriculture).

5. Seven of the projects were sectorwide approaches in health (Bangladesh, Burkina Faso, Cambodia, Mauritania, Niger, Sri Lanka) that had either an explicit nutrition objective or component.

6. The 27 projects were approved in 20 countries; 12 of these countries had child stunting (height for age) of at least 30 percent, compared with a total of 47 developing countries overall with this average level of stunting (Shekar, Heaver, and Lee 2006, appendix 5.6).

7. Only 3 percent of projects in Europe and Central Asia were nutrition projects. For the remaining Regions, nutrition projects accounted for 12–14 percent of the HNP portfolio.

8. Bangladesh Health and Population, India Women and Child Development, Afghanistan Health Sector Emergency, Burkina Faso Health Sector Support and AIDS.

9. See, in particular, chapter 4 for a discussion of the health effects of water supply and sanitation interventions in Nepal.

10. The Bank's performance was rated satisfactory for 57 percent of the closed projects, and the borrower's performance only slightly better (64 percent).

11. World Bank 2004b. Note, however, that these figures are based on a comparison of a baseline total goiter rate among both schoolchildren and pregnant women and a follow-up measurement of schoolchildren only. This is an example of the very weak M&E in most of the nutrition portfolio. A 2001 study by IEG compared the performance of this project with two other iodine deficiency projects that promoted production, distribution, and consumption of iodized salt in China and Madagascar (Goh 2001). The study pointed to the extreme difficulty of getting results in Indonesia because of the large number of small salt producers that are difficult to regulate (70 percent of salt production comes from small salt farmers). In contrast, salt production and distribution is centrally controlled in China, while about six large producers in Madagascar produce 80 percent of the salt. That study found four key factors affecting the success of projects promoting iodized salt to combat iodine-deficiency disorders (IDD): (a) information and behavior change communication concerning IDD to raise the demand for iodized salt; (b) easy access; (c) industry compliance, through persuasion and alignment of incentives with the self-interests of the salt industry and consumers; and (d) quality control, since consumers cannot tell the extent of iodization.

12. In the *Sri Lanka Health Services Development* Project, low birthweight declined marginally, and an evaluation of one year of work by the nongovernmental organizations showed minimal impact; other indicators like the consumption of iodized salt were not measured. The *Mauritania Nutrition, Food Security and Social Mobilization Project*—a Learning and Innovation Loan that was supposed to test two different approaches to improved nutrition—did not do so; malnutrition was reduced 16 percent in two urban areas (though the data being compared are from a lean month and a normal season, so this may be exaggerated) and *increased* in rural areas by 6–8 percent; anemia among pregnant women and consumption of iodized sale were not measured. (Mauritania also experienced a major drought and locust infestation during project implementation.) The *Bangladesh National Nutrition Program* did not collect baseline data until two years before the project closed, and found that some of the targets that had been set were already achieved at baseline; project monitoring data suggest a decline in severe protein-energy malnutrition (PEM) from 24 to 16 percent from 2004 to 2006, and moderate PEM from 30 to 25 percent. There was substantial evidence of increased knowledge and change in some behaviors, however. Finally, there was no discernable improvement in malnutrition indicators in Andhra Pradesh, India, during the *Economic Restructuring Project*. (Source: Implementation Completion Reports.)

Appendix G

1. ESW is an activity that "(a) involves analytic effort; (b) is undertaken with the intent of influencing an external client's policies and/or programs; and (c) represents the views of the Bank (that is, not attributed to individual authors)." (IEG 2008h, p. 1)

2. Of this amount, $27.7 million was from the Bank budget and $15.1 million was financed from trust funds. Fiscal 2000 is the starting point for this review, because before that date ESW was not systematically tracked in the Bank's internal information systems.

3. The *Reaching the Poor with HNP Services* Project was partly financed by the Bank's research support budget, partly as knowledge management through the World Bank Institute and the HNP anchor, in addition to the Bill and Melinda Gates Foundation and the governments of Netherlands and Sweden. The only part of the exercise captured as official ESW were a few dissemination activities.

4. This total excludes obvious duplicates (for example, when a research working paper was also published as a book chapter). See the discussion in appendix H. One reason for the difference is that ESW for fiscal 1997–99 is not in the official database. However, because of the elapsed time, analytic work from those years was also more difficult to locate, despite an exhaustive search conducted by IEG.

5. The distribution of HNP ESW is slightly more skewed toward regional ESW and less to the country level, compared to the distribution for all sectors combined (country-level, 78 percent; regional, 17 percent; global, 5 percent) (IEG 2008h).

6. The results tracking framework for ESW was introduced in 2004; all ESW with a budget > $50,000 had to include a statement of objectives as of fiscal 2004, and in 2005, this was expanded to include all ESW. While the share of HNP ESW with an objective of informing lending may seem low (51 percent), it is actually greater than for ESW Bank-wide (41 percent with an objective of informing lending) (IEG 2008h).

7. While most PERs are managed outside the HNP sector, in some cases PERs have been sponsored by the HNP sector.

Appendix J

1. The 1997 HNP Strategy, *Health, Nutrition, and Population Sector Strategy Paper* (World Bank 1997b), July 3, 1997, called for (a) improving health, nutrition, and population outcomes for the poor; (b) enhancing the performance of health care systems; and (c) securing sustainable health care financing. This was to be achieved through (i) sharpening strategic directions; (ii) achieving greater impact; (iii) empowering HNP staff; and (iv) building partnerships.

2. For example, the Global Fund to Fight AIDS, Tuberculosis and Malaria (GFATM), the Global Alliance for Vaccines and Immunization (GAVI), the Bill and Melinda Gates Foundation, and the U.S. President's Emergency Plan for AIDS Relief (PEPFAR).

3. For example, the International Health Partnership, for which the Bank, jointly with the World Health Organization (WHO), provides the secretariat.

4. See, for example, the investigative study cited in endnote 6.

5. Even in low-income countries, total official development assistance for health is less than 30 percent of total expenditures.

6. An example of a country application of the Reaching the Poor work is the investigative study of utilization of health services and patient satisfaction for the poor in selected states in India, which has led to a range of reforms including management training, new staffing and service patterns, provision of essential drugs, and repair of equipment and facilities. This program resulted in increased utilization of all types of health facilities (improving absolute levels of utilization among the poorest 40 percent of the population) and improved patient satisfaction at lower-level project facilities (as opposed to hospitals) for the poor.

7. The establishment of two regional hubs in Africa (in Dakar and Nairobi) and recruitment of 10 high-level experts with a strong health systems focus will be completed by the end of fiscal year 2009.

8. Management notes, however, that during a 2005 Board discussion of the report from the Committee on Development Effectiveness, *Committing to Results: Improving the Effectiveness of HIV/AIDS Assistance and Draft Management Response*, questions were raised about the IEG's [formerly Operations and Evaluation Department's] evaluation methodology of the Bank's HIV/AIDS assistance, and concerns were raised about IEG's tone.

9. IEG would like to clarify that the recent results for HIV/AIDS projects highlighted in the HNP evaluation post-date the 2005 HIV/AIDS evaluation, which covered results only through mid-2004 and did not include any completed projects from the Multi-Country HIV/AIDS Program. Further, IEG and management use the same harmonized criteria for rating projects in all sectors, including HIV/AIDS.

10. The Portfolio Improvement Action Plan includes an analysis of the critical obstacles to project improvement, changes needed to upgrade projects, and measures to restructure or cancel if needed. Additional financial and/or technical support to achieve these improvements is an explicit part of the plan.

Koh Toch Health Center in Kampot Province, Cambodia. The Cambodia Disease Control and Health Department Project supported investments in improved health infrastructure and in control of major communicable disease killers—malaria, TB, and HIV/AIDS. Photo courtesy of Martha Ainsworth.

Adeyi, O., E. Baris, S. Chakraborty, T. Novotny, and R. Pavis. 2003. *Averting AIDS Crises in Eastern Europe and Central Asia—A Regional Support Strategy*. Washington, DC: World Bank.

Ainsworth, Martha, and Manisha Modi. 2009. "Overview of the Health, Nutrition, and Population Portfolio, FY1970–2006." IEG Working Paper. IEG, Washington, DC.

Akin, John S., Nancy Birdsall, and David M. De Ferranti. 1987. *Financing Health Services in Developing Countries: An Agenda for Reform*. World Bank Policy Study. Washington, DC: World Bank.

Armecin, Graeme, Jere R. Behrman, Paulita Duazo, Sharon Ghuman, Socorro Gultiano, Elizabeth M. King, and Nanette Lee. 2006. "Early Childhood Development through an Integrated Program: Evidence from the Philippines." World Bank Policy Research Working Paper No. 3922. World Bank, Washington, DC.

Aziz, K., B. Hoque, K. Hasan, M. Patwary, S. Huttly, M. Rahaman, and R. Feachem. 1990. "Reduction in Diarrhoeal Diseases in Children in Rural Bangladesh by Environmental and Behavioural Modifications." *Transactions of the Royal Society of Tropical Medicine and Hygiene* 84: 433–38.

Bustreo, Flavia, A. Harding, and H. Axelsson. 2003. "Can Developing Countries Achieve Adequate Improvements in Child Health Outcomes Without Engaging the Private Sector?" *Bulletin of the World Health Organization* 81(12): 886–94.

Bryce, Jennifer, Cesar G. Victora, Jean-Pierre Habicht, Robert E. Black, and Robert W. Scherpbier on behalf of the MCE-IMCI Technical Advisers. 2005. "Programmatic Pathways to Child Survival: Results of a Multi-Country Evaluation of Integrated Management of Childhood Illness." *Health Policy and Planning*, December 20, Supplement 1: i5–i17.

Cassels, Andrew. 1997. *A Guide to Sector-Wide Approaches for Health Development: Concepts, Issues and Working Arrangements*. WHO, Danish International Development Agency (DANIDA), Department for International Development (U.K.), European Commission. Geneva: WHO.

Castro-Leal, F., J. Dayton, L. Demery, and K. Mehra. 1999. "Public Social Spending in Africa: Do the Poor Benefit?" *World Bank Research Observer* 14(1): 49–72.

Charmarbagwala, Rubiana, Martin Ranger, Hugh Waddington, and Howard Nial White. 2004. "The Determinants of Child Health and Nutrition: A Meta-analysis." IEG Working Paper. IEG, Washington, DC.

Claeson, Mariam, Charles C. Griffin, Timothy A. Johnston, Mildred McLachlan, Agnes L.B. Soucat, Adam Wagstaff, and Abdo Yazbeck. 2002. "Health, Nutrition, and Population." In *A Sourcebook for Poverty Reduction Strategies*, ed. Jeni Klugman. Washington, DC: World Bank.

Cotlear, Daniel. 2000. "Peru: Reforming Health Care for the Poor." World Bank Human Development Department, LCSHD Paper Series No. 57. World Bank, Washington, DC.

COWI, Goss Gilroy, Inc., and EPOS. 2007. *Joint External Evaluation of the Health Sector in Tanzania, 1999–2006*. Copenhagen: Ministry of Foreign Affairs of Denmark.

Curtis, Val, and Sandy Cairncross. 2003. "Effect of Washing Hands with Soap on Diarrhea Risk in the Community: A Systematic Review." *Lancet Infectious Diseases* 3: 275–81.

Daniels, D.L., S.N. Cousens, L.N. Makoae, and R.G. Feachem. 1990. "A Case-Control Study of the Impact of Improved Sanitation on Diarrhea Morbidity in Lesotho." *Bulletin of the World Health Organization* 68(4): 455–63.

Dye, Christopher, Catherine Watt, and others. 2004. "The Effect of Tuberculosis Control in China." *The Lancet* 364: 417–22.

Elmendorf, A. Edward, and Flora Nankhuni. Forthcoming. "Evaluation of the World Bank's Support for Health, Nutrition and Population: Malawi Case Study." IEG Working Paper. IEG, Washington, DC.

Ergo, Alex, Meera Shekar, and Davidson R. Gwatkin. 2008. "Inequalities in Malnutrition in Low- and Middle-Income Countries: Updated and Expanded Estimates." Country Reports on HNP and Poverty. World Bank, Washington, DC.

Esrey, S.A., and J-P. Habicht. 1985. *The Impact of Improved Water Supplies and Excreta Disposal Facilities on Diarrheal Morbidity, Growth, and Mortality among Children.* Cornell International Nutrition Monograph Series 15. Ithaca, NY: Division of Nutritional Sciences, Cornell University.

Esrey, S.A., J.B. Potash, L. Roberts, and C. Shiff. 1991. "Effects of Improved Water Supply and Sanitation on Ascariasis, Diarrhea, Dracunculiasis, Hookworm Infection, Schistosomiasis, and Trachoma." *Bulletin of the World Health Organization* 69(5): 609–21.

Fair, Mollie. Forthcoming. "Review of the Portfolio of Population Lending, 1997–2006." IEG Working Paper. IEG, Washington, DC.

———. 2008. "From Population Lending to HNP Results: The Evolution of the World Bank's Strategies in Health, Nutrition, and Population." IEG Working Paper No. 2008/3. IEG, Washington, DC.

Fewtrell, Lorna, Rachel B. Kaufmann, David Kay, Wayne Enanoria, Laurence Haller, and John M. Colford, Jr. 2005. "Water, Sanitation and Hygiene Interventions to Reduce Diarrhea in Less Developed Countries: A Systematic Review and Meta-analysis." *Lancet Infectious Diseases* 5: 42–52.

Filmer, Deon. 2003. "The Incidence of Public Expenditures in Health and Education." Background Note to *World Development Report 2004: Making Services Work for Poor People.* World Bank, Washington, DC.

Freeman, Peter, and Kavita Mathur. 2008. "The Health Benefits of Transport Projects: A Review of the World Bank Transport Sector Lending Portfolio." IEG Working Paper No. 2008/2. IEG, Washington, DC.

G8. 2000. "G8 Summit Communiqué." Okinawa, Japan, July 23.

Gakidou, Emmanuela, Rafael Lozano, Eduardo Gonzales-Pier, Jesse Abbott-Klafter, Jeremy T. Barofsky, Chloe Bryson-Cahn, Dennis M. Feehan, Diana K. Lee, Hector Hernandez-Llamas, and Christopher J.L. Murray. 2006. "Assessing the Effect of the 2001–06 Mexican Health Reform: An Interim Report Card." *The Lancet* 368: 1920–35.

Giugale, Marcelo, Vincente Fretes-Chibils, and John L. Newman. 2006. *An Opportunity for a Different Peru: Prosperous, Equitable, and Governable.* Washington, DC: World Bank.

Goh, Chorching. 2001. "An Analysis of Combating Iodine Deficiency: Case Studies of China, Indonesia, and Madagascar." IEG Working Paper No. 18. IEG, Washington, DC.

Golladay, Frederick, and Bernhard Liese. 1980. "Health Problems and Policies in Developing Countries." World Bank Staff Working Paper No. 412. World Bank, Washington, DC.

Gonzalez-Rosetti, Alejandra. Forthcoming. "Evaluation of the World Bank's Support for Health, Nutrition, and Population: Egypt Case Study." IEG Working Paper. IEG, Washington, DC.

Gottret, P., and G. Schieber. 2006. *Health Financing Revisited: A Practitioner's Guide.* Washington, DC: World Bank.

Grosh, M., and J. Muñoz. 1996. "A Manual for Planning and Implementing the Living Standards Measurement Study." Survey Living Standards Measurement Study Working Paper No. 126. World Bank, Washington, DC.

Gwatkin, Davidson, and M. Guillot. 2000. *The Burden of Disease among the Global Poor.* Washington, DC: World Bank.

Gwatkin, Davidson, Adam Wagstaff, and Abdo Yazbeck. 2005. *Reaching the Poor with Health Services: What Works, What Doesn't and Why.* Washington, DC: World Bank.

Gwatkin, Davidson, Shea Rutstein, Kiersten Johnson, Rohini Pande, and Adam Wagstaff. 2000. *Socio-Economic Differences in Health, Nutrition, and Population.* Washington, DC: World Bank.

Hammond, Allen L., William J. Kramer, Robert S. Katz, Julia T. Tran, and Courtland Walker. 2007. *The Next 4 Billion: Market Size and Business Strategy at the Base of the Pyramid.* Washington, DC: World Resources Institute and IFC.

Harrold, Peter, and others. 1995. "The Broad Sector Approach to Investment Lending: Sector Investment Programs," World Bank Discussion Paper No. 302, Africa Technical Department Series. World Bank, Washington, DC.

Homedes, Núria, Antonio Ugalde, and Joan Rovira Forns. 2005. "The World Bank, Pharmaceutical Policies, and Health Reforms in Latin America." *International Journal of Health Services* 35(4): 691–717.

Huttly, S.R.A., S.S. Morris, and V. Pisani. 1997. "Prevention of Diarrhea in Young Children in Developing Countries." *Bulletin of the World Health Organization* 75(2): 163–74.

IEG (Independent Evaluation Group). Forthcoming. "Nepal: Rural Water Supply and Sanitation Project." Project Performance Assessment Report. IEG, World Bank, Washington, DC.

———. 2009a. "Eritrea: Health Project and HIV/AIDS, Malaria, STD and TB Control Project (HAMSET)." Project Performance Assessment Report. IEG, World Bank, Washington, DC.

———. 2009b. "Peru: Basic Health and Nutrition Project and Health Reform Project." Project Performance Assessment Report. IEG, World Bank, Washington, DC.

———. 2008a. *Annual Review of Development Effectiveness 2008: Shared Global Challenges.* IEG Study Series. Washington, DC: World Bank.

———. 2008b. "Egypt: Population Project." Project Performance Assessment Report. IEG, World Bank, Washington, DC.

———. 2008c. "Egypt: Schistosomiasis Control Project." Project Performance Assessment Report. IEG, World Bank, Washington, DC.

———. 2008d. "Kyrgyz Republic: Health Reform I and II." Project Performance Assessment Report. IEG, World Bank, Washington, DC.

———. 2008e. "The Population and Reproductive Health Capacity Building Program (PRHCBP)." Global Program Review. IEG, Washington, DC.

———. 2008f. *Public Sector Reform: What Works and Why?* IEG Study Series. Washington, DC: World Bank.

———. 2008g. "Romania: Roads II Project." Project Performance Assessment Report. IEG, World Bank, Washington, DC.

———. 2008h. *Using Knowledge to Improve Development Effectiveness: An Evaluation of World Bank Economic and Sector Work and Technical Assistance, 2000–2006.* IEG Study Series. Washington, DC: World Bank.

———. 2008i. *What Works in Water Supply and Sanitation? Lessons from Impact Evaluation.* IEG Study Series. Washington, DC: World Bank.

———. 2007a. *A Decade of Action in Transport: An Evaluation of World Bank Assistance to the Transport Sector, 1995–2005.* IEG Study Series. Washington, DC: World Bank.

———. 2007b. *Development Results in Middle-Income Countries.* IEG Study Series. Washington, DC: World Bank.

———. 2007c. "Ghana: AIDS Response Project (GARFUND)." Project Performance Assessment Report. IEG, World Bank, Washington, DC.

———. 2007d. "Ghana: Second Health and Population Project and Health Sector Support Project." Project Performance Assessment Report. IEG, Washington, DC.

———. 2007e. "Medicines for Malaria Venture." Global Program Review. IEG, Washington, DC.

———. 2007f. "Russian Federation: Health Reform Pilot Project." Project Performance Assessment Report. IEG, Washington, DC.

———. 2007g. *Unlocking the Development Potential of Regional Programs.* IEG Study Series. Washington, DC: World Bank.

———. 2006a. *Annual Review of Development Effectiveness 2006: Getting Results.* IEG Study Series. Washington, DC: World Bank.

———. 2006b. "Bangladesh: Fourth Population and Health Project and Health and Population Program Project." Project Performance Assessment Report. IEG, Washington, DC.

———. 2006c. *Engaging with Fragile States: An IEG Review of World Bank Support to Low-Income Countries Under Stress.* IEG Study Series. Washington, DC: World Bank.

———. 2006d. "Vietnam: Population and Family Health Project." Project Performance Assessment Report. IEG, Washington, DC.

———. 2005a. *Committing to Results: Improving the Effectiveness of HIV/AIDS Assistance. An OED Evaluation of the World Bank's Assistance for HIV/AIDS Control.* IEG Study Series. Washington, DC: World Bank.

———. 2005b. *Maintaining Momentum to 2015? An Impact Evaluation of Interventions to Improve Maternal and Child Health and Nutrition in Bangladesh.* IEG Study Series. Washington, DC: World Bank.

———. 2005c. *The Effectiveness of World Bank Support for Community-Based and -Driven Development.* IEG Study Series. Washington, DC: World Bank.

———. 2004a. *Addressing the Challenges of Globalization. An Independent Evaluation of the World Bank's Approach to Global Programs.* IEG Study Series. Washington, DC: World Bank.

———. 2004b. "Cambodia: Disease Control and Health Development Project." Project Performance Assessment Report. IEG, Washington, DC.

———. 2002a. *Bridging Troubled Waters: Assessing the World Bank Water Resources Strategy.* IEG Study Series. Washington, DC: World Bank.

———. 2002b. *Social Funds: Assessing Effectiveness.* IEG Study Series. Washington, DC: World Bank.

———. 1999. *Investing in Health: Development Effectiveness in the Health, Nutrition, and Population Sector*. IEG Study Series. Washington, DC: World Bank.

———. 1998. *Nongovernmental Organizations in Bank-Supported Projects*. IEG Study Series. Washington, DC: World Bank.

———. 1992. *Population and the World Bank: Implications from Eight Case Studies*. Washington, DC: World Bank.

IEG-IFC. 2008. *Biennial Report on Operations Evaluation in IFC 2008*. Washington, DC: World Bank.

IFC. 2007a. *The Business of Health in Africa: Partnering with the Private Sector to Improve People's Lives*. Washington, DC: IFC, The World Bank Group.

———. 2007b. *Annual Report*. Washington, DC: IFC, The World Bank Group.

———. 2007c. "IFC: Innovation for Better Health in Developing Countries—Investing in Life Sciences in Emerging Markets." Brochure. IFC, Washington, DC.

———. 2007. "Technical Briefing to the Board of Directors." Health and Education Department. IFC, The World Bank Group, Washington, DC.

———. 2006. "Smart Lessons from Africa," Johannesburg, South Africa. IFC, Washington, DC.

———. 2004. "Strategic Directions." IFC, Washington DC.

———. 2002. "Investing in Private Health Care: Strategic Directions for IFC." Health and Education Department. IFC, Washington, DC.

———. 1998. *Beyond 2000*. Washington, DC: World Bank.

———. 1982. *Annual Report*. Washington, DC: World Bank.

IFC Health Care Best Practice Group. 1999. "Investing in Private Health Care: A Note on Strategic Directions for IFC." IFC, Washington, DC. Photocopy.

Institute for Health Sector Development. 2004. "Private Sector Participation in Health." London.

Jalan, Jyotsna, and Martin Ravallion. 2003. "Does Piped Water Reduce Diarrhea for Children in Rural India?" *Journal of Econometrics* 112: 153–73.

Jamison, D.T. 2006. "Investing in Health." In *Disease Control Priorities in Developing Countries,* 2d ed. Washington, DC: Oxford University Press for the World Bank.

Jamison, D.T., J.G. Breman, A.R. Measham, G. Alleyne, M. Claeson, D.B. Evans, P. Jha, A. Mills, and P. Musgrove. 2006a. *Priorities in Health*. Washington, DC: World Bank.

Jamison, Dean T., Joel G. Breman, Anthony R. Measham, George Alleyne, Mariam Claeson, David B. Evans, Prabhat Jha, Anne Mills and Philip Musgrove, eds. 2006b. *Disease Control Priorities in Developing Countries*, 2d ed. Washington, DC: The World Bank. www.dcp2.org/pubs/DCP.

Jamison, Dean T., W.H. Mosley, A. R. Measham, and J.L. Bobadilla. 1993. *Disease Control Priorities in Developing Countries*. New York and Washington, DC: Oxford University Press for the World Bank.

Jha, P., and F. Chaloupka. 2000. *Tobacco Control in Developing Countries*. New York: Oxford University Press.

Johnston, Timothy. 2002. "Supporting a Healthy Transition: Lessons from Early World Bank Experience in Eastern Europe." IEG Working Paper Series. IEG, Washington, DC.

Kapur, Devesh, John Lewis, and Richard Webb. 1997. *The World Bank: Its First Half Century*. Washington, DC: The Brookings Institution.

Keutsch, G.T., O. Fontaine, A. Ghargava, C. Boschi-Pinto, Z.A. Bhutta, E. Gotuzzo, J. Rivera, J. Chow, A. Shhid-Salles, and R. Laxminarayan. 2006. "Diarrheal Diseases." In Disease *Control Priorities in Developing Countries,* 2d ed., ed. D. Jamison and others. New York: Oxford University Press.

King, Timothy. 2007. "Family Planning and the World Bank in Jamaica." In *The Global Family Planning Revolution: Three Decades of Population Policies and Programs*, ed. Warren C. Robinson and John A. Ross. Washington, DC: World Bank.

Klugman, Jeni, ed. 2002. *A Sourcebook for Poverty Reduction Strategies*. Washington, DC: World Bank.

Kutzin, Joseph. 1999. "Analysis of Kyrgyz Health Expenditures." World Bank. Photocopy.

Kyrgyz Ministry of Health, WHO Regional Office for Europe, World Bank, DFID, and USAID/ZdravPlus Program. 2000. "Review of Sanitary Epidemiological Services in Kyrgyz Republic." Report of the Interagency Mission to the Kyrgyz Republic.

Lele, Uma, Naveen Sarna, Ramesh Govindaraj, and Yianni Konstantopoulos. 2004. "Global Health Programs, Millennium Development Goals, and the World Bank's Role." IEG Working Paper Series. Case study for *Addressing the Challenges of Globalization*. IEG, Washington, DC.

Levine, Ruth, and the What Works Working Group, with Molly Kinder. 2004. *Millions Saved: Proven Successes in Global Health.* Washington, DC: Center for Global Development.

Lewis, Maureen. 2002. "Informal Health Payments in Eastern Europe and the Former Soviet Union: Issues, Trends, and Policy Explanations." In *Funding Health Care: Options for Europe*, ed. E. Mossialos, A. Dixon, J. Figueras, and J. Kutzin. Buckingham, U.K.: Open University Press.

———. 2000. *Who Is Paying for Health Care in Eastern Europe and Central Asia?* Human Development Sector Unit, Europe and Central Asia Region. Washington, DC: World Bank.

Loevinsohn, Benjamin, and Aakanksha Pande. 2006. "Measuring Results: A Review of Monitoring and Evaluation in HNP Operations in South Asia and Some Practical Suggestions for Implementation." South Asia Human Development Unit, World Bank, Washington, DC.

Lopez, Alan D., Colin D. Mathers, Majid Ezzati, Dean T. Jamison, and Christopher J. L. Murray. 2006. "Global and Regional Burden of Disease and Risk Factors, 2001: Systematic Analysis of Population Health Data." *The Lancet* 367: 1747–57.

Lutalo, Martin. 2006. "HIV/AIDS Getting Results: IFC Against Aids—Protecting People and Profitability." IFC, Washington, DC.

Mahal, A., J. Sing, F. Afridi, V. Lamba, A. Gumber, and V. Selvaraju. 2000. "Who Benefits from Public Health Spending in India?" National Council for Applied Economic Research, New Delhi.

Maikisch, Harald. 2007. "Lessons from Practice: Public-Private Collaboration Workshop in Podgorica, Montenegro." Presented at the Workshop, Sept. 17–18.

Martin, Gayle. 2009. "Portfolio Review of World Bank Lending for Communicable Disease Control." IEG Working Paper Series. IEG, Washington, DC.

Michaud, Catherine. 2003. "Development Assistance for Health (DAH): Recent Trends and Resource Allocation." Paper prepared for the Second Consultation, Commission on Macroeconomics and Health. WHO, Geneva.

Mills, Anne, R. Brugha, K. Hanson, and B. McPake. 2002. "What Can Be Done about the Private Health Sector in Low-Income Countries?" *Bulletin of the World Health Organization* 80(4): 325–30.

MDB (Multilateral Development Banks), ECG (Evaluation Cooperation Group), and WGPSE (Working Group on Private Sector Evaluation). 2006. "MDB-ECG Good-Practice Standards for Evaluation of Private Sector Investment Operations," 3d ed. ECG-WGPSE.

Nankhuni, Flora. Forthcoming. "Health Outcomes among the Poor in Countries Receiving World Bank Support." IEG Working Paper, IEG, Washington, DC.

Nankhuni, Flora, and Manisha Modi. 2008. "Analysis of Trends in Staffing of the World Bank's HNP Sector." HNP Evaluation Note. IEG, Washington, DC.

Narayan, Deepa, and Patti Petesch. 2002. *Voices of the Poor: From Many Lands.* New York: Oxford University Press for the World Bank.

Nassim, Janet. "Special Programme of Research, Development, and Research Training in Human Reproduction." World Bank Policy Research Working Paper No. 26. World Bank, Washington, DC.

Nikolic, Irina A., and Harald Maikisch. 2006. *Public-Private Partnerships and Collaboration in the Health Sector: An Overview with Case Studies from Recent European Experience.* World Bank Health, Nutrition and Population (HNP) Discussion Paper. Washington, DC: World Bank.

O'Donnell, O., E. van Doorslaer, R. Rannan-Eliya, A. Somanathan, S. Adhikari, D. Harbianto, C. Garg, P. Hanvoravongchai, M. Huq, A. Karan, G. Leung, C. Wan Ng, B. Raj Pande, K. Tin, K. TIsayaticom, L. Trisnantoro, Y. Zhang, and Y. Zhao. 2007. "The Incidence of Public Spending on Healthcare: Comparative Evidence from Asia." *World Bank Economic Review* 21(1): 93–123.

Over, Mead, Elliot Marseille, Julian Gold, Peter Heywood, Subhash Hira, and Indrani Gupta. 2004. *HIV/AIDS Treatment and Prevention in India: Modeling the Costs and Consequences.* Washington, DC: World Bank.

Overbey, Lisa. 2008. "The Health Benefits of Water Supply and Sanitation Projects: A Review of the World Bank's Lending Portfolio." IEG Working Paper No. 2008/1. IEG, Washington, DC.

PAHO (Pan-American Health Organization). 2007. *Health in the Americas 2007.* Vol. I. Scientific and Technical Publication #622. Washington, DC: PAHO.

Revenga, Ana, Mead Over, Wiwat Peerapatanapokin, Sombat Thanprasertsuk, Emiko Masaki, Viroj Tangcharoensathien, and Julian Gold. 2006. *The Economics of Effective AIDS Treatment: Evaluating Policy Options for Thailand.* Washington, DC: World Bank.

Robinson, Warren C., and John A. Ross, eds. 2007. *The Global Family Planning Revolution: Three Decades of Population Policies and Programs*. Washington, DC: World Bank.

Roll Back Malaria Partnership Secretariat. 2005. *Global Strategic Plan 2005–2015*. Geneva: Roll Back Malaria Partnership Secretariat.

Sahn, D., and S. Younger. 2000. "Expenditure Incidence in Africa: Microeconomic Evidence." *Fiscal Studies* 21(3): 321–48.

Schieber, George J. 1997. *Innovations in Health Care Financing: Proceedings of a World Bank Conference, March 10–11, 1997*. Washington, DC: World Bank.

Shaw, R. Paul. Forthcoming. "Evaluation of the World Bank's Support for Health, Nutrition, and Population: Nepal Case Study." IEG Working Paper. IEG, Washington, DC.

Shekar, Meera, Richard Heaver, and Yi-Koung Lee. 2006. *Repositioning Nutrition as Central to Development: A Strategy for Large-Scale Action*. Directions in Development Series. Washington, DC: World Bank.

Sinha, Shampa, and Judith Gaubatz. 2009. "Have Country Assistance Strategies Capitalized on Intersectoral Linkages to Improve Health Outcomes among the Poor?" IEG Working Paper. IEG, Washington, DC.

Strina, A., S. Carincross, M.L. Barreto, C. Larrea, and M.S. Prado. 2003. "Childhood Diarrhea and Observed Hygiene Behavior in Salvador, Brazil." *American Journal of Epidemiology* 157(11): 1032–38.

Subramanian, Savitha, David Peters, and Jeffrey Willis. 2006. *How Are Health Services, Financing, and Status Evaluated? An Analysis of Implementation Completion Reports of World Bank Assistance in Health*. HNP Discussion Paper. Washington, DC: World Bank.

UNAIDS (Joint United Nations Progam on AIDS). 2008. *Report on the Global AIDS Epidemic 2008*. Geneva: UNAIDS.

UNECA (United Nations Economic Commission for Africa), UNICEF (United Nations Children's Fund), and World Bank. 1998. *Addis Ababa Consensus on Principles of Cost Sharing in Education and Health*. New York: UNICEF.

UNICEF. (United Nations Children's Fund). 2006. *State of the World's Children*. New York: UNICEF.

Vaillancourt, Denise. Forthcoming. "World Bank Support for Sectorwide Approaches in Health: A Comparative Study of IEG Evaluations of Health SWAps in Five Countries." IEG Working Paper. IEG, Washington, DC.

VanDerslice, James, and John Briscoe. 1995. "Environmental Interventions in Developing Countries: Interactions and Their Implications." *American Journal of Epidemiology* 141(2): 135–44.

Van de Walle, D. 1995. "The Distribution of Subsidies through Public Health Services in Indonesia." In *Public Spending and the Poor*, ed. Dominique Van De Walle and Kimberley Neads. Washington, DC: World Bank.

Villar Uribe, Manuela. Forthcoming. "Pilot Projects, Impact Evaluation, and the Quality of Monitoring and Evaluation in the Health, Nutrition, and Population Portfolio." IEG Working Paper. IEG, Washington, DC.

Wagstaff, Adam, and Mariam Claeson. 2004. *The Millennium Development Goals for Health: Rising to the Challenges*. Washington, DC: World Bank.

Wagstaff, Adam, and Shengchao Yu. 2007. "Do Health Sector Reforms Have Their Intended Impacts? The World Bank's Health VIII Project in Gansu Province, China." *Journal of Health Economics* 26(3): 505–35.

Walt, Gill, and Kent Buse. 2006. "Global Cooperation in International Public Health." In *International Public Health: Disease, Programs, Systems, and Policies*, 2d ed. Sudbury, MA: Jones and Bartlett.

White, Arlette Campbell, Thomas W. Merrick, and Abdo S. Yazbeck. 2006. *Reproductive Health: The Missing Millennium Development Goal*. Washington, DC: World Bank.

Wood, Bernard, Dorte Kabell, Nansozi Muwanga, and Francisco Sagasti. 2008. *Synthesis Report on the First Phase of the Evaluation of the Implementation of the Paris Declaration*. Copenhagen: Kabell Konsulting ApS.

World Bank. 2009. "Implementation of the World Bank's Strategy for Health, Nutrition, and Population (HNP) Results: Achievements, Challenges, and the Way Forward—Progress Report." SecM2009-0147. World Bank, Washington, DC.

———. 2008a. *Global Monitoring Report*. Washington, DC: World Bank.

———. 2008b. "Implementation Completion and Results Report on a Credit in the Amount of SDR 41.3 Million (US$60 Million Equivalent) to the Republic of Madagascar for a Second Health Sector Support Project." World Bank, Washington, DC.

———. 2008c. "Implementation Completion and Results Report on a Proposed Credit in the Amount of SDR 39.2 Million (US$50.0 Million Equivalent) to the Republic of Cameroon for a Multi-Sectoral HIV/AIDS Project." World Bank, Washington, DC.

———. 2008d. "Implementation Completion and Results Report on a Credit in the Amount of SDR 38.8 Million (US$50 Million Equivalent) to the Republic of Kenya for a Decentralized Reproductive Health and HIV/AIDS Project." World Bank, Washington, DC.

———. 2008e. "Implementation Completion and Results Report on a Credit in the Amount Of SDR 41.3 Million (US$60 Million Equivalent) to the Republic of Madagascar for a Second Health Sector Support Project." World Bank, Washington, DC.

———. 2008f. *Safe, Clean, and Affordable: Transport for Development. The World Bank Group's Transport Business Strategy for 2008–2012.* Washington, DC: World Bank.

———. 2007a. *Healthy Development: The World Bank Strategy for Health, Nutrition, and Population Results.* Washington, DC: World Bank.

———. 2007b. "Implementation Completion Report on a Credit in the Amount of US$50 Million to the National AIDS Control Council, Government of Kenya for a HIV/AIDS Disaster Response Project." World Bank, Washington, DC.

———. 2007c. "Implementation Completion and Results Report on a Credit in the Amount of SDR 11.8 Million (US$14.7 million equivalent) to the Republic of Senegal in Support of the First Phase Nutrition Enhancement Program." World Bank, Washington, DC.

———. 2007d. "Implementation Completion and Results Report on a Credit in the Amount of SDR 68.50 Million (US$92.0 Million Equivalent) to the People's Republic of Bangladesh for a National Nutrition Project." World Bank, Washington, DC.

———. 2007e. "Implementation Completion and Results Report on a Loan in the Amount of US$30.0 Million to the Bolivarian Republic of Venezuela for a Caracas Metropolitan Health Services Project." World Bank, Washington, DC.

———. 2007f. *Malawi Public Expenditures Review.* Washington, DC: World Bank.

———. 2007g. *Population Issues in the 21st Century: The Role of the World Bank.* HNP Discussion Paper. Washington, DC: World Bank.

———. 2006a. "Implementation Completion Report on a Credit in the Amount of US$96.7 million to India for a Tuberculosis Control Project." Report No. 34692. World Bank, Washington, DC.

———. 2006b. *A New Social Contract for Peru.* World Bank Country Study. Washington, DC: World Bank.

———. 2006c. *Repositioning Nutrition as Central to Development: A Strategy for Large-Scale Action.* Washington, DC: World Bank.

———. 2005a. *Reaching the Poor with Health, Nutrition, and Population Services—What Works, What Doesn't, and Why,* ed. D. R. Gwatkin, A. Wagstaff, and A.S. Yazbeck. Washington, DC: World Bank.

———. 2005b. *Rolling Back Malaria: The World Bank Global Strategy & Booster Program.* Washington, DC: World Bank.

———. 2005c. *The World Bank's Global HIV/AIDS Program of Action.* Washington, DC: World Bank.

———. 2004a. *Addressing HIV/AIDS in East Asia and the Pacific.* Washington, DC: World Bank.

———. 2004b. "Implementation Completion Report on a Loan in the Amount of US$18.8 million to the Republic of Indonesia for the Intensified Iodine Deficiency Control Project." World Bank, Washington, DC.

———. 2004c. *Improving Health, Nutrition, and Population Outcomes in Sub-Saharan Africa—The Role of the World Bank.* Washington, DC: World Bank.

———. 2004d.*Water Resources Sector Strategy: Strategic Directions for World Bank Engagement.* Washington, DC: World Bank.

———. 2004e. *The World Bank Group's Program for Water Supply and Sanitation.* Water Supply and Sanitation Sector Board. Washington, DC: World Bank.

———. 2003a. *Averting AIDS Crises in Eastern Europe and Central Asia.* Washington, DC: World Bank.

———. 2003b. *World Development Report 2004: Making Services Work for Poor People.* Washington, DC: World Bank.

———. 2002. *Cities on the Move: A World Bank Urban Transport Strategy Review.* Washington, DC: World Bank.

———. 2001a. *HIV/AIDS in the Caribbean: Issues and Options.* Washington, DC: World Bank.

———. 2001b. *Kyrgyz Republic: Review of Social Policy and Expenditures. Vol. 1: Overview of Health, Education, and Social Protection Issues.* Report No. 22354-KZ. Washington, DC: World Bank.

———. 2001c. *World Development Report 2000/2001: Attacking Poverty.* Washington, DC: World Bank.

———. 2000a. *Intensifying Action against AIDS in Africa.* Washington, DC: World Bank.

———. 2000b. *World Bank Strategy for Health, Nutrition, and Population in East Asia and the Pacific Region.* Washington, DC: World Bank.

———. 1999a. *A Health Sector Strategy for the Europe and Central Asia Region.* Washington, DC: World Bank.

———. 1999b. *Intensifying Action against HIV/AIDS in Africa.* Washington, DC: World Bank.

———. 1999c. *Population and the World Bank: Adapting to Change.* Washington, DC: World Bank.

———. 1998a. *Assessing Aid: What Works, What Doesn't and Why.* World Bank Policy Research Report. Washington, DC: World Bank.

———. 1997a. *Confronting AIDS: Public Priorities in a Global Epidemic.* Washington, DC: World Bank.

———. 1997b. *Health, Nutrition, and Population Sector Strategy Paper.* Health, Nutrition, and Population Family, Human Development Network. Washington, DC: World Bank.

———. 1996a. *Poverty Reduction and the World Bank: Progress and Challenges in the 1990s.* Washington, DC: World Bank.

———. 1996b. *Sustainable Transport: Priorities for Policy Reform.* Washington, DC: World Bank.

———. 1996c. *World Bank Participation Sourcebook.* Washington, DC: World Bank.

———. 1994a. *Better Health in Africa.* Washington, DC: World Bank.

———. 1994b. *The Broad Sector Approach to Investment Lending: Sector Investment Programs.* Washington, DC: World Bank.

———. 1993a. "Peru: Poverty Assessment and Social Policies and Programs for the Poor." World Bank Report No. 11191-PE. World Bank, Washington, DC.

———. 1993b. *Water Resources Management: A World Bank Policy Paper.* Washington, DC: World Bank.

———. 1993c. *World Development Report 1993: Investing in Health.* Washington, DC: World Bank.

———. 1989. *Sub-Saharan Africa: from Crisis to Sustainable Development.* Washington, DC: World Bank.

———. 1988. *Acquired Immunodeficiency Syndrome (AIDS): The Bank's Agenda for Action.* Washington, DC: World Bank.

———. 1987. *Financing Health Services in Developing Countries: An Agenda for Reform.* Washington, DC: World Bank.

———. 1986a. *Financing Health Services in Developing Countries: An Agenda for Reform.* Washington, DC: World Bank.

———. 1986b. *Poverty and Hunger: Issues and Options for Food Security in Developing Countries.* Washington, DC: World Bank.

———. 1984. *World Development Report 1984: Population and Development.* Washington, DC: World Bank.

———. 1980a. *Health Sector Policy Paper.* Washington, DC: World Bank.

———. 1980b. *World Development Report 1980: Poverty and Human Development.* Washington, DC: World Bank.

———. 1975. *Health Sector Policy Paper.* Washington, DC: World Bank.

———. 1974. *Population Policies and Economic Development.* Washington, DC: World Bank.

———. 1973. *Nutrition Policy: Policy Guidelines for Bank Nutrition Activities.* Sector Program Paper. Washington, DC: World Bank.

———. 1972a. *Possible Bank Actions on Malnutrition Problems.* Washington, DC: World Bank.

———. 1972b. *Sectoral Programs and Policies Paper.* Washington, DC: World Bank.

World Bank Group. 2007. *Detailed Implementation Review: India Health Sector, 2006–2007.* Volume I. Washington, DC: World Bank.

———. 2002. *Private Sector Development Strategy: Directions for the World Bank Group.* Washington, DC: World Bank.

WHO. 2008. *World Malaria Report 2008.* WHO: Geneva.

———. 2004. *World Report on Road Traffic Injury Prevention.* WHO: Geneva.

———. 2003. *The World Health Report 2003—Shaping the Future.* WHO: Geneva.

———. 2002. *World Health Report: Attributable Mortality by Risk Factor, Level of Development and Sex, Statistical Annex.* WHO: Geneva.

———. 2002. *The World Health Report 2002—Reducing Risks, Promoting Healthy Life.* WHO: Geneva.

———. 2000. *The World Health Report 2000: Health Systems: Improving Performance.* WHO: Geneva.

WHO/Department of Control of Neglected Tropical Diseases. 2006. "Neglected Tropical Diseases, Hidden Successes, Emerging Opportunities." <http://whqlibdoc.who.int/hq/2006/WHO_CDS_NTD _2006.2_eng.pdf>.

WHO and World Bank. 2004. *World Report on Road Traffic Injury Prevention*. Geneva: WHO.

Xianyi, Chen, Wang Liying, Cai Jiming, Zhou Xiaonong, Zheng Jiang, Guo Jiagang, Wu Xiaohua, D. Engels, and Chen Minggang. 2005. "Schistosomiasis Control in China: The Impact of a 10-Year World Bank Loan Project (1992–2001)." *Bulletin of the World Health Organization* 83(1): 43–48.

Yazbeck, Abdo S. 2009. *Attacking Inequality in the Health Sector: A Synthesis of Evidence and Tools*. Washington, DC: World Bank.

Zaky, Hassan H.M., Sherine Shawky, Faten Abdel Fattah, and Eman El-Hadary. 2007. "Evaluation of the Impact of the Provider Incentive Payments on Reproductive Health Services: Egypt's Health Sector Reform Programme." Report written for the Ministry of Health and Population, Central Administration for Technical Support and Projects. Funded by the Reproductive Health and Research Department, WHO, Geneva.

Zimmerman, Michale B., Pieter L. Jooste, and Chandrakant S. Pandav. 2008. "Iodine Deficiency Disorders." *The Lancet* 372: 1251–62.

Zwane, Alix P., and Michael Kremer. 2007. "What Works in Fighting Diarrheal Diseases in Developing Countries? A Critical Review." Center for International Development (CID) Working Paper, No. 140. Center for International Development, Harvard University, Cambridge, Massachusetts.